The Big Flip

JOURNALISM AND POLITICAL COMMUNICATION UNBOUND

Series editors: Daniel Kreiss, University of North Carolina at Chapel Hill, and Nik Usher, University of San Diego

Journalism and Political Communication Unbound seeks to be a high-profile book series that reaches far beyond the academy to an interested public of policymakers, journalists, public intellectuals, and citizens eager to make sense of contemporary politics and media. "Unbound" in the series title has multiple meanings: It refers to the unbinding of borders between the fields of communication, political communication, and journalism, as well as related disciplines such as political science, sociology, and science and technology studies; it highlights the ways traditional frameworks for scholarship have disintegrated in the wake of changing digital technologies and new social, political, economic, and cultural dynamics; and it reflects the unbinding of media in a hybrid world of flows across mediums.

OTHER BOOKS IN THE SERIES:

Journalism Research That Matters
Valérie Bélair-Gagnon and Nikki Usher

Voices for Transgender Equality: Making Change in the Networked Public Sphere
Thomas J Billard

Reckoning: Journalism's Limits and Possibilities
Candis Callison and Mary Lynn Young

News After Trump: Journalism's Crisis of Relevance in a Changed Media Culture
Matt Carlson, Sue Robinson, and Seth C. Lewis

Press Freedom and the (Crooked) Path Toward Democracy: Lessons from Journalists in East Africa
Meghan Sobel Cohen and Karen McIntyre Hopkinson

Data-Driven Campaigning and Political Parties: Five Advanced Democracies Compared
Katharine Dommett, Glenn Kefford, and Simon Kruschinski

Borderland: Decolonizing the Words of War
Chrisanthi Giotis

Not Your Parents' Politics: Understanding Young People's Political Expression on Social Media
Neta Kligler-Vilenchik and Ioana Literat

Movement Media: In Pursuit of Solidarity
Rachel Kuo

The Politics of Force: Media and the Construction of Police Brutality
Regina G. Lawrence

Connective Action and the Rise of the Far-Right: Platforms, Politics, and the Crisis of Democracy
Steven Livingston and Michael Miller

Authoritarian Journalism: Controlling the News in Post-Conflict Rwanda
Ruth Moon

Apocalyptic Authoritarianism: Climate Crisis, Media, and Power
Hanna E. Morris

Imagined Audiences: How Journalists Perceive and Pursue the Public
Jacob L. Nelson

Pop Culture, Politics, and the News: Entertainment Journalism in the Polarized Media Landscape
Joel Penney

The Big Flip: Racial Demographic Change and the Future of American Democracy
Andrew Ifedapo Thompson

The Invented State: Policy Misperceptions in the American Public
Emily Thorson

Democracy Lives in Darkness: How and Why People Keep Their Politics a Secret
Emily Van Duyn

Media and January 6th
Khadijah Costley White, Daniel Kreiss, Shannon C. McGregor, and Rebekah Tromble

Building Theory in Political Communication: The Politics-Media-Politics Approach
Gadi Wolfsfeld, Tamir Sheafer, and Scott Althaus

Capturing News, Capturing Democracy: Trump and the Voice of America
Kate Wright, Martin Scott, and Mel Bunce

Weapons of Mass Deception: How Right-wing Media Wage Information Warfare and Undermine American Democracy
Yunkang Yang

The Big Flip

Racial Demographic Change and the Future of American Democracy

ANDREW IFEDAPO THOMPSON

OXFORD
UNIVERSITY PRESS

OXFORD
UNIVERSITY PRESS

Oxford University Press is a department of the University of Oxford.
It furthers the University's objective of excellence in research, scholarship,
and education by publishing worldwide. Oxford is a registered trade mark of
Oxford University Press in the UK and in certain other countries.

Published in the United States of America by Oxford University Press
198 Madison Avenue, New York, NY 10016, United States of America.

CIP data is on file at the Library of Congress.

ISBN 9780197822142

ISBN 9780197822135 (hbk.)

DOI: 10.1093/9780197822173.001.0001

Printed by Integrated Books International, United States of America

The manufacturer's authorized representative in the EU for product safety is
Oxford University Press España S.A. of Parque Empresarial San Fernando de Henares,
Avenida de Castilla, 2 – 28830 Madrid (www.oup.es/en or product.safety@oup.com).
OUP España S.A. also acts as importer into Spain of products made by the manufacturer.

MIX
Paper
FSC FSC® C183721

Dedicated to Nova Thompson

Contents

Acknowledgments

This work, this text, and these ideas would not have been possible without them being lifted up by my loved ones. Thank you, Mom, Dad, Jonathan, Lissy, Curt, Angela, Julian, Vic, Kaelin, Roman, Jake, Wilson, Malia, Tyler, and so many others.

1

Introducing the Big Flip

The following statement comes from Tucker Carlson, a political pundit on Fox News:

> The great replacement. Yeah. It's not a conspiracy theory. It's their electoral strategy. And we know that because they say it all the time.

Here he is directly responding to a mass shooting in Buffalo, New York. The shooter had one clear motive: rebelling against a sense of threat they felt was coming from racial demographic change in the United States.

...

On May 15, 2022, an eighteen-year-old entered a grocery store, Tops, with a modified Bushmaster XM-15, an automatic gun similar to the AR-15. He live streamed the entire event on Twitch. Pulling up in his car, he first shot and killed the store security guard. Then he shot three other people on his run into the building through the front door. It initially looked to be an indiscriminate mass shooting; everyone he saw, he opened fire on. Running through the front of the market, he shot four other people multiple times. As a woman lay bleeding on the ground from multiple gunshot wounds, he aimed and shot her again. At this point in the live stream, he reloaded his gun. Through his camera, viewers of his Twitch stream could read a few words that were written on his rifle: *niggers*, *Dylann Roof*, *John Earnest*, and *SYGAOWN*. These four words, and the ideas behind them, are intimately connected. They all pertain to the "Great Replacement" conspiracy.

Near the end of the massacre, he pointed his gun at a person huddled behind the checkout counter; realizing quickly that this person was White, he immediately aimed his gun away, exclaiming, "Sorry!"

...

In total, this man in Buffalo killed ten people and injured another three. Everyone killed in this mass shooting was a Black American. This was his

The Big Flip. Andrew Ifedapo Thompson, Oxford University Press. © Oxford University Press (2026).
DOI: 10.1093/9780197822173.003.0001

explicit murderous intention. He was motivated by ideas and messages about the Great Replacement, like those described below again by Tucker Carlson:

> Here's what we do know for a fact. There is a strong political component to the Democratic Party's immigration policy. We're not guessing this. We know this and we know it because they have said so.
>
> They've said it again and again and again. They've written books on it and monographs and magazine articles. They have bragged about it endlessly. They talk about it on cable news constantly and they say out loud, we are doing this because it helps us to win elections. That's not something that is said once. It's something that's gloated about again and again and again and we think that's wrong.
>
> (Carlson 2022)

Political elites like Tucker Carlson have been arguing that the changes in the United States are deliberate, political, and a threat to the racial composition of the country. These narratives connect directly to the words written on the Buffalo shooter's rifle, which I describe next.

The Words on the Rifle

niggers | *Dylann Roof* | *John Earnest* | *SYGAOWN*

The first word is a heinous racial slur toward Black Americans, the hatred directed at the people killed in Buffalo; the second is the name of a White supremacist who killed nine Black Americans in a church in South Carolina; the third, a White supremacist who killed one woman and injured three others in a synagogue; the fourth and final term is an acronym for the statement "Stop your genocide against our White nations." These words attempted to elevate the White supremacists who had committed previous massacres. All of these words are related to the so-called Great Replacement conspiracy theory.

Extremists who subscribe to this idea express concern about the changes happening in the United States, specifically the racial demographic changes: White Americans are projected to become a minority by mid-century. They feel a sense of racial threat from this prospect, thinking they will wield less influence in society. To these extremists, the shrinking number of Whites is politically driven. Through their fear, they infer that political elites are deliberately shrinking the number of White Americans through immigration, dissuading White Americans from having children, and increasing birth rates for people of color—the same sentiments Tucker Carlson advocates.

These ideas are central to the manifesto posted online by the Buffalo shooter. The threat he felt from the changing United States motivated him to kill Black Americans, who he perceived were responsible for his conspiratorial idea of "White genocide." Racial threat led to the development of extremist ideology, and murder followed from that. This type of fear is a major concern for domestic terrorism. As the country diversifies, there will likely be increases in these same forms of violence, discrimination, and hatred toward racial minorities.

The coverage of this event resulted in a pervasive discussion about far-right, White supremacist extremism. For a punctuated moment, media outlets covered the origins and role of the Great Replacement conspiracy in driving far-right extremism. Others correctly connected it directly to the White supremacists whose names were written on the gun:

> Leslie Gardner, a 63-year-old woman who has lived in the majority-Black neighborhood around the Tops store her entire life, said that as an older Black resident, she sees the incident as the latest in a long string of white supremacist violence in Buffalo and across the nation.
>
> "There's anger, which is natural, but people my age, we've seen it all," Gardner said. "We've heard it from our parents and our grandparents that this is our legacy, our legacy of survival, our legacy of being abused and brutalized." The shooting for her is "another Dylann Roof... another lynching, another Emmett Till situation."
>
> (Maccaskill and Sheets 2022)

Two major points were missed in the initial days of coverage of this attack: It was linked to a recent string of White supremacist terrorism, and the conditions for these ideas and actions are growing.

The Canary in the Coalmine

On June 17, 2015, a White man walked into Emanuel African Methodist Episcopal Church in Charleston, South Carolina, and shot and killed nine Black Americans in the midst of Bible study. This was his intention.

On his social media accounts, he would often display the Confederate flag, the Rhodesian flag to lionize the brutal British colony, and other White supremacist iconography. Online he would often exclaim that "blacks are taking over the world," and in a manifesto he published online shortly before his terrorist attack, he wrote, "I chose Charleston because it is [the] most historic city in my state, and at one time had the highest ratio of blacks to Whites in the country" (Bernstein, Horwitz, and Holley 2015). This White supremacist sought to start another civil war in the United States. He wanted to and tried to kill as many Black Americans as he could. This, he thought, would "awaken" White Americans to the Great Replacement conspiracy he thought was actively underway, but it launched a larger conversation about Confederate symbols throughout the American South.

People who initiated this conversation sought to move the historical conversation away from lionizing historical figures who supported slavery—in short, they argued that Confederate statues are anti-Black. On a public level, these ideas resonated quite widely, but they also led to public backlash. A series of political elites opposed the removal of Confederate statues and similar figures; further, there was a growing public sentiment among some White Americans that was similar. Even the mere discussion of Confederate figures was viewed as threatening among this set of White Americans. Their anger eventually rose to a fever pitch, and throughout the country, White supremacists and other far-right ideologues organized in reaction to this symbolic conversation about the history of the United States. They felt threatened, so they mobilized a rally in 2017.

The rally came to be known as Unite the Right. It was a direct response to the outcry from the attack on the Black Episcopal church in Charleston, South Carolina. Pundits who defended White supremacists' violent, racist, and anti-democratic actions would often explain these actors away as "lone-wolves" (Ajinkya 2012). They argued that these were mentally disturbed individuals who were not widely represented in public. An additional claim was that there was no coordination among ideologically similar people—in short, that White supremacists were unitary individuals with no wider grounding in American politics. But the magnitude of the Unite the Right rally turned this idea on its head. To the entire country, it was a grand public demonstration of White supremacy.

The event, which spanned days, was one of the first contemporary displays of wide-ranging authoritarian sentiments among a larger share of

Americans. The motivation behind it was strongly and overtly a reaction to the campaign to take down Confederate statues in the American South. The removal of these statues was a threat to and rallying call for far-right groups. To them, American culture was changing in ways that would fundamentally alter their identities and way of life. Droves of angry White men and some women converged on Charlottesville, Virginia, to make their grievances known. These marches turned violent, resulting in the murder of a counter-protestor.

The most visceral display of this authoritarian ideation was a march held on the night of August 11, 2017. Hundreds of Unite the Right protestors carried tiki torches and chanted in unison, "Jews will not replace us." This phrase deserves attention. It was at once an assertion of anti-Semitism and an expression of racial threat from other racial minorities. The chants were about the Great Replacement conspiracy but from a slightly different point of focus, asserting that there is a cabal of elite Jewish Americans who are orchestrating a replacement of White Americans with people of color and that this band of elites is intentionally threatening the status and power of White Americans. This conspiracy connects to the idea of Jews encouraging mixed-race families, increased immigration, increased birth rates among people of color, and decreased birth rates among White Americans. It posits that Jews are trying to replace an "us" who are the rightful (White) Americans.

A major throughline connects all three of these extremist moments. The Buffalo shooter's SYGAOWN, the Charleston shooter's "Blacks are taking over the world," and the Unite the Right's chant "Jews will not replace us" all connect to a larger narrative. They call to the declining numbers of White Americans and increasing numbers of Americans of color: the majority-minority flip, which in this book I call the *big flip*. These Americans feel that their identity and general position in society are in danger, and they assume that their group will not be able to exercise the same influence in American society.

There is a major and important dynamic necessary to understanding the connection of these three events. The views expressed in Charleston, Charlottesville, and Buffalo are not limited to a small set of extremists in the American public. They represent what happens when a sense of threat motivates political violence. But extremists are not the only Americans who hold these anti-democratic views in reaction to the big flip; *many* other Americans hold these same latent ideas about the world. These sentiments and ideas abound in the mass American public, particularly among White Americans. Throughout this same public, this same sense of threat is leading to changing ideas about American society and, most critically, changing American politics and ideas of democracy. Threat is the starting place of this book; the question of the future of American democracy is its conclusion.

Extremism without Extremists

Rising support for anti-democratic ideas among the public has been given increasing attention among pollsters. The following is from a testimony from Michael German:

> An Associated Press/NORC Center for Public Affairs poll conducted before the Buffalo shooting indicated that almost one-third of Americans agreed with the statement that "a group of people is trying to replace native-born Americans with immigrants for electoral gains." Twenty-nine percent of Americans believed immigration increases are "leading to native-born Americans losing economic, political, and cultural influence," according to the poll.
>
> A recent Yahoo/YouGov poll found that fifty-four percent of Fox News viewers believe that "a group of people in this country are trying to replace native-born Americans with immigrants and people of color who share their political views."
>
> (German 2022)

Negative and fearful perceptions of racial demographic change span outside of how Americans think about other racial groups. Their ideas of changes to racial groups extend to questions of the function of American democracy. The big flip has a strong pull on how Americans think about their government and representation. Racial threat shifts how Americans consider the democratic process. It shapes the future prospects of authoritarianism in the United States by making fearful White Americans more comfortable with it—because the alternative is a system of government in which they have less influence. In a growing capacity, the Great Replacement conspiracy is leading some Americans to want to overturn American democracy.

The American Story of Racial Threat

The big flip is the majority-minority flip in racial demographics, and the threat elicited from this change leads some Americans to the idea of flipping democracy. The first concept I advance in this book is this: Racially threatened sentiments are not limited to extremists—specifically, we should think about them on a wider public level. Anti-democratic ideas are made more palatable and widespread by a racial threat. They can thus be held by seemingly less extreme Americans.

The declining number of White Americans is a well-documented and researched phenomenon. When introduced to information about the big flip, White Americans become concerned along the same lines that I described: They worry that their ways of life will fundamentally change, their status will decrease, and they will be more subject to discrimination.

In one of the first works examining psychological reactions to information about the majority-minority flip, Craig and Richeson find that simply telling White Americans about it leads them to express more negative attitudes toward Americans of color. They conclude the following:

> The present research provides a detailed examination of how the perceived loss of majority status by Whites in an increasingly diverse country affects the expression of racial bias. This research provides insight into how Whites may react to the impending demographic shift and highlights potential for perceived threat and intergroup hostility in a nation on the precipice of arguably the greatest change in racial make-up since the Immigration and Nationality Act of 1965.
>
> (2014a)

There are important historical precedents for the perceived racial threat in American politics; it did not simply emerge in relation to the national demographic trends of the country. It was initially established as a concept that concerned local changes to racial group sizes. For example, the idea of "White flight" is from racial threat; it describes the mass exodus of White Americans in reaction to the ethnic or racial diversification of an area they previously lived in (Rossell 1975; Frey 1979; Crowder 2000; Woldoff 2011). A series of these changes occurred in light of integration across the United States in the mid-twentieth century.

Limited Racial Threat

Racial threat has long been connected to negative racial attitudes as well as views about the social safety net, immigration, refugee rights, and other policy attitudes. These feelings previously have been connected to different advocacy for policy views. Discussions of crime and policies like affirmative action were ostensibly not about race and Black Americans. Political scientist Martin Gilens describes these issues as being "nominally nonracial policy issues" (Gilens 1995). On their face, they were not about race, but when crime was debated, elites and members of the public could talk about levels of crime, inner-city gun violence, and a host of other ideas, and these concepts would connect to ideas of race in the minds of some. These policy areas became so connected to race that attitudes about racial groups would motivate support for the policy. Americans' opinions about Black Americans would determine whether they supported affirmative action.

Similarly, immigration policy was another place where deeper racial concerns converged with conventional conservative politics. Restrictive immigration positions were national in their scope and intentionally focused on building up commerce in the United States. Debates over this policy position maintained a smaller scope; they were effectively quibbles over how exactly to approach the idea of immigration. The answer to the question "How should we approach immigration to the United States?" was essentially to allow either more or fewer immigrants into the country, and this was anchored in ideas of how it might benefit the national economy. Prior to the mainstreaming of far-right ideas, these were areas where there was convergence between the moderate wings and the extreme, ethnonationalist wings of the Republican Party.

Importantly, both of these sets of policy attitudes and the discussions surrounding them legitimized democracy by advancing different policies instead of questioning the system. For example, despite being the leader of the party that emphasized restrictive immigration policy, George W. Bush sought to pass the Comprehensive Immigration Reform Act of 2007 (Pear and Hulse 2007). This bipartisan-supported bill would have provided a path to citizenship for more than twelve million undocumented immigrants, but the legislation eventually died in the Senate after receiving bipartisan opposition from further Right and Left senators.

Further to this point, strategies used by elites to activate racial threat in the public worked to deepen the connection of race to variant issues.

For decades, political elites have used racial dog whistles to signal to their most racially resentful supporters that certain issues would benefit Black Americans and other racial minorities, thereby leading to encroachment on their social status and power. They did this to get these supporters to turn out and support their campaigns (Mendelberg 2001; Thompson and Busby 2021).

Importantly, racial threat and its ability to further enflame negative racial sentiments have maintained a malleable connection to politics. They are not necessarily connected to a given policy unless elites and other members of the public make the connections. In other words, affirmative action does not need to be associated with feelings about Black Americans; it can easily be reframed to concern another group (e.g., women) or issue (e.g., helping to lift Americans out of poverty). Under this same dynamic, racial threat has shifted in its orientation from policy to democracy as a whole. Elite political messaging and overall changes to the political landscape are the major causes of this shift (Bartels 2022).

Whereas Americans' racial views once determined their support for particular policy areas, I find and show systematically that they now determine their support for American democracy. These debates have veered away from being about policy and legitimizing the democratic system of government and steered toward contesting the very idea and existence of American democracy. They do not concern how the government should approach immigration; they concern how immigration could affect all of American society. In short, they greatly raise the stakes of politics, moving it from a policy debate to an existential debate about the future of the American democratic system. The sense of racial threat from demographic changes increases the perception that American democracy will benefit Americans of color more than White Americans. This expressed threat then leads to a change in the understanding and representation of American democracy, decreasing White Americans' support for the processes of democracy and the system as a whole.

I argue that this is a distinct issue for White Americans who are threatened by their numbers diminishing over time. Concerning power in the functional role of democracy, this calls out a fundamental tension in democratic theory between direct democracy and representative democracy. Sizes of political and social groups are vital to both systems of democracy, but particularly under direct democracy do they reign supreme. James Madison expressed concerns over the domination of groups within the idea of the tyranny of the majority. White Americans assume that when they become a numerical minority through a shifting American racial demography, they will be less able to exercise their views in politics through either direct or representative means. As such, this shifting role of projected group size leads to increased tension with the democratic system itself.

That is, White Americans will no longer have the numbers, so democracy, a system that requires majorities to succeed, will not work solely through Whites turning out in politics. It cannot be White dominated anymore, and people of color will have more numerical influence in politics—insofar as both Americans of color and White Americans turn out proportionally to their population numbers.

Theoretically, this dilemma pertains to overall public commitment (particularly White Americans' commitment) to the system of democracy. It requires, at times, a give-and-take dynamic wherein one's political interests are not always met or one's political party loses. Despite this operating as a core tenant of democracy, the United States has been White dominant since its origin, so White Americans have not needed to consider the possibility of conceding power.

Hooker describes this well in her book, theorizing that White Americans have deep difficulty with conceding power in the midst of supremacy in American democracy. This is because, under American democracy, they have never historically had to consider conceding a sizable portion of their power at any point. The big flip calls this into question—at the very least—on a numerical level.

She writes, "'American democracy [continually] gives more weight to the views and votes of White Americans than to the views and votes of racial and ethnic minorities. Race—more than class, and more than any other demographic characteristic—determines who wins and who loses in American democracy.' The result is that whites as a group have been theoretically confronted with the possibility of sharing political rule with nonwhites but have rarely had to experience it in practice" (Hooker 2023). In essence, American democratic practices, norms, and perceptions of the system as a whole have overtly and implicitly catered to White Americans. From this very consistency, White Americans have been conditioned to think that the system will forever cater to them, thereby making it de facto supportive of White supremacy. The changing racial demographics in the United States means, at the very least, that Americans of color will have greater numbers over time. This would mean that if they are mobilized, the group as a whole could affect democratic practices more than they had in the past—assuming that people of color have similar political interests that also differ from White Americans' interests, which is a tall assumption. Despite the many moving legs of this prospect of American politics, the mere intimation of a reduced amount of power for White interests greatly affects how Whites think about American democracy. I will show consistently that activating attitudes about the big flip sizably change contemporary public attitudes about American democracy, both on the levels of its processes and on the system as a whole. This has immense implications for the efficacy and strength of American democracy, which we have just begun to see; below I describe how the dynamics of democratic erosion from the big flip are already happening.

The Logical Conclusion of Racial Threat

The recent culmination of threat and anti-democratic sentiment within American national politics was the January 6 insurrection. On this day, President Trump held a rally on the National Mall in Washington, DC, bringing together his supporters from all over the country. The intention was simple: to contest the results of the 2020 election, which Biden had rightfully won. Trump said in a variety of ways that the election was stolen, albeit with no evidence. He riled up his supporters to march down to the Capitol building, where the election results were being certified in Congress later that day. They did as he had instructed.

After marching down to the Capitol, the protestors chanted and screamed at Capitol police. Phrases like "Hang Mike Pence" surged through the crowd. Eventually they came to barricades that Capitol police had put up to prevent them from coming any closer to the building, likely without any anticipation of the possibility of breach. The Capitol had last been breached by the British in 1814 (Holpuch 2021).

The mob collectively pushed at these barriers with the explicit intention of storming the Capitol; they were encouraged and prodded by then-President Trump. After some strain, they were able to first breach the barriers and then pass police into the chambers of the US Capitol. Again, their intention was to stop the certification of the election; for some of these insurrectionists, it was to harm and potentially kill members of Congress they viewed as their enemies. A series of disparate events of January 6 have been covered and discussed. Below, I bring them together.

At this point, many are familiar with Jacob Chansley, the January 6 rioter who wore a fur headdress with horns, but many are unaware that this same man gave a speech on the raided Senate floor about rooting out traitors. He also delivered a note to the Capitol building addressed to Mike Pence that read "It's Only a Matter of Time. Justice is Coming" (Vargas 2023). He has since been sentenced to forty-one months in prison for obstructing an official proceeding. With the insurrection well underway, President Trump tweeted, "Mike Pence didn't have the courage to do what should have been done" ("Trump's Tweet about Pence Seen as Critical Moment during Riot," n.d.), further fanning the flames of the insurrectionists. It has since been released that the vice president's security detail called loved ones to say their final goodbyes because they thought they would die in the moment. Reflecting on supporters who were heavily armed, many of whom were part of the far-right groups such as the Proud Boys and Oath Keepers, Donald Trump exclaimed, "They're not here to hurt me" and "I don't fucking care that they have weapons" (Lahut 2022). Capitol police discovered an "unoccupied red pickup truck with Alabama tags containing a trove of weapons, including an M4 carbine assault rifle, loaded magazines of ammunition, and components to make 11 Molotov cocktails" ("1–1:03 p.m.: Session Begins," n.d.). Ashli Babbitt, an insurrectionist who was shot and later died, has since become a martyr to many in the far right (Biesecker 2022).

This event was one of the first major displays of contesting the legitimate results of an election in the history of the United States. Understandably, a great deal of attention has been given to how elites either facilitated or legitimized the mass of disgruntled Republican extremists to invade the Capitol building. Media outlets have given attention to stories about who the insurrectionists are and what potential ideas motivated them to storm the Capitol. But beyond the motivations of those investigated, beyond the rhetoric of elites, beyond even the variant examples of individualized violence, there is a larger, systematic story at work about the insurrectionists. This story is strongly aligned with the big flip.

In a crucial study that describes the characteristics of the insurrectionists, a team of scholars shows that there is one clear throughline that is most predictive of participation—racial threat (Pape 2021). This study helps to identify the origins of insurrectionists. The origin points that were tested included whether they live in a rural community, their distance from Washington, DC, and a host of other variables. Ultimately, researchers found local decreases in White populations to be the major predictor of insurrectionists. Put statistically into the context of magnitude, as the population of White

Americans decreased in a local community by 1%, there was a 24% increased chance that an insurrectionist came from that community. Importantly, Pape's study finds declining White status to be at the heart of the insurrectionists' motivations. Most insurrectionists who traveled to the Capitol came from a community that had recently experienced a racial majority-minority flip, wherein White Americans recently became the minority.

This information is incredibly illuminating in describing the origin points of this extremist behavior. We can presume that many of the insurrectionists felt—or at the very least were around—a greater sense of racial threat than other Americans. We also know from research in political science, sociology, psychology, and other fields that these sorts of local demographic shifts lead to increased senses of threat and increased politically conservative attitudes (Key and Heard 1984; Giles and Hertz 1994; King and Wheelock 2007; Schlueter and Scheepers 2010; Glaser 1994; Kinder and Mendelberg 1995). On the ground, the feelings of the insurrectionists took many forms: They worried about the safety of their families because of racial stereotypes, worried they would have less influence in their local communities, and felt alienated by a changing culture in their towns. Scholars Darren Davis and David C. Wilson show that anti-Black attitudes and feelings of White Americans being the "besieged minority," consistently under threat of losing status in American society (Hochschild 2016), were potent drivers of insurrectionist sentiment (Davis and Wilson 2023).

Speaking generally to its function in public opinion, racial threat and the concerns about it take many forms; they can differ widely depending on the person who feels threatened.[1] Taking a step back and evaluating the development of anti-democratic attitudes across the mass public helps us paint a clearer picture of racial threat and its role in American democracy. The insurrectionists may have different feelings about exactly where the threat is coming from, but the important thing is that they agreed on the solution: to subvert American democracy if they felt that they were losing political power.

They saw the election as stolen for a variety of reasons that were racial in their orientation—because of people they saw as non-Americans casting illegitimate ballots, which was a strong component of the lie of the stolen election. They all agreed, and this led them to attempt to hurt (and likely kill) elected officials and ultimately overturn the election of President Joseph

[1] I show the breadth of this variation of racial threat within chapter 2.

Biden. This is where racial demographic change and US democracy converge strongly. In a variety of ways, the insurrectionists' concerns about racial minorities led them to action to overturn an election. They were so frightened that they were willing to tear down a long-standing pillar of democracy. Racial threat motivated these Americans to want to tear down the system they had once bought into because they thought it prevented them from winning in politics.

They assume that they will be in a weaker position in electoral politics because White Americans will be in the numerical minority following a racial demographic swing. Whether this weakening will happen is not predictable given the social nature of race and its politically contingent function (Levy and Myers 2021). Whiteness could change in its role and function. Parties themselves could shift their platforms to even more substantively accommodate these shifting sets of ideals, and, importantly, the size of any given group is not coextensive with political participation. That is, even if White Americans were a numerical minority, even a sizable minority, this does not explain their engagement with politics. There is a conceivable world wherein the White minority dominates politics because they turn out significantly more or consolidate political power by other institutional means. A telling and clear example of this comes in South Africa, which has seen decades-long White minority control of government (Manby 1995; Passemiers 2016).

The logic of Whites' loss of power simply through a slight diminishment in numbers is bunk. Yet the argument does not necessarily need to hold water for the threat to remain. It is a perception we need to take seriously. We know that a sense of threat has driven violent and authoritarian actions in the American public. We know that extremist groups use it as a tool for further recruitment of their members. We know that elites use it to inflame the concerns of their constituents in order to encourage them to turn out in elections. January 6 may be a canary in the coal mine for American democracy—the start of the contemporary explanation of the collapse of the United States' long-standing system of government. If racial threat is deeply connected to Americans' ideas of democracy, then what happens if more Americans feel threatened? The most immediate answer is that we will move closer to American authoritarianism. These diminishing White numbers would then reshape how much these Americans buy into the system of democracy.

How strongly the threat narrative from the big flip resonates will determine how deep a problem it is for American democracy. Within this book, I seek to identify this dynamic. First, I recount and document the contemporary origin points of racial threat in the American public in chapters 2 and 3. Second, I assess just how deeply racial threat is rooted in Americans' minds and how strong the connection is between threat and support for democracy. Third, I ask about the role of the major political parties in facilitating the spread of racial threat. Fourth, I ask whether the sense of racial threat from demographic change is felt among Americans of color in the same way it is among White Americans. And lastly, I offer propositions for how to curb the further spread of racial threat in the minds of all Americans.

Research shows that these racially threatened attitudes exist in the American public. In this book, I take them further. I ask the following questions: How widespread are these ideas of racial threat from the big flip? Do they connect as closely to anti-democratic attitudes as those we saw on January 6? Lastly, what can we expect if they spread further?

There is a strong, growing connection between these racially threatened ideas and anti-democratic views. Racial threat from racial demographic change is dangerous to the foundation of American democratic institutions. As the country changes, it shifts Americans' perceptions of who they think is being represented—as well as who they think wields enough power to win elections. I described this dynamic earlier. One crucial and understudied idea of racial threat is the view that racial minorities will have more influence over the processes of government. White Americans worry that their ability to influence politics will be a thing of the past. Importantly, these views are not far off from the sentiment that "Jews will not replace us." Feeling a sense of threat from demographic changes can relate to general anxiety about the changing world. This sense of threat does not need to be connected to larger conspiratorial ideas; however, the views and ideas that motivate this concern can easily become weaponized and then connected to notions that there is, in fact, a cabal looking to replace White Americans. Once these ideas are weaponized, they raise the stakes of politics exponentially. I show that these ideas can and do lead Americans to become more supportive of variant—and at times desperate—actions they think could curb the threat. These actions take the form of obstructing political opposition, increasing support for authoritarian leaders, and even increasing support for political violence.

The Importance of Norms in Politics

The public helps to set the standard for what is possible in politics. This is what political scientists call a *norm*. If the public maintains a norm of nonviolence, then violent political actions, such as the January 6 insurrection, will be only one-off political moments. They will be seen as extreme. The issue with norm maintenance in the public is when it does *not* find problems with authoritarian actions. When the public does not deem the action as bad and outside of what should be possible in politics, it shifts the window of what is possible in politics. The lack of sanctioning subtly gives legitimacy to those actions. Not holding authoritarians accountable for their authoritarian actions gives them further ability to move the boundary on what is allowed. For example, if a mayor arrests people who express opposition, and the public calls out this action as authoritarian and harmful, it signals to other representatives that they should avoid the same action. It shows other political elites that if they commit a similar action, they run the risk of being voted out of office. Conversely, if the public sees this mass arrest and does not react, then the opposite signal is sent. It suggests to leaders and the public alike that they can conduct similar actions—even "push the envelope" with more harmful authoritarian actions. As a whole, this example details how quickly norms of democracy can be shifted by public reactions.

Racial demographic change is a key part of the story of authoritarianism in the United States because the resulting perceived racial threat generates more support for further eroding American democracy. A driver of this is that some White Americans fear being unable to affect the outcome of elections because they won't wield an effective majority in democratic politics. This anticipation is not captured in the actual function of democratic politics in the United States because not all Americans participate, so a demographic minority does not necessarily function as a political minority. Media discussion, popular discourse, and even some scholarly discourse stop at this point of contention. Often, the fact that threat emerges from irrational or unfounded places leads to it being dismissed as not capturing political reality or the possible futures of US politics. In other words, because racial threat can be explained as an irrational phenomenon, it can be dismissed as unimportant within political discussion and coverage.

These dismissals miss the long-term implications that the mere existence of these views has for American democracy. Despite logical discontinuities in the source of the threat felt by the mass American public, many White Americans still feel threatened in the face of racial demographic change. Because this perception is a potent idea, it has a political truth to it. And as I show consistently throughout this book, these views have massive implications for how Americans think about and process democracy.

Perceptions matter in politics. They might not mesh with reality, but if someone believes that their perception describes the political world, then this perception will direct their political views and behavior. Many times, information to the contrary does little to satiate those perceptions. Perceptions are powerful drivers of politics, which many scholars have observed even more so with the spread of misinformation. If the majority-minority flip causes a sense of threat, there could be little to be said or done about these ideas because of how White Americans will rationalize their sense of threat. They might engage in what social psychologists call *cognitive dissonance*—applying more skepticism to information that challenges their sense of threat and less skepticism to information that confirms it.

The grand point of racial demographic change and threat comes from how democracy functions. Because the system requires a majority for victory and control of government, the shrinking White population leads threatened White Americans to infer that they will be less able to gain political power. From this position, they become less supportive of ideas of democracy.

Throughout this book, I show that perceptions of racial demographic change actually cause White Americans to become more anti-democratic. They assume that becoming a numerical minority will affect their ability to influence politics, and ultimately, I demonstrate that their perception of democracy is built upon the assumption of being able to exercise the most influence as the majority group. Once that narrative is called into question, their confidence in the system of democracy diminishes. Moreover, I show that they become more supportive of anti-democratic means of attaining and maintaining power—violence, obstructing political opposition, and questioning the legitimacy of democratic elections.

Here is one clear example of the connection between racial threat and anti-democratic views, just weeks before the Buffalo shooting. The Southern Poverty Law Center (SPLC) conducted a nationwide poll on the public support for the Great Replacement conspiracy. Ultimately, it found that seven in ten Republicans supported the idea. Among those who most strongly agreed, there was a deep connection between those views and grounded anti-democratic views about the legitimacy of the 2020 election and the January 6 insurrection.

The SPLC identifies a strong connection between the racially threatened ideas about the Great Replacement and anti-democratic ideas about the 2020 election. More than two-thirds of conspiracy believers also express strong authoritarian sentiments, and this confirms the central thrust of this book—Americans' threat-based views about racial demographic change have become intimately tied to their ideas of democracy. As time goes on, demographics shift, more messaging about these changes is made, and these authoritarian ideas are likely to increase among the public. In short, these senses of racial threat are a direct threat to American democracy.

In this book, I will further spell out the causes that can help explain this intimate connection between these two ideas. As I explore more thoroughly how these ideas pose a grand problem for democracy, a key theme I will emphasize throughout is just how these views can accumulate into bigger problems that unravel the fabric of American society.

There is a general understanding of how racial threat is bad for democracy, but so far we do not have a proper story about how these fears directly feed into views that erode democracy. This is an incredibly important point. Without it, we are unable to properly diagnose exactly how the threat is functioning. This can lead to speculation that could exacerbate the problem, an inability to anticipate how it is worsening, or an inability to devise steps to vitiate the sentiments of threat that erode democratic values.

In the story of how we arrived at this point, I identify a series of ideas that drive the backsliding of democracy in the United States. This is what social scientists call "identifying a mechanism." Specifically, I seek to determine and better articulate how the racial threat from racial demographic change directly affects how Americans think about democracy in the United States. I go about this in three parts in this book: past, present, and future.

I start in the past, discussing how Americans' historical ideas of race and the racial demographics of the United States have been shifted and molded over time. This then leads us to the present and the second part of this book, which involves a robust logical explanation of how threat activates authoritarian ideas in the minds of Americans currently. Finally, I bring the discussion of racial threat and democracy into the future of the country, providing potential ideas and suggestions for how to remedy the damaging effects of racial threat on American democracy.

2

The Big Flip and the Historical Struggle for Black Enfranchisement

At its core, the story of the big flip is the legacy of Black enfranchisement in the United States. When Americans think of people of color, they think of Black Americans because of their storied relationship with American democracy. Since the inception of the country, American democracy has persistently struggled with the role of Black Americans in society and politics. Gains and losses in Black Americans' rights have consistently challenged what American democracy means and how it ought to be interpreted. The original example of this is chattel slavery, which gravely contested the democratic norms and ideals the Founders put forth on paper. Thomas Jefferson referred to slavery as a "moral depravity." He described it as

> a hideous blot, as well from the heteromorph peculiarities of the race, as that, with them, physical compulsion to action must be substituted for the moral necessity which constrains the free laborer to work equally hard. We feel and deplore it morally and politically, and we look, without entire despair to some redeeming means not yet specifically foreseen.
>
> ("Letter from Thomas Jefferson to John Holmes, April 22, 1820. U.S. Capitol: Visitor Center," n.d.)

In other letters and correspondences, Thomas Jefferson expressed the belief that slavery was the greatest threat to the existence of American democracy. Yet despite his apparent opposition to slavery, he directly engaged in it as a slaveholder. Jefferson enslaved over six hundred people throughout his life, displaying bad faith by rhetorically opposing yet personally supporting it. William Cohen describes this incompatibility of values and action in detail:

> It seems paradoxical that Thomas Jefferson, one of the enduring heroes of American democracy, should have been the owner of more than 180

The Big Flip. Andrew Ifedapo Thompson, Oxford University Press. © Oxford University Press (2026).
DOI: 10.1093/9780197822173.003.0002

> slaves at the very time when he was proclaiming that all men were created equal and that they were "endowed by their Creator" with the "unalienable Rights" of "Life, Liberty and the pursuit of Happiness." Moreover, throughout his life he continued to hold that slavery was unjust and immoral. In 1785 he had used the phrase "avarice and oppression" to characterize the slaveholding interest, and he contrasted this with the "sacred side" of emancipation.
>
> (Cohen 1969, pp. 503)

Other Founders expressed similar ideas and difficulties with the institution of slavery. The irony of their stances, in most cases, is a throughline across their positions. The founders of American democracy were systematically subjugating Black Americans while asserting that they wanted to build up democratic ideals. In another telling example, Michael Signer describes James Madison's cognitive dissonance along these lines:

> Madison applied a different political philosophy to matters concerning the state to those concerning his own house. At the national level . . . he believed slavery presented an existential threat to a country premised on freedom. At Montpelier, with slaves he felt he treated well, he saw no such conflict.
>
> (Signer 2015)

Even Alexander Hamilton, who has been described as the "abolitionist founding father," has been shown by recent historians to have enslaved Black Americans (Chan 2004; Schuessler 2020). These many contradictions in maintaining democratic principles while restricting the human rights of Black people pervade the making of the early Republic, especially among the elites who so strongly championed democracy. Rogers Smith describes these competing political cultural traditions as central to the structure of the polity (Smith 1993). While democracy as a key theoretical foundation to American polity was put forth and articulated, so too were anti-democratic practices that limited the humanity of Black people living in the United States. To Smith, American politics has maintained these multiple traditions in tandem throughout its history. The "multiple traditions" run against one another on a theoretical level, but in practice they sit at the core of American political culture. While institutional slavery functioned from the inception of the polity and the Founders explained away their personal contradictions, early on in US history the question of the place of Black Americans was central to democracy. The avoidance of the question did not get rid of it, but merely suppressed it. To many White elites, Black Americans were not an existential problem for democracy, until they were. And with this contention came the Civil War.

The Struggle for Democracy and the Civil War

Early political elites recognized the massive human rights issue of slavery as an institution that limited claims on the function of American democracy. Millions of African Americans' lives and rights were suppressed while the new Republic was being touted, praised, and articulated as a rising beacon of democracy globally. The maintenance of slavery, but more deeply the importance of the rights of Black Americans, sat fundamentally at odds with democratic ideals. Quickly this became a point of contention in the polity due to widespread disagreement on how other Americans thought Black Americans ought to be treated. The suppression of this question could not exist for long because of how deeply anti-democratic the function and institution of slavery was. The nation could not exist in this contradiction. Either Black Americans were going to be recognized as they are—human—or they were going to be institutionally viewed as property from time immemorial. There was no in-between.

Abraham Lincoln described the existential crossroads that the nation was coming to in a speech at the Illinois State Capitol in 1858. He strongly emphasized the inherent contradiction in the divided views among the polity:

> We are now far into the fifth year, since a policy was initiated, with the avowed object, and confident promise, of putting an end to slavery agitation. Under the operation of that policy, that agitation has not only, not ceased, but has constantly augmented. In my opinion, it will not cease, until a crisis shall have been reached, and passed. "A house divided against itself cannot stand." I believe this government cannot endure, permanently half slave and half free.
>
> (Republican Party [Ill.] 1858)

Here Lincoln states that the United States could not continue to exist as a nation where half of it endorsed enslaving Black Americans and half opposed it. The institution of slavery and the general limitation of the humanity of Black Americans ran roughshod over the democratic norms and principles that so much of the country seemingly agreed upon. Democracy in America found itself coming to a head because of the question of Black enfranchisement. The question had not been forgotten in the early days of the Republic—the Founders were highly aware of slavery's stain on the country—it was simply suppressed until it no longer could be.

The war happened—as so many expected—leading to extreme consequences and the first moment in which American democracy nearly fractured. The Civil War pushed the country to the brink of dissolution. Equally important and often overlooked is the fact that the same Civil War offered an initial experience of freedom for Black Americans. In the midst of the war, Black Americans saw a fundamental shift in their societal role and perception. To this, Foner writes the following:

> The transformation of blacks' role within American society began during the Civil War. For the nearly four million slaves, for the tiny, despised black population of the free states, and for the free blacks of the South, the war held out the hope of a radical change in American race relations. Each of those groups took actions that helped propel a reluctant white America down the road but also to a constitutional recognition of the principle of civil and political equality regardless of race—a concept utterly unprecedented in the preceding two and a half centuries of American history.
> (1987, 863–64)

Despite being a full-fledged war that took the lives of roughly 2% of the entire country, the Civil War was one of Black Americans' first experiences of a fundamental shift in their role in American society. On the whole, this gives a point of comparison into just how brutalizing chattel slavery was for Black Americans. Participating in war was a reprieve from slavery.

This experience paints a bifurcated picture of the state of US democracy that persisted over time. On one end, Black Americans lived in marginalized, subjugated positions that did not recognize their humanity; on the other, White Americans benefited from Black labor and dehumanization, using it to elevate their sense of self in American society. The simple existence of the Civil War opened up the informal freedom of Black Americans; their very humanity had to be recognized amid their participation in the war effort.

Whites who supported the institution of slavery saw its eradication as a direct threat to their existence, which was in part due to the fact that their political identity was built on the subjugation of Black Americans.

A Union victory concluded the bloody conflict. This triumph was accompanied by a subsequent, albeit moderately paced, eradication of slavery and political enfranchisement of Black Americans. The decade and a half that followed the Civil War, known as Reconstruction, saw a whirlwind of federally enacted protections and advancements of Black Americans' rights over an extremely short period of political time. One of the first among these was the Reconstruction Act of 1867, which brought about the readmission of former Rebel states. This same act designated Southern states into five military-controlled zones. The purpose of the authority given to the military in each of these zones was the strict enforcement and maintenance of Black Americans' political rights.

During Reconstruction, Black Americans were able to politically mobilize in ways that were previously outside of the bounds of possibility:

> The advent of black suffrage inspired freedmen with a millennial sense of living at the dawn of a new era. Former slaves now stood on an equal footing with whites, a black speaker told a Savannah mass meeting, and before them lay "a field, too vast for contemplation." As in 1865 blacks found countless ways of pursuing aspirations for autonomy and equality and of seizing the opportunity to press for further change. Strikes broke out during the spring of 1867 among black longshoremen in the South's major port cities and quickly spread to other workers, including Richmond, Virginia, and Selma, Alabama, restaurant workers. Hundreds of South Carolina blacks refused to pay taxes to the existing state government, and there was an unsuccessful attempt to rescue chain gang prisoners at work on Mobile, Alabama's streets. Three blacks refused to leave a whites-only Richmond streetcar, and crowds flocked to the scene shouting, "Let's have our rights." In New Orleans, groups commandeered segregated horse-drawn streetcars and drove them around the city in triumph. By midsummer, integrated transportation had come to these and other cities.
>
> (Foner 1987)

Reconstruction was a brief yet vital period for the advancement of American democracy; nearly 20% of all constitutional amendments were passed during that time. Across the entire American polity, there was an institutional and informal reconsideration of the humanity of Black Americans. Black Americans across the country asserted their agency and power in as many ways as they could. During this period, American democracy expanded and started to formally include Black Americans.

However, the democratic expressions by Black Americans amid state-sanctioned support were not met with overwhelming White positivity. Instead, the newfound recognition of Black Americans' rights was threatening to many Whites, and the expansion of democracy generated strong White opposition. The reason for this opposition rested directly on expression of the ideals of American democracy—They were racist assertions about who American democracy ought to be for. Following Reconstruction, the period known as the "Redemption" era is historically defined by White backlash in government and widespread violence. The same sentiments that reinforced chattel slavery did not simply vanish with Reconstruction.

W. E. B. Du Bois describes the perceived stakes of this new democratic enfranchisement at the time. To many Whites, the threat from Black enfranchisement was existential: "It had been insistently and firmly believed by the best thought of the South: that if political power were given to Negroes it would result virtually in the overthrow of civilization" (2017, 524). Reconstruction led to fervent, violent opposition to the expansion of civil rights for Black Americans. These sentiments were anti-democratic in their nature. They were driven toward explicitly barring Black Americans from exercising their political power. Du Bois goes on to describe this:

> The South was impelled to brute force and deliberate deception in dealing with [Black Americans] because it had been astonished and disappointed not by Black's failure, but by his success and promise of greater success. (2017, 584)

Threat stretched beyond individual responses among White Americans. Those who acted on their anti-Black ideas and opposition to Reconstruction collectively organized. During the Redemption period, paramilitary groups began forming to harass and intimidate Black Americans and White sympathizers. Hate groups such as the Ku Klux Klan and the Red Shirts also garnered significant followings and exponential upticks in membership during this time in direct reaction to Black enfranchisement. Often improperly viewed simply as groups that mobilized to individually attack and intimidate Black Americans, these groups colluded to prevent Black Americans from participating in politics in a direct effort to keep them in a marginalized position in American society:

> The Klan was political in purpose, that the Klan's activities were aimed "against the Negro as a citizen-one attempting to be a voter and at times, the social equal of other men—rather than against the Negro as a violator of law or the infringer upon the rights of other men."
>
> (Shapiro 1964)

When the Klan first emerged onto the political scene post-Reconstruction, its express intention was to continue Black disenfranchisement by any means necessary. Put more directly, there was a want to return to the system of chattel slavery. The struggle for Black human rights was one that immediately took on a political role in the electoral system:

> The Klan attempted to create an atmosphere of terror in which Negro voters would be eliminated and victory in a crucial contest thereby assured for the Democrats. . . . Activity by the Klan in 1868 was closely associated the Democratic Party. It is impossible in many places to separate the violence engaged in by groups of Democrats from that of organized Klan's. In 1868 the Klan was a new organization in South Carolina. . . . The objectives of the Klan were clearly political. Confessed members avowed that the Klan aimed at the prevention of Negro voting and the disruption of the Union League.
>
> (Shapiro 1964)

Crucially, the Klan did not emerge out of fringe elements of the White South. It was a direct outgrowth of the racial threat that the White American public felt from the recent advancement of Black political rights—which, importantly, was the simple recognition of Black humanity and autonomy, nothing more (depicted in figure 2.1).

Extending onto the national stage of politics, Ulysses S. Grant recognized the Klan's central political goal of subjugating Black Americans by preventing participation. He announced his concern to the general American public in a special message. He stated that this goal was

> [b]y force and terror to prevent all political action not in accord with the views of the members; to deprive colored citizens of the right to bear arms

and of the right to a free ballot; to suppress schools in which colored children were taught; and to reduce the colored people to a condition closely akin to that of slavery.

("Special Message: The American Presidency Project," Peters and Woolley)

Figure 2.1 The Union as it was. The lost cause worse than slavery.

Figure credit: Library of Congress.

In reaction to the mounting support for the Klan and rampant anti-Black violence and murder, Grant worked to pass the Enforcement Act of 1870. This is colloquially known as either the Civil Rights Act of 1870 or the First Ku Klux Klan Act. The specific verbiage of the legislation "provided criminal penalties for individuals attempting to prevent African Americans from voting by using or threatening to use violence or engaging in other tactics" (Lynch 2021). That the national government took it upon itself to enforce Black political rights—and protect people from state and local violence—is a clear indicator of how rampant this violence was, and also how unprotected Black Americans were. Again, this was greeted with backlash.

Though it was passed rather quickly, the Enforcement Act was met with violent resistance:

> Whatever the constitutional and partisan ramifications of this legislation, it ran head-on into a long tradition of southern lawlessness . . . [Southern conservatives] accused federal judges of sending men to prison for no other crime than the exercise of their political rights under the Constitution. Southern Democrats believed indictments stemmed from personal and political vengeance rather than actual wrongdoing and that perjured witnesses and packed juries ensured convictions. This overblown rhetoric turned federal prisons into Bastilles and Justice Department officials and army officers into Persian satraps. The impassioned denunciations of the Enforcement Acts did not reflect their actual operation. US district attorneys and marshals confronted the same problems faced by state and local officials. Arresting Klansmen at first provided Republicans with some security, but many of the leaders successfully evaded capture. Bands of desperadoes intimidated deputy marshals and even assassinated witnesses. (Rable 2007)

Formalizing Black Disenfranchisement

There were concerted means of barring Black Americans' democratic enfranchisement through formal functions of government and policy. Immediately following Reconstruction, White opposition to Black enfranchisement led to legislating anti-democratic means of barring and disincentivizing Black participation. These codified policies were manifestations of the same anti-Blackness expressed through individuals and the Klan. They were simply consolidated into stronger, systematic forms of discrimination.

> In the 1890s, a generation after the great expansion in black voting and office-holding, legislatures and constitutional conventions controlled by white southern Democrats disenfranchised the South's black adult males, extinguishing voting rights for the great majority of African Americans.
> (Valelly 2004)

This same opposition found fertile ground in President Andrew Johnson's leadership due to the strong states' rights emphasis in his political ideology:

> Johnson had supported Lincoln's call to emancipate the slaves but viewed the role of the federal government in a starkly different light. Where Lincoln believed that the central government had an obligation to defend the integrity of the Union, individual rights, and the rule of law, Johnson was an unyielding proponent of states' rights and tight limits on federal power. He argued that the federal government should not interfere in local politics, even if the failure to do so left the freedmen disenfranchised.
> (Horwitz and Anderson 2009)

The conservative motivation of Johnson led to a situation where Black Americans were slated to lose their newfound enfranchisement. This is exactly what happened. As a president, he facilitated the early erosion of democratic rights gained by Black Americans. His presidency facilitated a retrenchment of White supremacy across the nation. The court case *Minor v. Happersett* further eroded Black Americans' democratic capabilities: "In Minor, the Supreme Court refused to rule that the 14th or 15th Amendments—or any other law or part of the Constitution—created a fundamental right to vote" (Smith, Anderson, and Rackaway 2015). As such, those who were formally granted citizenship were not also granted the ability to exercise their voting rights. In effect, citizenship did not equal voting rights per this Court ruling.

Additionally, in a series of informal ways under Johnson, Southern White Americans worked to disenfranchise Black Americans. This disenfranchisement set the stage for the end of Reconstruction—and a readvancement of White supremacy in the United States that formally occurred in the Compromise of 1877.

The Compromise led to the removal of federal military protection of Black Americans from White Americans across the South. As a result of the removal, there was little recourse to the retrenchment of Black disenfranchisement across Southern states. It led to the rampant spread of anti-Black violence across the region, committed by ordinary White Americans and government officials alike:

> One year later, the presidential election produced an electoral deadlock. In the end, Hayes assumed the presidency, but he owed southern members of Congress a favor for supporting him over Democrat Samuel Tilden. Hayes' part of the deal included ending Reconstruction and establishing local control in the South. The era of Jim Crow was born. Southern state governments were free to institute racially motivated laws including those that restricted African American ballot access. The arguments about access to the ballot for African Americans took on an urgent quality as a number of states crafted new laws. Thinly veiled by the pretense of neutrality, these laws often stripped the franchise from African American voters.
>
> (Smith, Anderson, and Rackaway 2015)

White opposition to Black enfranchisement within the South led to the establishment of policies that, again, in a different form from chattel slavery, disenfranchised and dehumanized Black Americans. Literacy tests, poll taxes, grandfather clauses, and White primaries are some of the most well known of these efforts. All were used to prevent Black Americans from participating in politics. Literacy tests were motivated by overwhelming, unshakable opposition to Black Americans engaging in politics. Poll taxes were another institutional form of anti-democratic restriction of political participation for Black Americans. They required the payment of a flat tax, which many Black Americans were unable to pay. One man from Georgia in the 1930s articulated his inability to exercise his right to vote: "Do you know I've never voted in my life, never been able to exercise my right as a citizen because of the poll tax? . . . I can't pay a poll tax, can't have a voice in my own government" (Federal Writers' Project, Regional Staff 2016). Southern states also used grandfather clauses, which gave voting rights to only those who had the ability to vote within a certain, arbitrary period—for example, January 1, 1867, which was prior to Reconstruction and thereby barred all Black Americans from participating (Pildes 2000).

These anti-democratic ideas reverberated throughout American politics in the Redemption period. Mississippi Senator James K. Vardaman asserted this directly: "I am just as much opposed to Booker T. Washington as a voter with all his Anglo-Saxon re-enforcements as I am to the cocoanut-headed, chocolate-colored typical little coon who blacks my shoes every morning. Neither is fit to perform the supreme function of citizenship" (Pollack 1947). For many White elites and the mass White public, uniform Black disenfranchisement was necessary for their sense of self. There were no exceptions to this rule. As the effort to bar Black Americans from exercising their political abilities mounted, elites took cues from one another and built out networks of anti-democratic policy.

Vardaman was among the most prominent of these anti-Black voices. He worked to maintain Mississippi's Constitution of 1890. This constitution was one of the first to introduce poll taxes and literacy tests, which then served as an outline for other states to follow. The explicit language of the constitution is presented next. The parameters for the literacy test appeared in section 241, which contains an immense number of stipulations for Mississippians' permission to vote.

> Every male inhabitant of this State, except idiots, insane persons and Indians not taxed, who is a citizen of the United States, twenty-one years old and upwards, who has resided in this State two years, and one year in the election district, or in the incorporated city or town, in which he offers to vote, and who is duly registered as provided in this article, and who has never been convicted of bribery, burglary, theft, arson, obtaining money or goods under false pretenses, perjury, forgery, embezzlement or bigamy, and who has paid, on or before the first day of February of the year in which he shall offer to vote, all taxes which may have been legally required of him, and which he has had an opportunity of paying according to law, for the two preceding years, and who shall produce to the officers holding the election satisfactory evidence that he has paid said taxes, is declared to be a qualified elector; but any minister of the gospel in charge of an organized church shall be entitled to vote after six months residence in the election district, if otherwise qualified.
>
> ("The Mississippi Constitution of 1890 as Originally Adopted," n.d.)

Shortly after this section comes the outline for poll taxes, in section 243:

> A uniform poll tax of two dollars, to be used in aid of the common schools, and for no other purpose, is hereby imposed on every male inhabitant of this State between the ages of twenty-one and sixty years, except persons who are deaf and dumb or blind, or who are maimed by loss of hand or foot; said tax to be a lien only upon taxable property. The board of supervisors of any county may, for the purpose of aiding the common schools in that county, increase the poll tax in said county, but in no case shall the entire poll tax exceed in any one year three dollars on each poll. No criminal proceedings shall be allowed to enforce the collection of the poll tax.
>
> ("The Mississippi Constitution of 1890 as Originally Adopted," n.d.)

Despite the immense amount of jargon used to shirk the explicitly anti-Black and anti-democratic nature of these voting requirements, Southern elites were well aware of their intention.

Vardaman offered praise for this constitution in 1900. He asserted the clear purpose behind it, refusing to mince his words: "There is no use to equivocate or lie about the matter. Mississippi's constitutional convention of 1890 was held for no other purpose than to eliminate the nigger from politics—not the ignorant and vicious, as some apologists would have you believe, but the nigger. Let the world know it just as it is.... In Mississippi, we have in our constitution legislated against the racial peculiarities of the Negro.... When that device fails, we will resort to something else" (McMillen 1990).

The race-neutral language of Mississippi's Constitution offered a framework for other states to emulate. South Carolina adopted similar language in 1895, and Oklahoma in 1907. Regarding South Carolina's Constitution, D. D. Wallace observed the clear connection it had to Mississippi's:

> The Mississippi plan or something better was all that was in sight or ever had any chance of success [for the South Carolina Constitution of 1895]. The essence of this plan as originated in the present constitution of Mississippi is that the registration officer is allowed to refuse registration to illiterate voters whom he judges unable to understand any clause of the constitution he may read to them, and to accord the right to those whom he judges able to understand. The object is, of course, to disfranchise the

> ignorant negro, while retaining the illiterate white vote, and in this the scheme has not failed.
>
> (Wallace 1896)

These policy changes also lent themselves to replication across states on a deeper level when Mississippi's constitutional amendments were protected by the Supreme Court. In the 1898 case *Williams v. Mississippi*, the plaintiff, Henry Williams, asserted that Mississippi's voting laws defined in the 1890 constitution were intended to suppress the Black vote.

In yet another iteration of reinforcing Black disenfranchisement, the Court ruled 9–0 rejecting Williams's argument. Joseph McKenna's opinion provides a summary of the Court's view: "The constitution of Mississippi and its statutes do not on their face discriminate between the races, and it has not been shown that their actual administration was evil; only that evil was possible under them" (United States Congress 1900). Black political disenfranchisement worked its way up from local to state levels to federal codification.

Historian Rayford Logan coined the term *the Nadir* to describe the end of Reconstruction as the point when "the Negro's status in the United States [reached its lowest point]" (Logan 1997). Scientific racism and phrenology emerged at the same time to justify the continued brutality toward Black Americans. Anti-Black violence rose exponentially. Lynchings, beatings, and other random acts of violence occurred on a large scale. Ida B. Wells recounts the direct, political orientation of all the anti-Black violence happening in this period as a reaction to the formal political enfranchisement of Black Americans:

> Just as the lynch-law regime came to a close in the West, a new mob movement started in the South. This was wholly political, its purpose being to suppress the colored vote by intimidation and murder. Thousands of assassins banded together under the name of Ku Klux Klans, "Midnight Raiders," "Knights of the Golden Circle," et cetera. They spread a reign of terror by beating, shooting and killing colored people. In a few years, the purpose was accomplished, and the black vote was suppressed.
>
> (Barnett 2002)

The mass-scale anti-Black sentiments that were expressed in light of Reconstruction were bolstered and encouraged by Southern political elites. These elites went to extensive lengths to further systematize anti-Black sentiment. Ben Tillman, a Southern Democratic senator and one-term governor of South Carolina, asserted this explicitly: "We have done our level best [to prevent blacks from voting] . . . we have scratched our heads to find out how we could eliminate the last one of them. We stuffed ballot boxes. We shot them. We are not ashamed of it" (Logan 1997).

Every one of these instances demonstrates how central the question of Black enfranchisement was to the way that White Americans processed their ideas about democracy. It was not enough that Whites had civil and political rights; they needed to subvert the autonomy of Black Americans to fully buy in to democracy. When Black Americans gained political enfranchisement, many Southern Whites took it as an affront to their position in democracy. They saw their power decrease.

Because American democracy was established amid the mounting solidification of chattel slavery, many White Americans read the democratic principles to be a system that existed to elevate their status. In short, they believed in a Herrenvolk democracy, which represented Whites exclusively (Vickery 1974; T. Anderson 2019).

Citizens and elites alike made strong efforts to advance their idea of the United States as a Herrenvolk democracy. In North Carolina in 1898, the White residents of Wilmington County went as far as to publish a White Declaration of Independence:

> Believing that the Constitution of the United States contemplated a government to be carried on by an enlightened people; believing that its framers did not anticipate the *enfranchisement* of an ignorant population of African origin; and believing that the men of the State of North Carolina who joined in forming the Union did not contemplate for their descendants a subjection to an inferior race . . . [w]e, the undersigned citizens of the city of Wilmington and county of New Hanover, do hereby declare that we will no longer be ruled, and will never again be ruled, by men of African origin. This condition we have in part endured because we felt that the consequences of the war of secession were such to deprive us of the fair consideration of many of our countrymen.
>
> (Raleigh News and Observer 1898)

The writers of this declaration specifically point out that it was Black enfranchisement they had such strong opposition to. Anti-Black, anti-democratic attitudes were inflamed in the midst of Reconstruction, leading to the Redemption era. And this mass opposition that was coordinated between citizens and elites ushered in the Jim Crow era. Quite well known in American history, Jim Crow laws were defined by widespread, institutional disenfranchisement of Black Americans within the South.

Institutionalizing Black Disenfranchisement

The era of Jim Crow is defined by the alignment between ordinary White Americans and elites in their deepening of restricting Black Americans' human rights. Bridging the Black Nadir and Redemption era, when violence against Black Americans was rampant, Epperly et al. (2020) provide an explanation for the shift toward using the state capacity to bar Black Americans from politics:

> Ad hoc and often violent suppression is more likely when internal political or state capacity to implement formal legal techniques is lacking, and when external actors present constraints. When internal capacities increase and external constraints decrease, elites will choose legislative, centralized, typically non-violent approaches to suppression. . . .
>
> The use of violence reflected both a lack of political and state capacity and the federal stance as guarantor of black voting rights. Once internal capacities were present and external constraints were removed, Southern Democrats shifted to centralized bureaucratically-implemented voter suppression, which reduced political lynchings.
>
> (Epperly et al. 2020)

At the onset of Reconstruction, some political elites opposed the institutionalizing anti-democratic, anti-Black policy. However, over time, with both pressure from the public and the increased capacity of federal and state governments to engage in suppression efforts, Jim Crow soon became the law of the land. In other words, the necessary conditions were met for the rebirth of state-sanctioned Black dehumanization. More specifically, this rebirth can be defined by the rolling back of the political power of Black Americans.

The heart of the matter was democracy. It was about who ought to be represented and have their voices heard among the American public.

Black Americans' political agency, to many White Americans at the time of Reconstruction, sat in diametrical opposition to their views of what American democracy was. For some, the United States was explicitly a Herrenvolk democracy. To others, the consideration of Black American suffrage was implicitly uncomfortable. Political elites helped to encourage and facilitate both of these sets of attitudes—the lion's share of these elites were Southern conservative Democrats.

Over time, anti-Black disenfranchisement became more institutionalized. Reconstruction caused a significant backlash that led to further codification of the dehumanization of Black Americans in systems of government. Jim Crow represented a deepening of White supremacy. The rise of Jim Crow was defined by "the enormous promise of emancipation, the revolution of Reconstruction (national rebirth, birthright citizenship, the franchise, black institution building, and perhaps the most promising and most threatening development of all, the sudden expression of black political power), and its tragic unraveling at the hands of a recalcitrant South and an ever more indifferent North" (Gates 2019).

Adolph Reed Jr. also goes about articulating the institutional logic of Jim Crow:

> Segregation, Lofgren argues, was not a major focal point for southern or black politics until it became an element of reassertion of planter and merchant class power after the defeat of Reconstruction and the Populist insurgency at the end of the nineteenth century. As a systematic social order, its purpose was to impose through law and social regulation a doctrine of white supremacy that established boundaries on the politically thinkable in much the same way that anti-communism would nationally during the post–World War II decades. It is worthy of note as well that the victorious ruling class didn't impose the regime in most places until blacks (and many poor or working-class whites) had been taken out of the political equation by disfranchising them.
>
> (Reed 2022)

The logic of Jim Crow was the prevention of the political rights of Black Americans. Its express purpose was to consistently dehumanize Black Americans while also reinforcing entry barriers to the political system. On both of these fronts, it was a distinctly anti-democratic system that was a direct outgrowth of slavery. The connection between these two eras cannot and should not be understated. They feed directly into one another. The intention of the deepening anti-democratic informal and formal institutions was to replicate the same White supremacist political and social system that had been established in the time of chattel slavery.

The long arc of White supremacy over Black Americans—from chattel slavery to informal, rampant violence to Jim Crow—often fails to capture the main influence behind its maintenance: the perception of the racial threat that Black Americans posed, specifically in the context of democracy, where Black Americans could exercise their voices and thereby defend their humanity. Jim Crow was part of an intention. If it was not Jim Crow, it would have been another institution that limited the capacity of Black Americans. After the first Jim Crow law passed, other anti-democratic systems cropped up to disenfranchise:

> [The first Jim Crow legislation passed in 1891] also provided for the first effective enforcement of the poll tax requirement for voting and made more generally applicable the stringent registration and election laws of 1889–1890. Therefore, it would appear that the passage of bona fide "Jim Crow" legislation went hand in hand with the adoption of indirect restrictions on Negro suffrage. This action was probably considered necessary in view of the avowed opposition of Negro leaders to such legislation.
>
> (Folmsbee 1949)

The legal repeal of Jim Crow did not rid the United States of the anti-Black sentiment that pervaded the public. It was institutionalized, not limited to the formal systems that it birthed. This idea has been described metaphorically as "old poison, new bottles," meaning that the same negative attitudes that were deeply held and supported in American society were simply placed into different institutions. The reaction to *Brown v. Board of Education II* decades later showed this to be true. The same anti-Black sentiments that came out following Reconstruction reemerged in reaction to another moment of Black enfranchisement. Below is an editorial comment made in the *Daily News* in Jackson, Mississippi, in the wake of the *Brown v. Board II* decision in 1954.

> Human blood may stain Southern soil in many places because of this decision, but the dark red stains of that blood will be on the marble steps of the United States Supreme Court building.
>
> (Mohamed 2022)

The threat of violence here is exactly in line with other statements made by Southern White elites in the wake of Black enfranchisement in the form of the Reconstruction amendments. Elite Harry Byrd, governor of Virginia, began immediately organizing resistance to the ruling: "If we can organize the Southern States for massive resistance to this order, I think that in time the rest of the country will realize that racial integration is not going to be accepted in the South" (Day 2015).

After this moment, the battle for Black Americans' civil rights raged on. Some initially viewed it as a victory, but protections for Black citizens' rights had not yet been codified in law. *Brown* also activated more overt White resentment across the country that had since been dormant or simply kept more private. In institutions that were required to integrate Black students, White parents and school administrators reacted with violent aggression. One of the most egregious of these reactions came in Prince Edward County, Virginia. On May 1, 1959, the entire county closed its public school system and opened private schools exclusively for White students funded by state taxes and tax credits (Brookover 1993).

The Long Civil Rights Movement for Black Americans' Rights

Reactions to the *Brown* decision were clear indicators that the struggle was not going to conclude even with federal institutions ruling. Confidence in the Supreme Court eroded in light of *Brown*. Locally and nationally, anti-Black, anti-democratic sentiment led to similar instances like those in Prince Edward County. Droves of White Americans worked to prevent integration for as long as they could.

Many saw these reactions as indicators to continue pressing civil rights legislation. With the continuation of a groundswell of Black activism, lobbying efforts, and pressure from some political elites (especially President Lyndon Johnson), the Civil Rights Act was eventually passed in 1964. It was the most sweeping legislation protecting civil rights since the Reconstruction acts nearly a century prior. The protections outlined in the Act prevented discrimination in public places and among employers, facilitating the integration of schools and other public spaces.

Bill Moyers's reflection on the passing of the Civil Rights Act offers insight into what President Johnson correctly perceived as a Southern political realignment:

> The night that the Civil Rights Act of 1964 was passed, I found [Lyndon Johnson] in the bedroom, exceedingly depressed. The headline of the bulldog edition of the *Washington Post* said, "Johnson Signs Civil Rights Act." The airwaves were full of discussions about how unprecedented this was and historic, and yet he was depressed. I asked him why.
>
> He said, "I think we've just delivered the South to the Republican Party for the rest of my life, and yours."
>
> (Gittinger and Fisher 2004; Gold 2009; Johnson 2014)

Resistance to Black Americans' civil rights took shape in reorienting the country's political map. Previously, the South was solidly Democratic, due to the strong control of conservative Democrats, who often mobilized White voters by appealing to the racial threat from Black Americans. This support echoed from Reconstruction onward. After the passing of this legislation, Southern conservative representatives defected from the Democratic Party to the Republican Party because of Democrats' new advocacy for Black civil rights.

Empirically, scholars have found grand support for the idea that the transition among voters was entirely due to anti-Black sentiment: "We conclude that defection among racially conservative whites just after Democrats introduce sweeping Civil Rights legislation explains essentially all of the party's losses in the region. We find essentially no role for either income growth in the region or (non-race-related) policy preferences in explaining why Democrats 'lost' the South" (Kuziemko and Washington 2018).

Civil rights of Black Americans, as they were established in the Act of 1964, were persistently in the crosshairs of GOP elites. Richard Nixon, in a secret meeting with Strom Thurmond, asserted that it was his intention to "retard civil rights enforcement" (Perlstein 2009). Over time, this anti-Black resentment was fueled by political strategizing. The Southern Strategy, used by the Nixon campaign, was the most prominent of these national approaches to weaponizing anti-Black sentiments for the sake of politics. Coverage of this idea in *The New York Times* in 1970 brought out the clear intention even at that point in time:

> Sterilized and scientific as are the terms by which Kevin Phillips plots the emerging Republican majority, its common denominator is hostility to blacks and browns among slipping Democrats and abandonment of the Democratic party because of its identification with the colored minorities.
>
> (Boyd 1970)

This eventually became a blueprint for Republican political strategizing, especially for but not limited to the South. Republican elites adapted these messages over time. Norms of discourse changed in the American public, so elites adapted their language. The appeals were still able to work because the underlying senses of threat remain—they are still used in contemporary political discourse (Mendelberg 2001; Thompson and Busby 2021).

Lee Atwater in 1981 described the evolution of the use of this terminology in a now infamous statement:

> You start out in 1954 by saying, "Nigger, nigger, nigger." By 1968 you can't say "nigger"—that hurts you, backfires. So you say stuff like, uh, forced busing, states' rights, and all that stuff, and you're getting so abstract. Now, you're talking about cutting taxes, and all these things you're talking about are totally economic things and a byproduct of them is, blacks get hurt worse than whites.
>
> (Perlstein 2012)

While these strategy changes were being made, ideology was also being adapted in the Republican Party. At length, Jacquelyn Hall describes how these changes occurred:

> Reworking that narrative for their own purposes, these new "color-blind conservatives" ignored the complexity and dynamism of the [civil rights] movement, its growing focus on structural inequality, and its "radical reconstruction" goals. Instead, they insisted that color blindness—defined as the elimination of racial classifications and the establishment of formal equality before the law—was the movement's singular objective, the principle for which King and the Brown decision, in particular, stood. They admitted that racism, understood as individual bigotry, did exist—"in the distant past" and primarily in the South—a concession that surely would

> have taken the Old Right by surprise. But after legalized Jim Crow was dismantled, such irrationalities diminished to insignificance.
>
> In the absence of overtly discriminatory laws and with the waning of conscious bias, American institutions became basically fair. Free to compete in a market-driven society, African Americans thereafter bore the onus of their own failure or success. If stark group inequalities persisted, black attitudes, behavior, and family structures were to blame. The race-conscious remedies devised in the late 1960s and 1970s to implement the movement's victories, such as majority-minority voting districts, minority business set-asides, affirmative action, and two-way busing, were not the handiwork of the authentic civil rights movement at all. . . . In fact, the remedies themselves became the cause of our problems, creating resentment among whites, subverting self-reliance among blacks, and encouraging "balkanization" when nationalism and assimilation should be our goals. It was up to color-blind conservatives to restore the original purpose of civil rights laws, which was to prevent isolated acts of wrongdoing against individuals, rather than, as many civil rights activists and legal experts claimed, to redress present, institutionalized manifestations of historical injustices against blacks as a group.
>
> (Hall 2005)

In the decades that followed the civil rights movement, "color-blind conservatism" was an ideology adopted by the GOP for strategic purposes that dovetailed with the persistent use of racial messaging among party elites. This primarily took off on a national level from the 1970s through the 1990s. The ideology offered cover for elites to consistently use anti-Black messaging, often in implicit ways and with plausible deniability. Continuing with the concepts articulated by Atwater, the GOP could turn out base voters by making racial appeals, and when criticized for the use of these messages, they could shield themselves by claiming that they were not referring to race in their statements. Most politically savvy people, both oppositional to and supportive of the anti-Black message, knew what was meant, but elites could attempt to claim nonracial intention.

> As one longtime student of welfare reform observed, Republicans were exploiting the anger of middle-class taxpayers who believed that their tax dollars were going to the undeserving poor, particularly "young women, without education, who are long-term dependents and whose dependency

> is passed on from generation to generation." The unspoken subtext of this outlook was the belief that "these women are inner-city substance-abusing blacks spawning a criminal class."
>
> (Carter 1999)

This strategy was used to mobilize and turn out racially resentful White Americans. It kept in motion the anti-Black, anti-democratic sentiments that had existed from the inception of color-blind conservatism, and it shifted the conversation away from who Americans thought to be deserving of government assistance and, on a deeper level, who they thought ought to be represented.

At their core, these anti-Black sentiments were dispersed for the decades that followed the civil rights movement. They remained under the surface and implicit, however, and emerged in a strong, albeit initially overlooked, reaction to the election of Barack Obama, who was very much an actualization of the long civil rights movement that had begun in Reconstruction.

3

The Big Flip in Recent Years

Obama's victory in 2008 was momentous. He overcame seemingly impossible odds to win the presidency and ushered in a new era in American politics. The conclusion of the 2008 presidential election indicated that times were changing for droves of Americans. Media coverage and focus were rightfully on the excitement as described above. Jubilation seemed to pervade the polity:

> African-Americans wept and danced in the streets on Tuesday night, declaring that a once-reluctant nation had finally lived up to its democratic promise. Strangers of all colors exulted in small towns and big cities. And white voters marveled at what they had wrought in turning a page on the country's bitter racial history. "It brought tears to my eyes to see the lines," said Bob Haskins, a black maintenance worker at an Atlanta church, where scores of college students voted on Tuesday. "For these young folks, this is a calling. Everything that Martin Luther King talked about is coming true today."
>
> (Swarns 2008)

Americans celebrated through the night into the morning on the night of the election; many schools were canceled or delayed the following day. These emotions were palpable and reasonably focused on in the national narrative. However, just below the surface, there was a bubbling undercurrent of angry Americans. They were angry about the same thing this other large share of the country was elated about—the newly elected president's identity.

Obama was elected on November 4, 2008. The following week, something else happened that received no attention within the larger conversation of politics. The main White supremacist website at the time, Stormfront, crashed because it could not handle the exponential uptick in traffic from new users. The website for the League of the South, a secessionist group, experienced a jump in hits from fifty thousand to three hundred thousand directly following the election (Jonsson 2008). *Something* was happening.

The Big Flip. Andrew Ifedapo Thompson, Oxford University Press. © Oxford University Press (2026).
DOI: 10.1093/9780197822173.003.0003

A sizable, albeit quiet, portion of Americans were being driven toward extreme White supremacist ideas. Why? The answer is clear, given the timing of the increase in website traffic: because Obama represented a change they thought was coming to America—and did not like it in the least. To many, Obama was the culmination of the racial component of the great American experiment. He was the big flip embodied as a sole individual. I map the history of this idea and the subsequent fallout from Obama's legacy within this chapter. Both of these components set the stage for how deeply tied the big flip has become to American democracy.

The Great American Experiment

There is a storied history of the connection between race and democracy within the United States. Since its founding, the idea that the country is a "great experiment" has persisted:

> The social, and especially the political institutions of the United States, have, for the whole of the current century, been the subject in Europe, not merely of curious speculation, but of the deepest interest. We have been regarded as engaged in trying a great experiment, involving not merely the future fate and welfare of this Western continent, but the hopes and prospects of the whole human race. Is it possible for a Government to be permanently maintained without privileged classes, without a standing army, and without either hereditary or self-appointed rulers? Is the democratic principle of equal rights, general suffrage, and government by a majority, capable of being carried into practical operation, and that, too, over a large extent of country?
>
> (New-York Daily Tribune 1860)

Despite the grand irony that this statement comes just years before the Civil War, some of this sentiment taps into the fact that the United States was one of the first heterogeneous/multiracial democracies in the West. There was a variety of competing interests and perspectives in the country that were not represented in other democracies established around the same time in Europe. One core question on the persistence of the American experiment is this: Can the country persist and thrive when there are so many different ideas, viewpoints, and perspectives present?

Over time, there have been multiple instances where the American experiment has been put under strain. At these moments, competing interests within the public have been perceived to be potentially too strong to reconcile; the role of race has been central to many of these moments—the Civil War, Reconstruction, and the civil rights movement, just to name a few. Within the background of these historical moments was a simple yet powerful point. The contention that motivated these moments was the expansion of rights for racially marginalized Americans, namely Black Americans. The Civil War was fought over slavery and the enfranchisement of Black Americans; Reconstruction and the civil rights movement were the continuation of the same struggle, with the explicit intention of further realizing the political rights of Black Americans. These previous historical moments considered the representation of the preexisting racial population in the country; in short, they were struggles over how different racial groups *should* be thought about and treated throughout the United States. None of these events threatened the composition of the country. They did not deal with groups changing size nor the political implications of those changing sizes.

This is how the big flip functions as a historical departure from the function of race in the United States. It represents a realization of the United States as a melting pot, which initially started as an abstraction in American culture.

The Melting Pot

One of the first major cultural descriptions of racial demographic change in America was a metaphor: the melting pot. The idea was used to describe how there was, and would continue to be, a blending of race and culture as time marched on. Central to the melting pot metaphor was that, eventually, the United States would be a cornucopia of racially mixed people. Americans would essentially be indistinguishable from one another because of the racial blending that was predicted to occur.

The origin of the idea of the melting pot comes from a 1908 play by the same name (Kraus 1999; Zangwill 2017). Through these ideas and the mythology that surrounded the melting pot, the multicultural orientation of the United States started to become more apparent. However, for many decades, on a national level, this idea was an abstraction. It did not hold water in the minds of many Americans. Though they might have agreed that the melting was slated to occur in the future, their family and friends did not change drastically; they lived in relatively racially homogeneous communities, and their racial lives were stable. Starting in the 1990s, significantly more coverage and attention were given to the actual future of racial demographics.

This metaphor for the changing landscape of the United States took off in the 1990s (Fuchs 1990; McDonald 2007; Jacoby 2009). *Time Magazine* gave a cover to this idea, presenting an image of a woman who represented a multi-hyphenate, mixed future of the country. This piece covered the changing landscape of the United States through interracial marriage and immigration. It identified both of these dynamics as causes of the "new face" of the country. For example, an article describes issues of racial discrimination that interracial couples experience:

> Intolerance need not be that blatant to inflict wounds. If Tony Jeffreys, 34, and Alice Sakuda Flores, 28, have a child, that hypothetical Japanese-Filipino-German-Irish-Buddhist-Catholic-American will become flesh and blood. In their one year of marriage, Tony says, "I've heard friends say stupid stuff about Asians right in front of Alice. It is real hypocritical because a lot of them have Mexican or black girlfriends or wives." Sometimes the more subtle the rejection, the sharper the sting. Says Candy Mills, 29, the daughter of black and Native American parents, who is married to Gabe Grosz, a white European immigrant: "I know that people are tolerating me, not accepting me."
>
> Such pain is evidence that America has yet to harvest the full rewards of its founding principles. The land of immigrants may be giving way to a land of hyphenations, but the hyphen still divides even as it compounds. Those who intermarry have perhaps the strongest sense of what it will take to return America to an unhyphenated whole. "It's American culture that we all share," says Mills. "We should capitalize on that." Perhaps her two Native American–black-white-Hungarian-French-Catholic-Jewish-American children will lead the way.
>
> (*Time Magazine* 1993).

The ultimate point that this narrative leads to is the melting pot. At some point in the future, there would be so many "hyphenated" Americans that their hyphens would not matter. Despite larger cultural agreement on the legitimacy of this idea, it was hotly debated in public. The melting pot implied assimilation. Under this view, Americans would abandon their different—and apparently divisive—cultural identities for the larger moniker of "American" after enough melting.

The contrasting perspective that emerged at the same time was multiculturalism, which today aligns closely with views of diversity and inclusion. Multiculturalism states that there should not necessarily be a blending and melting as the country diversifies, but that each cultural group brings something unique to bear in the United States. America as a *salad bowl* was the alternative metaphor that this perspective advanced. It sat in direct contrast to the melting pot. The difference between these two perspectives about the changing country became a political battleground at the time; the question they both asked was "How is America going to look as time goes on?"

Arthur Schlesinger was a major thought leader in advocating for the idea of the melting pot, arguing against multiculturalism in his book *The Disuniting of America: Reflections on a Multicultural Society*:

> In 1974, after testimony from ethnic spokesmen denouncing the melting pot as a conspiracy to homogenize America, Congress passed the Ethnic Heritage Studies Program Act—a statute that, by applying the ethnic ideology to all Americans, compromised the historic right of Americans to decide their ethnic identities for themselves. The act ignored those millions of Americans—surely a majority—who refused identification with any particular ethnic group.
>
> The ethnic upsurge (it can hardly be called a revival because it was unprecedented) began as a gesture of protest against the Anglocentric culture. It became a cult, and today it threatens to become a counter-revolution against the original theory of America as "one people," a common culture, a single nation.
>
> (Schlesinger 1998, 56)

Within a later part of his book, he asserts even more overtly his support for advancing the idea of the melting pot:

> The American synthesis has an inevitable Anglo-Saxon coloration, but it is no longer an exercise in Anglo-Saxon domination. The republic embodies ideals that transcend ethnic, religious, and political lines. It is an experiment, reasonably successful for a while, in creating a common identity for people of diverse races, religions, languages, cultures. But the experiment

> can continue to succeed only so long as Americans continue to believe in the goal. If the republic now turns away from Washington's old goal of "one people," what is its future?—disintegration of the national community, apartheid, Balkanization, tribalization?
>
> (Schlesinger 1998)

Schlesinger offered a strong reaction to the diversification of the United States, instead arguing for one where assimilation to an "American" identity was key to keeping the country together. And like the arguments he leveled, much of the conversation around American racial demographic change in the 1990s was high theory. It was speculative in nature. Academics and public intellectuals argued about how the country might change in the coming years and how these changes ought to be considered, with little evidence. The larger American public, while clearly discussed in the debate, was not as present in the conversation because it was not being held in a wider setting. More to this point, many Americans at the time did not care because there were no real stakes.

For these reasons, they could not conceptualize how the United States might look different in the future. In the 1990s, the melting pot future was quite distant to many Americans. This perspective was soon to change. Two key events strongly shifted the American public's perception of racial demographic change, making the big flip much more real and salient. The first event happened via the 2010 Census and the projections that surrounded it, and the second event was the election of Barack Obama.

Measuring the Big Flip through the Census

The year 2000 was the initial moment that the changing nature of the United States became real for some, but not many. Census analysts made large projections about how the country was slated to shift in racial demographics (Grieco 2001; Prewitt 2002). These sentiments were calcified a decade later, with projections following the subsequent census. When the 2010 Census data were first released, the information they provided was fairly innocuous to the public. The highlighted results touched on the general orientation of the country along gender, racial, and age-related lines. At the point of its release, there were a few controversies — namely, counting undocumented immigrants and the use of the word *Negro* in the survey for Black Americans (Stonecipher 2010; D. Cohn 2010). However, once more analyses of the data were conducted, something revealing about racial demographics was discovered: Researchers found that if trends continued as they had over the previous decade, White Americans were projected to become a numerical minority by mid-century (Lopez 2005; Census 2011). This came as a surprise to experts, policymakers, and eventually the mass American public. It was the first real indicator of the big flip.

Gradually the American public became more aware of these changes, and the inferences about the country's future came with it. The narrative of the majority-minority flip caught fire soon after analysts articulated the projections. It rose to such a level of prominence that researchers began testing how simply describing it would shift Americans' views of the world. Two psychologists, Maureen Craig and Jennifer Richeson, were among the first to test how this projected racial demographic change affected how Americans considered race. In a series of studies they conducted from 2010 to 2013, they found that White Americans would express fear and concern when they learned of these census projections. These studies also showed that White Americans primed to consider the flip expressed more negative views toward racial minorities—and that these same Americans would become more supportive of conservative ideas and policy. In short, they showed that the census projections caused White Americans to feel a sense of racial threat. The effects of their senses were nebulous. Projections shifted their attitudes, but these studies were limited in what they said about how the threat could shift ideas throughout American society. They could articulate how Americans thought about racial demographic changes, though not about how their thoughts could shift over time. Because these projections about the future of the country were simply projections when they first emerged in American discourse, the sense of racial threat they prompted did not have a "bite." White Americans expressed a feeling of threat without a place to ground it. Another event accentuated this reaction about the future. The second event, which led to an increased sense of the magnitude of racial demographic change, was the role of Barack Obama.

The Big Flip Embodied: The Legacy of Obama

The election of President Barack Obama was a monumental moment for representation in the presidency. However, in the early days of the 2008 Democratic primaries, there was skepticism about Obama's ability to win, and concern about his safety. Because he was a prominent Black candidate, many perceived him to be in grave danger among the more racist elements of the American public. Analysts expressed caution:

> "There is no question that the possibility of violence directed at presidential candidates, especially Obama, is the elephant in the middle of the room," says Peter Fenn, adjunct professor of political management at George Washington University, to describe the media's careful coverage of the issue. "There is a hypersensitivity about this issue. And in one sense, there should be because you don't want to put the idea out there. But you also get overanalysis, like with Hillary's comments about RFK [Robert F. Kennedy]."
>
> (Baram 2008)

Supporters expressed similar concerns:

> There is a hushed worry on the minds of many supporters of Senator Barack Obama, echoing in conversations from state to state, rally to rally: Will he be safe? In Colorado, two sisters say they pray daily for his safety. In New Mexico, a daughter says she persuaded her mother to still vote for Mr. Obama, even though the mother feared that winning would put him in danger. And at a rally here, a woman expressed worries that a message of hope and change, in addition to his race, made him more vulnerable to violence.
>
> (Zeleny 2008)

It was clear that Obama's racial identity was driving how Americans across the country were thinking about him and judging his candidacy. As Telser and Sears describe, these views were at the core for Democrats, both those who contested the candidacy of a Black man and those who wanted it:

> Barack Obama was unambiguously judged by his race throughout the primary season. Racial predispositions, in fact, were readily accessible when either positive or negative evaluations of Barack Obama were being expressed way back in 2007. Moreover, the racially resentful expressed these predispositions by strongly opposing his candidacy for the nomination from the campaign's onset. Yet after Obama established himself as a viable and electable candidate after Iowa, the least resentful also began to vote their racial predispositions in support for him. The upshot was

> a pattern of racialized momentum, whereby Obama's activation of the heretofore largely unnoticed liberal side of the racial resentment dimension won him the Democratic nomination.
>
> (Tesler and Sears 2010, 51)

When Obama won the Democratic primary, the feat was met with elation and a cautious optimism about the future—again, both about his candidacy and also about his safety on the national platform. Voters and political historians alike saw this as a grand moment in and of itself, regardless of what was to happen in the general election.

> Watching Obama speak, I found it hard to believe that this was the USA. I flashed back to a scene fifty-odd years ago: I was four years old, on a family trip to Florida, and caused a minor scene in a bus station when I wandered over and took a drink from the water fountain marked "Colored." (I could read the sign, but had no idea what it meant.) I'd grown up during the civil rights movement, had heard Martin Luther King speak. And here was an African-American who had risen higher than any non-white person in any Western country, and moreover had done so in a nation that has never, with the exception of the Irish John Kennedy, elected a president from even its white minorities—no Jews, no Poles, no Italians—and had nominated only one other, the hapless Michael Dukakis.
>
> (Weinberger 2008)

When Obama ultimately got into the fray of the general election, there was further doubt cast about whether he could win over Americans on the whole. Obama's race and the outward perception of it were clearly crucial to this story. Many of the concerns were projections about the views of other Americans. They stemmed from perceptions of racism. Voters were claiming that they didn't want to vote for Obama or they perceived that his chances were nil because many voters would oppose him as a Black man. Then, even in the face of his victory, there was fear that he could inevitably lose his life over vitriol and hatred. When he won the primaries, some worries were quelled. When he then won the 2008 presidential election, there was another, greater moment of triumph. Americans'—especially Black Americans'—perceptions of what was possible shifted in this one moment. Many viewed racial barriers to be overtaken once and for all; their worries about Obama's candidacy and appeal to Americans were shattered. The highest position in the country was finally opened to more Americans than it had been during any time in history.

The following day, news stations reported mass elation among the public. Obama's victory radiated across the nation and the world. *The New York Times* cover read "Obama: Racial Barrier Falls in Decisive Victory." Further, in the same front-page article, the first sentence read, "Barack Hussein Obama was elected the 44th president of the United States on Tuesday, sweeping away the last racial barrier in American politics with ease as the country chose him as its first [Black] chief executive" (Nagourney 2008). Race was front and center in reflections on this election, but with jubilation. Obama had overtaken a barrier for so many Americans, and especially so for Black Americans.

Media coverage tapped into the elation of many Americans; for so many this was a moment of triumph, relief, excitement, and hope. They did not know what the future held, but insofar as Obama was elected, history had been made. Obama's candidacy was no longer a concern. Neither was his potential for electability. However, the things many Americans were previously concerned about did *not* go away. The relief and mischaracterization of Obama's victory led some to conclude that the United States was post-racial (i.e., beyond the idea of race in society) in light of the 2008 election (Schorr 2008; Dawson and Bobo 2009; Love and Tosolt 2010; Tesler 2016).

The Angry and Overlooked Undercurrent

There was also an undercurrent of racially resentful Americans who were more emboldened and threatened than ever before. This was, for them, a historical moment as well. Disdain was festering, primarily among White Americans, which stemmed from a sense of fear that came after the election. Some media gave attention to far-right and White supremacist voices in the time leading up to the election too. For example, *Rolling Stone* covered White supremacists who favored Obama's election for reasons they believed would favor White supremacy recruitment.

One interview with a White supremacist stands out in detailing this exact motivation. He says the following:

> Obama might be a better candidate for our cause because he's racially conscious. One of our big things in the National Alliance is to raise the racial

> consciousness of our people. Young whites in universities, they've been stripped of any kind of racial identity. Obama may be a racist in a positive sense for his people—that will awaken a lot of the whites, knock some sense into them. . . . Perhaps the best thing for the white race is to have a black president. My only problem with Obama is perhaps he's not black enough.
>
> (Peisner 2009)

This undercurrent of Americans was arguably more mobilized than ever before. The norms of politics seemed to be changing, and, even more threatening, Obama had a great deal of public support at the time of his election. Because of these conditions, instead of expressing their disdain aloud, these aggrieved Americans kept their views quiet and more implicit.

The most visceral example of the mobilization of these disgruntled Americans happened in a place where they could maintain anonymity. It took place on Stormfront, a White supremacist website, in the days that followed the election. Stormfront was a forum among the first corners of the Internet where supremacists congregated and strategized en masse. Just a few days after the 2008 election, the website crashed because it could not handle the exponential uptick in traffic. Given the timing, there are no other effective alternative explanations: Obama was at the core of this wave of racial resentment—as a person and as an indicator of a changing country.

Droves of threatened Americans were becoming more partial to—or at the very least were introduced to—White supremacist ideology. A Black man in the White House was threatening to these Americans because he contested their idea of American society. He was also a representation of what they feared was to come throughout the country: White Americans receding a position of power, and Americans of color, namely Black Americans, subverting that power. Obama really did represent a change to these Americans, but a *bad* change.

A Growing Opposition to a Changing Country

The threat felt from Obama came from projections about the future and from his person. So threat, for these Americans, existed in both the present and the future. Moreover, it did not go away in the years that followed his election.

Over time, the threat turned into political organizing, which then consolidated into a substantive political movement—the Tea Party, which was a direct outgrowth of the many intersecting racially resentful sentiments.

Far-right elements of conservative ideology took great issue with the direction they saw the country to be headed in, many components that call to the big flip. These members' grievances were articulated at what they perceived to be "bad policy." These policies that they opposed were implicitly racial in their orientation. Political scientists Vanessa Williamson, Theda Skocpol, and John Coggin summarize these components of the support surrounding the movement within its early days:

> We find that the Tea Party is a new incarnation of longstanding strands in US conservatism. The anger of grassroots Tea Partiers about new federal social programs such as the Affordable Care Act coexists with considerable acceptance, even warmth, toward long-standing federal social programs like Social Security and Medicare, to which Tea Partiers feel legitimately entitled. Opposition is concentrated on resentment of perceived federal government "handouts" to "undeserving" groups, the definition of which seems heavily influenced by racial and ethnic stereotypes. More broadly, Tea Party concerns exist within the context of anxieties about racial, ethnic, and generational changes in American society.
>
> (Williamson, Skocpol, and Coggin 2011, 26)

One of the most prominent views that was woven throughout Tea Party ideology was the idea that there are "makers" and "takers" in American society. The makers do the work, while the takers free-ride off of their labor (Fortuna 2019). Going further, the makers are people who deserve assistance and representation, and the takers are Americans who take advantage of the system of government and other Americans for the sake of their own gain. These ideas were designed to be implicitly racial, and they also tapped into long-standing racial stereotypes—such as, for example, the "welfare queen" stereotype, which characterizes Black women as lazy people who take advantage of welfare programs instead of working (Hancock 2004). So, many of these "undeserving Americans" or "takers" were people of color, though heavily stereotyped to be Black Americans. People of color were the exact people who were increasing in population (according to the census) and gaining greater positions of power (e.g., Obama's victory).

Exactly as Williamson, Skocpol, and Coggin (2011) describe, a great deal of the fear that motivated Tea Party support was a sense of racial threat about the future of the United States. It emerged directly after the election of Barack Obama because these fears became much more palpable in light of the first Black president. Reports of racially motivated assaults by Tea Party members abounded in the early days of the movement:

> A Latino advocacy group has launched an online campaign pressuring top Republican leaders to apologize for "inciting Tea Party racism." The group Cuéntame (Spanish for "tell me") posted a video and petition late Wednesday to its Facebook page in response to ongoing reports that members of the conservative Tea Party movement formed a mob around members of Congress on Saturday in protest of their vote to overhaul health care. Venerable civil rights leader, Rep. John Lewis, a Democrat from Georgia, along with fellow African-American Congressman Andre Carson, a Democrat from Indiana, say they were both called n***er as they returned from hearing President Barack Obama address Congress at the Capitol.
>
> (L. Hill 2010)

The behavior of Tea Party members and affiliates carried on to such an extent that the NAACP made a resolution specifically about the movement:

> Tea Party protestors have engaged in explicitly racist behavior, displayed signs and posters intended to degrade people of color generally and President Barack Obama specifically; and
>
> WHEREAS, Tea Party members have used racial epithets and verbally and physically abused African-American congressmen and others, and have been charged with making dangerous threats against duly elected public officials; and
>
> WHEREAS, some Tea Party leaders and spokespersons have apologized for and encouraged such racist behavior, rather than fully repudiating it; and
>
> WHEREAS, hard-core white supremacist organizations have participated in and on occasion led Tea Party protests, all while searching for recruits in the fertile racist milieu of the Tea Party movement; and
>
> WHEREAS, Tea Party movement is a threat to the pursuit of human rights, justice and equality for all.

> THEREFORE, BE IT RESOLVED, that the NAACP will educate its membership and the community that this movement is not just about higher taxes and limited government, but something that could evolve and become more dangerous for that small percentage of people who really think our country has been taken away from them. (NAACP 2010)

From its inception, the Tea Party was focused on the changing role of race in the United States. It set the stage for a contentious 2010 midterm, during which the movement pushed a series of candidates whose platforms were in line with conservative Tea Party ideology or candidates who were Tea Party members.

Back and Forth on the National Level

Republicans shellacked Democrats in 2010 (Harris and MacAskill 2010; Weisman 2010). Nearly 35% of all voters in the 2010 midterms were Tea Party supporters, and 32% of all candidates who won elections were Tea Party–backed. On the whole, it is estimated that Tea Party protests held from 2009 to 2010 led to about three to five million votes for Republican candidates. This electoral event left the Democratic Party scrambling about the future of the party's power. It seemed to be a clear repudiation of Obama's agenda. The racial resentment that motivated Tea Party support was a major driver of this immense swing in electoral politics. Republicans took back the House of Representatives essentially because of the Tea Party and massive disdain toward Obama (Karpowitz et al. 2011; Olver 2011).

The grand swing in support on a national scale left Democrats considering Obama's prospects for the future. The year 2010 was the backlash to Obama, and the chances of a second term were under heavy scrutiny. The function and role of his presidency could have been just a one-off moment for representation and, ultimately, just a flash in the pan (Goldman 2010). Pundits and members of the public were expressing ideas that Obama's legacy as the first Black president was grand but lacked staying power because he might not be able to win reelection in 2012.

These considerations about Obama's potential for reelection persisted from 2010 onward, leading to the 2012 election against Republican nominee

Mitt Romney. Obama won handily despite the consistent Republican opposition in leadership.

> And even Obama's pre-election appeals to cooperation are wrapped in an I'm-still-the-president tone that suggests that Americans will be looking at two opposing camps glaring at each other across the barricades—gridlock all around.
>
> Here's John Boehner, the likely speaker if Republicans take the House, offering his plans for Obama's agenda: "We're going to do everything—and I mean everything we can do—to kill it, stop it, slow it down, whatever we can."
>
> Senate Minority Leader Mitch McConnell summed up his plan to National Journal: "The single most important thing we want to achieve is for President Obama to be a one-term president."
>
> (Barr 2010)

Also, despite the clear backlash his presidency received in 2010 and the prominent role of the Tea Party, Obama still defeated Romney in the 2012 presidential election. This was a major signal for Republicans. Again, this election was about Obama but also not *just* about Obama. It was about the coalition he built, the fact that he was the first Black president, and the fact that he had fervent opposition to him among both Republican elites and Republican voters. His reelection was a reaffirmation of the politics of the big flip.

Twice, the fear of the changing country was not enough to mobilize sufficient opposition to the Obama campaign. So in response to this, Republican elites scrambled in the period following the 2012 election. They needed to reorient their strategy out of concern that they were missing political changes afoot in the country. Out of this re-strategizing came the Growth and Opportunity Project, colloquially known as the 2012 GOP autopsy, a report describing the need to change the Republican party strategy. This was a turning point for all of American politics because it ultimately set the trajectory for major upheaval in the entire system.

A Big Fork in the Road

The 2012 election showed the GOP that it was at a critical juncture. It needed to adjust to the changing racial dynamics of the United States or else. The "or else" here was an existential threat to the party. Some leaders presumed that if they were not able to appeal more effectively to Americans of color, they would then lose consistently on a national scale indefinitely to the Democratic Party. Reflecting on the 2012 loss, the autopsy report articulates this very concern:

> The nation's demographic changes add to the urgency of recognizing how precarious our position has become.
>
> America is changing demographically, and unless Republicans are able to grow our appeal the way GOP governors have done, the changes tilt the playing field even more in the Democratic direction.
>
> In 1980, exit polls tell us that the electorate was 88 percent white. In 2012, it was 72 percent white. Hispanics made up 7 percent of the electorate in 2000, 8 percent in 2004, 9 percent in 2008 and 10 percent in 2012. According to the Pew Hispanic Center, in 2050, whites will be 47 percent of the country while Hispanics will grow to 29 percent and Asians to 9 percent.
>
> If we want ethnic minority voters to support Republicans, we have to engage them and show our sincerity.
>
> (Franke-Ruta 2013; Barbour et al. 2013)

The report identified the big flip as a massive problem for the party. The conclusion was simple: Either the GOP changes its platform or suffers the consequences of the future. Even more to the point of Obama and the big flip, the report explicitly articulates the political implications of the changing country and how Obama's wins were indicators of the potential future:

> Unless the RNC gets serious about tackling this problem, we will lose future elections; the data demonstrates this. In both 2008 and 2012, President Obama won a combined 80 percent of the votes of all minority voters, including not only African Americans but also Hispanics, Asians, and others. The minority groups that President Obama carried with 80 percent of the vote in 2012 are on track to become a majority of the nation's population by 2050. Today these minority groups make up 37 percent of the population, and they cast a record 28 percent of the votes in the 2012 presidential election, according to the election exit polls, an increase of 2 percentage points from 2008. We have to work harder at engaging demographic partners and allies. One outside group that has been particularly successful at engaging its community and increasing its Republican support is the Republican Jewish Coalition. We should incorporate some of its tactics in our efforts.

> By 2050, the Hispanic share of the U.S. population could be as high as 29 percent, up from 17 percent now. The African American proportion of the population is projected to rise slightly to 14.7 percent, while the Asian share is projected to increase to approximately 9 percent from its current 5.1 percent. Non-Hispanic whites, 63 percent of the current population, will decrease to half or slightly less than half of the population by 2050.
> (Barbour et al. 2013)

Obama was an indicator of what was to come for the Democratic Party. GOP elites presumed he had built a legacy and coalition with staying power. Due to the strength of this legacy, the future was apparently certain for the Democratic Party. It could appeal to, mobilize, and motivate Americans of color in ways that the Republican Party, at that point, could not. Republicans had defined the party around the idea of White identity, and their voting bloc was shrinking.

The GOP found itself at a fork in the road. The narrative spelled out in the autopsy report was that the party had one possible option in the face of the changing country: Adapt the party platform to appeal more to racial minorities. Alternatively, the narrative presumed that the Republican Party would consistently lose on the national level. This perspective did not account for the larger alternative—one that would contest the actual system it existed within. In other words, the autopsy only considered system-legitimizing alternatives. The alternative called the entire system of government into question, which changed the rules of the game. At its core, this perspective was anti-democratic.

Two Choices, Two Widely Different Conclusions for American Democracy

In light of perceptions of the big flip, there were essentially two directions that the Republican Party could go. As the Obama coalition demonstrated, the party was in trouble on a national level. If party members did not adjust their strategies, they could end up losing elections consistently. The 2012 autopsy report helped to articulate an *expansionist* party strategy, while the emergence of the Tea Party in 2010 showed a *restrictionist* strategy. I describe the theoretical origins of both of these strategies below.

Choice #1: An Expanding Party

The expansionist perspective is grounded in democratic theory—namely, building coalitions to represent diverse sets of interests. One of the most prominent places this idea of representative democracy comes from is "Federalist 10." Madison writes that American democracy facilitates the practice of coalition building, and because of the size of the republic, only the best candidates will be selected by the public:

> In the first place, it is to be remarked that, however small the republic may be, the representatives must be raised to a certain number, in order to guard against the cabals of a few; and that, however large it may be, they must be limited to a certain number, in order to guard against the confusion of a multitude. Hence, the number of representatives in the two cases not being in proportion to that of the two constituents, and being proportionally greater in the small republic, it follows that, if the proportion of fit characters be not less in the large than in the small republic, the former will present a greater option, and consequently a greater probability of a fit choice.
>
> In the next place, as each representative will be chosen by a greater number of citizens in the large than in the small republic, it will be more difficult for unworthy candidates to practice with success the vicious arts by which elections are too often carried; and the suffrages of the people being more free, will be more likely to centre in men who possess the most attractive merit and the most diffusive and established characters.
>
> (Hamilton, Madison, and Jay 2008)

The expansionist perspective outlined in the autopsy report and other places was the realization of Madison's idea of the republic. In light of the shifting country, the party would need to adjust, bringing about a more wide-ranging platform and candidates that appeal to these changes. In response to the big flip, the expansionist GOP approach embodies and emboldens democratic principles.

This approach called for appealing more to racial minorities as a point of strategizing racial demographic change for the Republican Party. Elites emphasized that they should particularly focus on Latinx Americans. To bring in more voters, they would need to expand their ideas of what it meant to be a Republican, advance more diverse candidates, and adjust the party platform, just to name a few ideas. The intention behind this would be to expand the scope of the party in order to compete with newly galvanized Democrats on the national level. As stated many times in the autopsy, this perspective was meant to avoid certain death for the GOP as they knew it. However, this perspective was founded on the idea of the party succeeding through democratic means. In other words, the elites who theorized the future of the party in the autopsy only considered whether they would be able to appeal to racial minorities by adjusting the party platform and turning them out. The expansionist approach to racial demographic change was rooted in legitimizing the system of democracy. Alternatively, the restrictionist approach to Republican Party strategizing sat in direct opposition to expansion. At its core, it was antithetical to the function, norms, and practices of democracy. This moment in the GOP set up the party for the future.

Choice #2: A Restrictive Approach

Overall, party members who subscribed to the restrictionist perspective saw the big flip as a threat to the future of the party. They wanted to keep the GOP in power but did not agree that expanding the party appeal was the proper way to secure power into the future. Instead, they saw that they ought to double down on their base while restricting the newer incoming voters, many of whom were people of color. Their perspective was markedly antidemocratic, and it meshes with the historical function of conservative parties in Western politics.

Ziblatt argues that conservative parties could not authoritatively acquire power amid democratization. So, to secure power, they had to concede ground to democratic politics and norms.

> Conservative parties faced a dilemma in the post-1848 world. To gain power meant reaching across the great abyss of voters deploying electoral strategies to win "the numbers game." By making appeals to voters in such a way, these politicians, however, would alter the very inegalitarian and hierarchical world that mid-century conservatives sought to preserve... Too much adaptation was precisely what conservatives sought to avoid. How to preserve their world, their interests, and power while participating in politics was the essence of the "conservative dilemma" after 1848.
>
> (Ziblatt 2017)

Conservative aristocrats and parties came to adhere to democratic principles because they saw utility in using the system to maintain power. They intentionally capitulated to the system of government because they saw its usefulness. That is, they only wanted democracy insofar as it worked for them. Crucial to the restrictionists' perspective is that if democracy no longer serves them, then they can move in any direction they think can help consolidate their power.

A Republican restrictionist approach to racial demographic change is essentially "playing dirty." The approach involved bucking the rules of the democratic game of elections to contest the perceived growing power of the Democratic opposition. It also accentuated ideas of racial threat to incline more supporters to turn out for elections *and* support shifting the rules of the game. Those who subscribed or were at least partial to the restrictionist approach did not want to take any chances about the future of the GOP. For them, maintaining power was crucial for the party, and they needed to do it by any means necessary. They could do this by contesting the outcomes of elections if they lost, sowing doubt about the electoral process among voters, encouraging restrictive measures for likely non-GOP voters, and even going so far as to encourage violence in order to throw a wrench into politics when needed. For the restrictionists, no strategy was off the table. They just needed to maintain power.

The Big Fork

The fork in the road for Republicans left party elites with these two disparate solutions to the big flip. Following the 2012 election, GOP party elites were in great deliberation about how to proceed. They had lost the White House twice and were concerned that a third loss in a row would tank voters' confidence in the party.

> [In the 2012 Election] minorities were 26% of the vote, but are 51% of live births. Republicans do not have to abandon their principles, but they absolutely must mend fences. . . . This will require creativity. But time is running out.
>
> (R. Martin 2015)

The GOP was soul-searching following Obama's reelection. They knew that they needed to orient for the party's future. This is where recharting the path for the 2016 presidential election came into play—in particular, the lead-up to it. The 2016 Republican primaries were a battleground for competing ideas on the party's future. A host of candidates in the Republican presidential primaries embodied different approaches to how the GOP would handle the changing racial demographics of the United States.

The Battle of Ideas

The entire nomination process for the Republican presidential candidate was essentially the battleground for the ideas that the Republican Party was grappling with at the time surrounding the big flip. The candidates that either adhered to or embodied the expansionist approach were Jeb Bush and Marco Rubio. In contrast, the restrictionist candidates were Ted Cruz and Donald Trump. When the race for the 2016 primaries first began, there was a near consensus about who the front-runner was going to be: Jeb Bush (Enten 2015).

He brought legacy because he a part of the Bush family, which many believed he could use to his advantage. His policy positions were moderate compared to many other candidates, and he spoke Spanish and was somewhat tied to Latinx communities during his time in Florida (Cadava 2015; Killingsworth 2015).

> Over several decades, Bush has become unusually well versed in US–Latin American relations and the interests of Latino communities in the United States. This is perhaps the main reason he'll be a more appealing candidate among conservative Latinos than most others in the field.
>
> (Cadava 2015)

In total, Jeb Bush was the clear expansionist candidate answer to racial demographic change. He could court establishment Republican voters, namely moderate White conservative voters, and, presumably, bring in new Latinx voters into the GOP. party fold.

In a similar way, Marco Rubio brought to bear a somewhat moderated ideological and policy platform. The major difference between him and Bush was that Rubio brought a descriptive advantage because he was a Latino candidate.

> The Florida senator, dynamic and bilingual, seems to embody a new generation of Latino leaders. But even if he wins the Republican presidential nomination, experts say, Rubio faces two daunting hurdles: the GOP's anti-immigrant rhetoric and his own retreat from comprehensive immigration reform two years ago.
>
> (King 2015)

Rubio's appeal—or at the very least perceived appeal—to Latinx voters was his identity. Within the framing of his candidacy, many described Marco Rubio's Cuban heritage as a boon to his running for office.

> One candidate, Marco Rubio, nurtured by the sprawling Cuban-American community here, bounces effortlessly between two cultures—fritas and hamburgers, Spanish and English—in a city so comfortably bilingual that news conferences pivot between the languages.
>
> (King 2015)

Despite some ideological differences, many made direct comparisons between Rubio and Bush throughout the primaries. In essence, both candidates called to the expansionist approach in different, moderated ways.

> [Scott] Walker's withdrawal did more than release his old supporters. It narrowed the choice for mainstream conservative donors, voters and officials who had been waiting on the sidelines. Without Mr. Walker in the race, the choice for mainstream conservatives started becoming clearer. Unless they are willing to support an anti-establishment candidate like Ted Cruz, it's down to Mr. Rubio and Mr. Bush.
>
> (N. Cohn 2015)

Both of these candidates targeted more of the moderate Republican voters. This dynamic was a potential issue in the GOP primaries. Far-right and extreme ideas are more likely to be considered in primaries, but they do not necessarily propel candidates to win (Hirano, Snyder, and Ting 2009; Woon 2018).

It was believed Rubio could bring in more Latinx voters because he could serve as a Republican with whom they more closely identified. His identity was an advantage not only for him but also for the potential bloc of voters he could mobilize. In short, some GOP elites thought he could court the Latinx Republican vote. His descriptive background was seen as a boon for his candidacy—*if* the party was moving in the expansionist direction. While Jeb Bush was not a disagreeable candidate to many Latinx voters, Rubio was seen as having a greater ability to bring them on board because he was a Cuban man. Bush and Rubio were expansionist candidates in their own unique ways.

The Restrictionists

On the other end, two candidates represented the restrictionist approach: Ted Cruz and Donald Trump. Again, the restrictive approach to GOP strategizing was to obstruct political opposition and to stir up negative sentiments in their base to mobilize them more effectively. Ted Cruz was the candidate for this approach, but in a way this ostensibly legitimized American political norms. He was pushing hard for the Evangelical vote and maintained far-right policy positions that were born out of his Christian identity and strong conservatism.

> Cruz doesn't propose remedies. He performs rants. He's not interested in collaboration or teamwork. His main use for other politicians, even in his party, is as foils and targets. Paul Ryan got a taste of that over the weekend, when Cruz, on NBC's "Meet the Press" asked if Ryan was a true conservative and dodged the question, withholding his blessing.
>
> (Bruni 2015)

Although he was a firebrand candidate, Ted Cruz fit more into the conventional conception of a Republican candidate. He was effectively an insider who had worked in Washington politics for most of his career. His radical positions came from his Evangelical background and, to many, were maintained to tap into his base.

Early discussion of the primaries in 2015 focused on Cruz's strong conservative positioning among Republican primary voters.

> Republican conservatives [have been] paying greater heed to Cruz, who seems to be positioning himself as the ultraconservative fallback—the rabble rouser in the bullpen—if angry voters rethink Trump or Carson and want an establishment-vilifying candidate with at least some government experience.
>
> (Bruni 2015)

A central theme emerged through this discussion of Cruz as an ultraconservative yet part of the establishment: He served as a candidate who fit the restrictionist mold in ways that did not overtly call the system of government into question. He was an establishment restrictionist. Cruz might subvert democratic practices in ways that were legal because of his background in law and time as a career politician. He had shown glimpses of the role he might carry out as president during his time in the Senate, where, at one point, he engaged in a kind of grandstanding to advocate for defunding Obamacare—even though it was not up for a vote (Roberts 2013). Cruz was the restrictionist who could appeal to Americans as being conventional despite *not* being so in practice. Donald Trump, on the other hand, made no concessions about being a restrictionist candidate, many times doubling down on this perspective.

Trump: A Restrictionist in Direct Opposition to the Big Flip

From the onset of his campaign for office, Donald Trump made clear how he was going to move as a candidate: He would intentionally stir up fear and anxiety about the changing country, emphasizing a nearly lost, bygone era of American society. This was apparent in his very first speech at his official campaign announcement.

> The US has become a dumping ground for everybody else's problems.
>
> [Applause]
>
> Thank you. It's true, and these are the best and the finest. When Mexico sends its people, they're not sending their best. They're not sending you. They're not sending you. They're sending people that have lots of problems, and they're bringing those problems with us. They're bringing drugs. They're bringing crime. They're rapists. And some, I assume, are good people.
>
> (Phillips 2021)

In many ways, he positioned himself as the direct opposition to the big flip. He was the candidate for those who felt an overt concern about the United States changing and who felt their cultural life, jobs, or security were threatened. Most of these positions were tied to diminishing numbers, status, and social cache of White Americans and the increasing numbers of

Americans of color. The position that Trump was advocating for, however, was clear: He would be the bulwark that these fearful voters could turn to, the candidate who could prevent the frightening changes from happening. Importantly, this theme carried from the onset to the remainder of his campaign. At various points, more attention was given to the theatrics of his position. For example, the media gave attention to how differently he spoke than other GOP candidates, how combative and joking he was to the opposition, and how he would essentially riff at his rallies. *FiveThirtyEight* found that, in the middle of the primaries, Trump was receiving 46% of all media coverage (Silver 2015).

In a similar way that the jubilation of Obama's election suppressed attention to the undercurrent of angry Americans, coverage of Trump's character masked the way he tapped into the sentiment of those same Americans. Put shortly, Trump's personality overshadowed the way that he was tapping into high levels of racial threat among members of the American public.

In the later days of the primaries, it became increasingly clear that Trump's restrictionist position was meshing with a sizable current of Republican voters. The sentiment of these voters was similar in nature to the categorical opposition to Obama—for example, increased support for the Tea Party and the White nationalist sentiments that were prompted at the beginning of Obama's tenure. Trump positioned himself strongly as pushing back against Obama without much justification for where this opposition was grounded. The lack of a clear ideological motivation was more evidence that it came from a symbolic place. Ideology did not matter. It was simply about the opposition to something that Obama embodied. Trump's position and the support he received came from the perception of Obama as an embodiment of the big flip.

To this, Rachel Blum writes the following:

> Voters who enthusiastically supported Trump were distinguished from other Republicans by their penchant to view ethnic and cultural outsiders as threats to their own status in American society.
>
> (Blum 2020, 60)

This campaign position, in tandem with overt racial signals, helped to spur on a set of Americans whose attitudes had previously not been captured. Further, the Obama presidential era had ushered in an apparent norm of post-racial politics. This foundationally set up a scenario where racially threatening language was not taken as seriously because many took it to be harmless.

There were large swaths of Americans who believed that race was an antiquated concept in politics—largely because Obama achieved what many viewed to be impossible. It led to a public blind spot, mostly among liberal White Americans, that precluded taking Trump's campaign and restrictionist position seriously.

The Public Blind Spot

The major problem of the public blind spot brought about by post-racial perceptions of the United States was that it led a large portion of Americans to presume it was impossible for Trump to win on the national stage. The perceived absurdity of his platform and person actually led to elevating his campaign. White liberal Americans viewed Trump as so far outside the norm that it was a farce. The position led liberal-leaning media outlets to cover the campaign as a series of gaffes. Statements Trump made in seriousness to his many supporters were framed and perceived to be speaking to a minority of Americans.

This bled into strategizing among Democrats.

> "I admit to being suckered into every narrative that predicted Trump's demise over and over," said Connecticut Senator Chris Murphy, a Clinton ally. "I admittedly was a pretty consistent skeptic that they were ultimately going to nominate this buffoon, so I probably came to the realization that he was the nominee as late as anybody."
>
> "I was in denial for a very long time," added former Vermont Governor Howard Dean, the one-time presidential candidate and DNC chair. "I tell people I was wrong for 52 weeks in a row starting in June."
>
> (Debenedetti 2016)

A similar willful ignorance and selective attention among the White liberal public and media outlets alike masked the perceived relevance of Donald Trump's campaign. Convinced by his restrictionist position, however, his supporters saw the repercussions of the big flip as *very* real. Racial threat was a key element to their support, coming from a perceived decline of the United States within the previous eight years. Obama was a sign of what was to come if Trump was not elected. Importantly, the big flip called to abstract ideas and perceptions more than to on-the-ground conditions. As such, the threat that was felt among supporters was coming from an immaterial place. This fed into the public blind spot. Supporters and Trump himself were referring to a symbolic loss that could not be assessed quantifiably. To many other Americans, these positions were absurd, so they did not take them seriously.

When Trump and supporters said that "no one respected" the United States anymore, or that the previous Obama years were a disaster, many of these ideas were coming from a place of racial threat. The inability to reconcile this motivation with their sense of the world led to a great deal of confusion the more that Trump rose in the primary polls.

The confusion and inability to explain what was happening rose once Trump won the GOP nomination. Skepticism in Trump's ability to win carried all the way up to the president. In his piece "My President Was Black," Ta-Nehisi Coates wrote of a conversation he had with President Obama:

> When I told Obama that I thought Trump's candidacy was an explicit reaction to the fact of a black president, he said he could see that, but then enumerated other explanations. When assessing Trump's chances, he was direct: He couldn't win.
>
> (Coates 2017)

More to this point, this idea motivated a good deal of academic work during this same time (Dawson and Bobo 2009; Lopez 2010; Love and Tosolt 2010; T. Lee 2011). The final nail in the coffin for this public blind spot came from the big flip, namely that Democrats misperceived a growing advantage over Republicans *because* the United States was slated to become a majority-minority nation—the same motivation behind the GOP's 2012 autopsy report that led to the fork in the road for Republicans. It led to the undervaluing of Trump's chance to win, and eventually set into place an idea that would threaten the future of American democracy.

4
Demographic Determinism

In the lead-up to the 2016 presidential election, there was a great deal of public confidence in two key ideas. The first idea was that Hillary Clinton was a shoo-in to win the election. This confidence among Democrats came from her position as an establishment politician, her prospect as the first woman to be nominated by the Democratic Party, and, as I described in chapter 2, the general understanding that Donald Trump was outside of the norms of conventional politics. There was also mounting confidence in the electoral map, both for the 2016 election and subsequent elections, strongly driven by the prospect of the big flip. We see this idea reinforced in the lead-up to election day. Clinton's victory was a forgone conclusion to many:

> Hillary Clinton is tied with Donald J. Trump in Georgia, catching up with him in South Carolina and generally showing strength in traditionally Republican parts of the South. It seems like the Democratic dream come true—demographic changes are turning Southern states purple.
>
> (Crespino 2016)

> The Republicans might not be able to keep up with Florida's demographic shift any longer: The early polls show Mrs. Clinton with consistent advantage of about four percentage points. Here's the unsurprising reason: Mr. Trump has alienated Hispanic voters, making the last decade of demographic shifts even more potent.
>
> (N. Cohn 2016)

The second idea came from the presumption that, by coupling Clinton's lead of the Democratic Party with demographic trends, the Democratic Party was put in a position to substantively dominate electoral politics for decades to come. It was simply the idea that demographics were destiny for Democrats.

The Big Flip. Andrew Ifedapo Thompson, Oxford University Press. © Oxford University Press (2026).
DOI: 10.1093/9780197822173.003.0004

MIKEY DAY: "Because of shifting demographics, there might never be another Republican president in this country."
DAVE CHAPPELLE: "Word? You ever been around this country before?"

(Saturday Night Live, 2016)
(SNL opening skit from early November 2016)

As I describe next, the confidence in the Democratic Party's future was consistently reaffirmed by a misperception I call *demographic determinism*: the idea that as the number of Americans of color increases and the number of White Americans decreases, the Democratic Party will be at an increasing and insurmountable advantage in electoral politics over the Republican Party.

Demographic Determinism in the Big Flip

Determinism as an idea originates from metaphysics, a subfield of philosophy. It involves a worldview about the order of events, either within the context of an individual or on a grander, global scale. Determinism is the presumption that events that occur in the world lead to a certain, determined outcome. Importantly, individuals can make choices on a smaller scale, but these choices, whatever they are and however they are made, still lead to the same outcome.

> Causal determinism is, roughly speaking, the idea that every event is necessitated by antecedent events and conditions together with the laws of nature.
>
> (Hoefer 2023)

Determinism can often emerge in the discussion of religion. For example, Christian ideas of determinism are evoked in common expressions such as "God has a plan" and "everything happens for a reason" (Gaskin 1993; Feinberg and Brown 2006; Rea 2011).

Demographic determinism is a slightly more complex idea built on core deterministic presumptions about the future of American politics. The idea takes the big flip as an irrefutable fact, then overlays partisan politics onto it. In an even more complex way, it reductively captures historical racial politics within the United States, then projects those same racial politics into the future.

The Logic of Demographic Determinism

Demographic determinism begins under the assumption that White Americans are soon going to be a numerical minority, while Americans of color will become the numerical majority across the United States. It is assumed that White Americans are taken to identify as mostly Republican, while Americans of color are seen as mostly Democrat. So, from the big flip, the conclusion becomes simple: The Democratic Party will be at a growing advantage over the Republican Party as time goes on. As the United States approaches the moment of the big flip, this party advantage will only increase; when the flip actually occurs, Democrats will become the preeminent political party.

This logic is what motivated the confidence in the Democrats' future within the weeks leading up to the 2016 presidential election. Also, despite Clinton's loss and Trump's victory in 2016, demographic determinism has not ceded in its importance to American politics. If anything, it has grown in significance and relevance to both Republicans and Democrats.

> The long-term Democratic bet on demographic destiny assumes that minority voters who support the party today will continue to in the future. But it also assumes that today's white Democrats will stay with the party as the context around them shifts.
>
> (Badger 2017)

> The Democrats are still relying on arc-of-history beliefs and long-term demographic trends.
>
> (Douthat 2017)

Demographic determinism has become a widespread idea. It holds weight across the American public. However, despite this prominence, it cannot be overstated that demographic determinism is a *misperception* about American politics. This misperception feeds directly into the logic of the idea itself. I will show that there are three underlying assumptions that drive the greater misperception of demographic determinism.

The Misperception of Demographic Determinism

There are three core components of how demographic determinism operates as a misperception. I call these the *three P's*: prediction, people of color (POC), and partisanship. All three of these concepts are linked but can be considered as separate, standalone ideas about racial demographic change in America. First, the misperception of prediction refers to the function of race within the United States. Demographic determinism does not account for the porousness and shifts of race within the country. Race as a social construct is affected by a variety of social changes. The meaning of race—and, on the whole, the identification with racial groups—shifts over time. A prime example of this porosity of race is the shifting idea of what it means to be White (Ignatiev 2008). In the late nineteenth century, a handful of European immigrant groups were not socially categorized as White within American racial politics. These were Irish, Italian, and Polish immigrants. Eventually, into the early twentieth century, these immigrant groups were incorporated into Whiteness, due to their increasing sizes and changing social norms (Ignatiev 2008).

Race does not adhere to a set of natural laws because it is a social construct. As such, it changes over time. It is *likely* to change, too, as society changes. To contextualize this idea, Omi and Winant write the following:

> As social beings, we must categorize people so as to be able to "navigate" in the world—to discern quickly who may be friend or foe, to position and situate ourselves within prevailing social hierarchies, and to provide clues that guide our social interactions with the individuals and groups we encounter.
>
> But while the act of categorizing people and assigning different attributes to such categories may be universal, the categories themselves are subject to enormous variation over historical time and space. The definitions, meanings, and overall coherence of prevailing social categories are always subject to multiple interpretations. No social category rises to the level of being understood as a fixed, objective, social fact . . .
>
> We assert that in the United States, race is a master category—a fundamental concept that has profoundly shaped, and continues to shape, the history, polity, economic structure, and culture of the United States.
>
> (Omi and Winant 2014, 105–6)

This component of race makes predictions about the future of racial groups near impossible. So, when discussions of the big flip emerge, even if we know that White Americans are shrinking in population size relative to Americans of color, we have less of a sense of *how* this will occur. More to this point, there is a likelihood that other groups could be brought into the fold of Whiteness over time (Wimmer 2013; Abascal 2020). This potential incorporation of groups and shifting of the meaning of race makes any kind of prediction near impossible.

> The majority-minority society is no certainty. Whether the United States becomes such a society in the next several decades depends on what we mean by the concept. In the narrow way that the Census Bureau has defined it—the point at which the number of Americans who declare themselves on the census to be non-Hispanic and unmixed white by race dips below 50 percent—it seems more likely than not to occur eventually.... Even so, the Census Bureau's way of collecting and compiling data probably exaggerates the imminence of this societal transition because of the categorization of individuals from mixed majority-minority backgrounds as not white.
>
> Yet even if the majority-minority society as defined by the Census Bureau is attained, it will not look like the conception most Americans today undoubtedly have of it. In this respect, the Census Bureau projections are deeply misleading. When confronted with projections that foresee whites as a future numerical minority, most Americans probably imagine ethnoracial groups that look approximately as discrete and distinct as they do now but with rather different relative sizes: relatively fewer whites, relatively more Asians, blacks, and Hispanics, in particular. That is to say, the projections establish a binary and therefore zero-sum situation: if individuals are not white, then they are minorities.
>
> (Alba 2018a)

Yet despite the shifting needle of race over time, institutions and scholars have made predictions about the future of race. They have interpreted race to be a fixed idea. This fixed idea led to the big flip becoming an established projection, and the sense of threat that comes with it. But, again, predicting the future of race in America motivates the misperception of demographic determinism because it presumes to know how the future of the United States will look.

The Historical Understanding of People of Color

Despite the malleability of race as a concept, on an institutional level it functions with a set of logic. Race within the United States has long functioned as a binary, notwithstanding the fact that there are a multitude of racial groups. The racial binary is a system; W. E. B. Du Bois and others referred to it as the "color line" (Sears and Savalei 2006; Du Bois 2015). The logic of the system is simple: White is on top, and Black is on bottom. All other racial groups are defined in relation to the two ends of the binary in this system. Juan Perea spells out this logic:

> Race in America consists, either exclusively or primarily, of only two constituent racial groups, Black and White. . . . In addition, the paradigm dictates that all other racial identities and groups in the United States are best understood through the Black/White binary paradigm.
>
> (Delgado and Stefancic 1998)

As a social system, the binary does not overtly exclude the existence of other racial groups. It does, however, define those groups directly in relation to Whiteness and Blackness. This means that all other racial minorities can maintain a strong sense of their identity, but when they enter into intergroup contact and politics, the racial binary filters how they are *perceived* as a group.

The Racial Binary through History

There are a variety of places where the binary emerges within US history that reinforce how many Americans think about the existence and function of different racial groups throughout the United States. The binary has been evoked in debate about the function of the US government. The former chair of the US Civil Rights Commission, Mary Francis Berry, stated, "[The United States is composed of] three nations, one Black, one White, and one in which people strive to be something other than Black to avoid the sting of White Supremacy."

In another place, in light of the riots in the summer of 1967, the Kerner Commission put out the now-famous Kerner Report on the drivers of these riots. The report concluded on one particular point:

> Our Nation is moving toward two societies, one black, one white—separate and unequal. Reaction to last summer's disorders has quickened the movement and deepened the division. Discrimination and segregation have long permeated much of American life; they now threaten the future of every American. This deepening racial division is not inevitable. The movement apart can be reversed. Choice is still possible. Our principal task is to define that choice and to press for a national resolution.
>
> (Disorders and Zelizer 2016)

In earlier iterations of the study of domestic American politics, the Black-White binary took the form and description of the "Negro Problem." Gunnar Myrdal describes this at length within his book *An American Dilemma: The Negro Problem and Modern American Democracy* (1995):

> To the great majority of white Americans the Negro problem has distinctly negative connotations. It suggests something difficult to settle and equally difficult to leave alone. It is embarrassing. It makes for moral uneasiness. The very presence of the Negro in America; his fate in this country through slavery, Civil War and Reconstruction; his recent career and his present status; his accommodation; his protest and his aspiration; in fact his entire biological, historical and social existence as a participant American represent to the ordinary white man in the North as well as in the South an anomaly in the very structure of American society. To many, this takes on the proportion of a menace—biological, economic, social, cultural, and, at times, political. This anxiety may be mingled with a feeling of individual and collective guilt. A few see the problem as a challenge to statesmanship. To all it is a trouble. (xlv)

On the existence of the United States, Myrdal emphasizes that Black Americans sit at the heart of the function of the nation. There is a moral quandary with Black Americans' marginal position, while the United States is claimed to be a shining beacon of equality and democracy. The work reinforces this moral dilemma. Reiterating the Black-White binary consistently, Myrdal asks how White Americans and the whole country reconcile articulating strong, Liberal ethics while so severely subjugating Black Americans—in short, keeping Black Americans on the bottom.

More to the point about the binary racial system, Andrew Hacker writes the following:

> America is inherently a "white" country in character, in structure, in culture. Needless to say, black Americans create lives of their own. Yet, as a people, they face boundaries and constrictions set by the white majority. (Hacker 2003)

The dynamic of the binary has persisted throughout the history of the United States—so much so that it maintains a historical legacy in how Americans think about the country. Speaking to the origins of this legacy, the political and economic system of slavery gave way to the social establishment of racial categorization that was reinforced through the formal abolition of slavery. The abolition of slavery led to a brief yet politically prosperous period for Black Americans known as Reconstruction. In the midst of this moment, then in a strong and concerted way immediately following it, there was a grand White backlash to the political enfranchisement of Black Americans. This period helped to further cement the social subjugation of Black Americans that persists to this day, despite evolution over time:

> The years during and after the Reconstruction Period saw whites coordinating to provide an informal social infrastructure (and to the extent legally permissible an institutional one as well) to maintain as much as possible the economic and political power previously guaranteed to them under slavery. (Acharya, Blackwell, and Sen 2016)

The current-day binary system is built on this political legacy. Racial relations between White and Black Americans have a strong, storied history that has cemented this national version of White supremacy.

Importantly and crucially, these relations do not exclude all other racial groups that exist in American society; the binary simply describes the poles of the racial structure of the United States (Alcoff 2003; Gonzalez-Sobrino and Goss 2019; Husain 2019; Patil 2021). All other racial groups fall in between the two poles of Whiteness and Blackness. The position of these groups is understood as relative to either Black or White polar ends. We see the binary system emerge in a variety of places: policy, historical understanding, and culture, to name a few. The historical rootedness of the Black-White binary is crucial to how Americans, namely White Americans, think about all other racial groups. Latinx and Asian

Americans have operated in a liminal space between the two polarities of the racial binary system.

Dixon describes how Hispanic and Asian Americans have drifted in between these ends of the racial system.

> Historically and culturally rooted racial/ethnic hierarchy differentially shapes whites' present-day threat of, contact with, and ultimately, prejudice toward blacks, Hispanics and Asians. Because Hispanics and Asians have been "whitened" to some extent and have ascended in this hierarchy, they represent less of a threat and have more comfortable interactions with whites than blacks.
>
> (Dixon 2006)

Racial triangulation theory, which is a scholarly amendment to how we think about the racial binary, abstractly describes how the drift between White and Black poles can occur. It addresses how Asian Americans function in between Whiteness and Blackness, introducing the important idea of foreignness to how we ought to consider race. Claire Jean Kim advances this idea by accounting for the Black-White binary:

> Asian Americans do not exist in a vacuum, isolated from other groups; to the contrary, Asian Americans have been racialized relative to, and in interaction with Whites and Blacks.... Asian Americans have been racially triangulated vis-à-vis Blacks and Whites, or located in the field of racial positions with reference to these other two points.
>
> (Kim 1999)

The functional role of the racial binary can lead to public conversations about race that imply relations between *only* Black and White Americans. Often this can come at the detriment and alienation of non-White and non-Black racial groups, who may feel left out of the discussion and meaning-making of race ("What It Means To Be Asian in America" 2022).

Blackness is the foundational position of racial marginalization that minority status in the United States is built upon. All other types of minority racial status are built off of it. Even stereotypes of Asian Americans sit in direct contrast to stereotypes of Black Americans. Motivations on the reason for this contrast abound:

> [Scholars suggest that] the model minority image was an elite class invention during the Civil Rights Movement to disunite African Americans

> and Asian Americans, to justify social inequality by holding African Americans and other disadvantaged groups to the model minority standard, and to dissolve the multiculturalism ideology.
>
> (Takaki 1993)

More recent instances have also evoked the model minority myth surrounding Asian Americans as an idea that has been used to drive a wedge between Asian Americans and Black Americans (Chow 2017). The logic of these events and ideas is simple: Asian Americans are examples of "good" racial minorities, and this implies that Black Americans ought to follow this model if they want to lift themselves up. Reinforcing the Black-White binary, author Frank Chin once stated, "Whites love us because we're not Black" (R. G. Lee 2010). The crucial feature of all of these examples is that the perceptions of other racial groups all stem from the Black-White binary paradigm in some respect.

For example, within policy debates over affirmative action, we also see how, theoretically and empirically, there is an understanding that this policy and others like it predominately affect Black Americans. Not only does rhetoric surrounding the issue reinforce the Black-White binary, but so too do the attitudes of many Americans (Gilens, Sniderman, and Kuklinski 1998; Menand 2020). Among other racially charged issues, namely welfare, attitudes toward Black Americans *specifically* are strongly predictive of whether other Americans support these issues.

In a study by political scientist Martin Gilens, he articulates the connection of Americans' views of African Americans to their views toward race-coded policy:

> Political issues such as crime and welfare are now widely viewed as "coded" issues that play upon race (or, more specifically, upon white Americans' negative views of blacks) without explicitly raising the "race card."
>
> (Gilens 1996)

The picture of the American public here is one that prioritizes the Black-White binary in how Americans think about race relations within a variety of different domains. Due to the history and function of the racial binary, Americans, for better or worse, often think in Black and White racial terms. One major issue with the Black-White binary I have already touched on is that it can often alienate non-Black racial minorities and fail to capture their experiences.

But another major, overlooked issue feeds into a misperception about race on a mass public level. Americans' pervasive view of the Black-White binary within all things concerning race is that it fuels a misperception of POC on the whole. The binary affects the image of who Americans think POC are, thus creating a limited framework. I argue and empirically show in chapter 5 that when Americans think of POC, they think of Black Americans predominately.

This identifies the core of the POC component of the second *P* of demographic determinism: Because Americans strongly associate the term *people of color* with *Black Americans*, they then also import all of the stereotypes about Black Americans onto this understanding. Threat from POC is filtered through the threat from Black Americans. The storied legacy of Black Americans' position in the racial binary system remains unshakable even in the changing country. As a misperception, this is a standalone idea, but when it interacts with the other two *P*'s (prediction and partisanship), it becomes a powerful idea that shifts ideas of democracy.

As such, when Americans, namely White Americans, think about the big flip and the growing percentage of POC, their minds specifically go to Black Americans, which is simply incorrect even in the predictions made about racial demographic changes. Perceptions of the big flip are therefore overdetermined by views of Black Americans. So the various stereotypes about Black Americans then feed into perceptions of the future of the country, motivating a sense of threat. I show that this misperception then leads to the third and final *P* in misperceptions, which stems directly from the second: that partisanship is directly connected to Black group identity.

The Colors of Partisanship

Partisanship, or the way people align with political parties, connects closely with racial identity in American politics. The connection between these two concepts has grown over time in a variety of respects (Mason 2018), especially in how they motivate each other. That is, stronger racial identity is tied to stronger partisanship, and vice versa. This discussion, however, has been limited to the way these forms of identity connect to one another in how Americans think about themselves. In other words, the discussion has been about how people express their identity. The connection between race and partisanship I highlight next is different—I refer to *perceptions*. Americans' views of how social groups relate to parties are tied to historical context, but they do not need to fully capture the party's makeup. Perceptions can be and often are couched within stereotypes (Rothschild et al. 2019). To put this into the form of a question, I ask: When people think of Democrats and Republicans, which racial groups come to mind?

Americans' perceptions of the racial identity of party members are historically driven. In the modern era of American political parties, the starting place for this comes from the racial realignment of the Democratic and Republican Party. The civil rights movement led to an institutional repositioning of Democrats and Republicans. In the mid-1960s, the Civil Rights Act and Voting Rights Act were fervently opposed by Southern Democrats on the grounds of racial resentment. Many Southern voters and elites opposed the political enfranchisement of Black Americans. As such, when the Civil Rights Act was passed, it led to a broad swath of Southern Democrats moving their affiliation. They left the party through the encouragement of defecting segregationists. Ultimately, they moved to the Republican Party and have stayed ever since.

> Indeed, the alignment among economic conservatism, GOP partisanship, and a conservative stance on civil rights at the mass and midlevels of the parties provided a permissive context for national party leaders to embrace an explicit alliance with southern whites. . . . The flip side of civil rights activists' success in forcing Democratic national elites to take a clear stand was that southern segregationists were now fully available for a new generation of Republican leaders and activists to mobilize, while economically conservative northern Republican voters' skepticism toward civil rights left them ready to embrace a racially conservative candidate.
>
> (Schickler 2016, 282, 284)

This partisan shift was cataclysmic for American politics and has stayed fixed ever since this political moment. It was crucial for how the parties relate to one another on a national. Republicans left, and in light of the Civil Rights Acts, Black Americans began aligning more closely to the Democratic Party. Scholars have recently shown that these affiliations among Black Americans operate on a social level. Ties between partisanship and Black racial identity have grown so closely connected that Black identity maps closely to Democratic partisan identity, irrespective of individual policy positions.

This connection, White and Laird show, has been a consistent component of Black politics in the post–civil rights political era:

> In the post–civil rights era, the racial politics of the Southern Strategy tarnished the relationship between Republicans and blacks. Over time and in response to changing commitments from the Democratic Party, Black Democratic Party support became normalized. In the twenty-first century, new social institutions like Black Twitter have emerged, offering new and developing in-group social tools for reinforcement of the now well-established Democratic partisan norm.
>
> (2020, 105)

Black Americans' social identity is tied to their Democratic partisan identity. Their party identity exists, at many points in time, irrespective of their policy positions because of the social identification with the party.

> Blacks' interpretations of the political parties' substantive policy positions may actually have their origins in the very norms that we believe underlie black political behavior. (2020, 156–57)

More to this point, and overlooked in political science until now, the effect of the civil rights movement was the starting place for racially coloring perceptions of Democrats and Republicans on a national level. Perceptions of these parties have been consistently colored in the public, and these shades have deepened over time. When Americans think of Democrats, they think of particular racial groups. They do the same thing when they think of Republicans. So the third *P* of misperceptions about the big flip is partisanship. To affirm this idea, in chapter 6 I show that reframing the big flip as an event that will benefit the Republican Party ultimately leads Republicans to express less racially threatened attitudes, voice more support for the Black Lives Matter movement, and become less anti-democratic.

Demographic Determinism

These three misperceptions—prediction, people of color, and partisanship—feed into a major problem for democracy. All three interact to create recipe for disaster in the minds of people who believe the three of them together. The idea extends from projections about the future of racial demographics within the United States. More specifically, it encapsulates why perceptions of the big flip can be so grand that they become a bane of American democracy. All three of these concepts combine to establish demographic determinism as the overarching misperception of the big flip.

Demographic determinism involves the enmeshment of prediction, people of color, and partisanship, which coalesce in a dangerous way for democracy. Crucially for Republicans and others who feel senses of threat from the Democratic Party, demographic determinism erodes their support for democracy. Next I detail how the larger sense of determinism is built on the three *P*'s.

First, on prediction. Demographic determinism is built on the idea that we can substantively predict what the future racial demographics of the United States will look like and how they will function. As I articulated, this is a misperception. It essentializes race as a fixed and natural category, which it is not. Race is bound to change into the future, and more specifically, White identification is bound to change as demographics change. As a result, it is effectively impossible to predict the number of White Americans into the future, or even *who* could identify as White into the future. To engage in anything of the sort is disingenuous to ideas and the structure of race in the United States.

Second, on POC. As a group, POC do not exist as a monolith in the United States. This assertion is a rhetorical truism at the current moment, but it does not mean this is how the ideas of POC operate in the minds of Americans. Black Americans are top the mind for many Americans when they think of POC. This misperception, working into the context of the big flip, leads to the presumption that when Americans are told that POC are soon to be the numerical majority, they assume that the groups who are growing at the greatest margin are Black Americans, which is untrue. Ironically, even in the context of the prediction misperception, this is a further misunderstanding. In all models of racial demographic change, Black Americans are stagnant in their growth. So the concern expressed about changing demographics in America comes from a misunderstanding about which groups are growing, causing more threat.

Last, the third misperception, partisanship, is built onto the previous two misperceptions, and with it Americans infer that Democrats will benefit from racial demographic change. They presume this because of the relationship between Democratic Party identity and Black Americans *exclusively*.

There are no other relationships that racial minority groups have with political parties that are as strong as the historical relationship between Black Americans and Democrats. But instead of making cognitive room for the prospect of different racial groups changing in size and not having as strong of an allegiance to Democrats, Americans use an incorrect cognitive shortcut. They infer that POC on the whole identify more closely with Democrats, which then leads them to assume that the big flip will benefit the Democratic Party as POC increase in population size.

Prediction, people of color, and partisan misperceptions together feed into attitudes toward American democracy. I show that predictions of the big flip largely motivate threat among the American public. These misperceptions drive negative attitudes about the future of American democracy by causing Americans, namely White Americans, to think they will be less able to exercise their voice under the current democratic system. And demographic determinism feeds into what I call the *big flip-out* over American democracy.

The Big Flip-Out

The big flip-out describes how racial threat erodes American public support for democracy. It involves who Americans think is slated to benefit from these demographic changes and win in the electoral system. As I have described above, the predominant assumption is that Democrats will greatly benefit because POC are perceived to identify more closely with the Democratic Party. This threatens Republicans, and threatened Republicans thus become less supportive of democracy because they think they will be unable to win in national politics into the future.

Throughout this book, I show that Americans' attitudes about democracy are closely tied to how likely they perceive their party to be able to win. Americans seem to be *contingent democrats*—supporting the system insofar as they think it will benefit themselves. For Republicans, demographic determinism calls into question their commitment to democracy. That is, the determinism makes the Republican Party believe it will be less able to win national elections because of the big flip. The shift then causes them to become more supportive of anti-democratic ideas like political violence, overturning elections, authoritarian-like leaders, and a host of other ideas that threaten the coherence and function of American democracy.

For Democrats, the same determinism motivates a confidence that can be politically stagnating. The perceived inevitability of these changes suggests to Democrats that the Democratic Party does not need to do anything in order to reap the benefits of the big flip.

The Institutional Origins of the Big Flip-Out

The dynamic of the big flip-out comes from two places. The first is driven by the structure and function of conservative parties in Western democracies. This origin point is historical in nature. Conservative parties have long existed under the auspices of securing power for economic elites. In transitioning from systems of government that consolidated power explicitly among landed elite, the movement in the West toward democratic representation caused elites to reorient their strategies to maintain their power. Democracy is ruled by the many; economic elites were the few. So economic elites needed to concede ground on their overt ability to rule, instead focusing their energies on working their power within the system of democracy. This transition was done for the sake of elites maintaining themselves in the long run.

Ziblatt describes the longer arc of this dynamic in Western Europe:

> Conservative parties faced a dilemma in the post-1848 world. To gain power meant reaching across the great abyss of voters deploying electoral strategies to win "the numbers game." By making appeals to voters in such a way, these politicians, however, would alter the very inegalitarian and hierarchical world that mid-century conservatives sought to preserve. At times nostalgic and at times simply resigned to inexorable change, conservative sentiment was captured by a leading British conservative in 1882, following Disraeli's death the year before; he described the descent of the old order as the "passing away of an epoch" and identified himself among "the last of the Conservatives."
>
> (Ziblatt 2017)

This same functional role of conservatism and democracy operated within the United States, driven only more, in part, by the institution of slavery. Race was another fold within the American social system that these economic elites could exploit in order to maintain their power. These elites in the United States sought to hold on to power through the system of democracy, but in order to facilitate this process, they worked to implement and valorize the valuation of race to embed differences among working-class White Americans and enslaved Black Americans, whom they could keep alienated from one another. There were already social benefits to the concept of Whiteness among working-class Whites, but conservative parties in the United States were also able to align their party platforms through different ways of reinforcing racial antipathy (Kilbride 2006).

This concept of the variant socioeconomic benefits of Whiteness has since been deemed the "wages of Whiteness." White Americans get social, material, and psychological benefits from their race, which are potent and powerful in how they are able to move around the world. These "wages" also work to differentiate Whites from minority racial groups.

White Americans could then use these wages to identify more closely to other White Americans than to Americans of color. This was especially the case for driving a wedge between White and Black Americans. To this, Du Bois wrote the following:

> Most persons do not realize how far [the view that common oppression would create interracial solidarity] failed to work in the South, and it failed to work because the theory of race was supplemented by a carefully planned and slowly evolved method, which drove such a wedge between the white and black workers that there probably are not today in the world two groups of workers with practically identical interests who hate and fear each other so deeply and persistently and who are kept so far apart that neither sees anything of common interest.
>
> (Du Bois 2017)

Wages of Whiteness were used to satiate the masses, and ostensibly align lower-class Whites with upper-class Whites under conservative parties. On the whole, the implementation and perpetuation of this system has been successful in aligning many White Americans' identities to conservativism.

The major point behind the history of this idea is that American conservative parties have only been tied to democratic practices insofar as they see the system as a viable option to maintain power. They have only been (lowercase *d*) democratic as long as they have taken the system to be a best-case scenario to maintain power. There have been feedback effects from the establishment of the conservative parties in the United States, but this institutional makeup alone did not set the country on an inevitable path toward the big flip-out; there have also been a series of decisions made by elites at critical junctures that have led the United States to this point in history.

Elite Strategizing and the Big Flip

The second place the big flip-out emerges from is party elites' decision-making. Political rhetoric and coalition-building are the two central areas wherein conservative elites have made decisions that have brought the United States to the big flip-out over democracy. On rhetorical levels, there is a history of conservatives using racially divisive messaging to mobilize their most racially resentful voter base. Racial messaging with this explicit purpose is a modern political phenomenon within American politics, which is mostly attributable to the recent enfranchisement of voters of color, namely Black voters, into conventional electoral politics.

Directly following the Civil Rights Acts in the mid-1960s, the Republican Party implemented the Southern Strategy. This term denotes rhetorical tactics the party used to generate fear and racial resentment among their base voters (Mendelberg 2001; Thompson and Busby 2021).

The GOP used this strategy as a means to mobilize and convince Republican voters to turn out to vote. It emphasizes a series of ideas about what would happen if Republicans were *not* elected to office. For example, some racial messaging paints the picture that Democrats do not care for the safety of White Americans, and if left to their own devices, they would allow "crime" (implicitly racialized as crime by Black Americans) to run rampant. This form of messaging reaffirms the partisan assumption latent within the three *P*'s. It associates Black Americans closely with the Democratic Party in a way where the party is perceived as kowtowing to the influence of Black Americans.

In contrast to the functional role of conservative parties described above, racial messaging has involved a series of rhetorical choices made by political actors. They were not constrained to use this rhetoric; they could have decided to use other rhetoric. Political elites made deliberate choices to use racially inflammatory rhetoric. With a similar agency, conservative elites have crafted their political platform to attract voters. In another way that reaffirms the party's connection to White Americans, many outreach efforts over the years have been racially homogeneous. To add, there have been instances where the party could have decided to make more eclectic, diverse platforms in order to attract Americans of color. However, collectively, the GOP has opted away from this prospect. Examples of this abound. Following the reelection of Obama, the GOP's growing sentiment that it needed to readjust its platform to accommodate more voters of color was at a fever pitch. Republicans could have gone the direction of changing the electorate and adjusting their messaging to bring more conservatively minded POC into the party. As I recount, the battle for the future of the party began here, carrying through the 2016 Republican primaries. They eventually decided, as a party, that opening up the party's platform was not the strategy they would take; instead, they emphasized a restrictionist position that would look to inflame their White base and prevent participation of the political opposition, which laid the foundation for what has become the big flip-out over American democracy. Conservative elites have sent implicit and explicit signals to Americans about the prospect and potential outcome of demographic determinism. Ultimately, these prospects call into question Americans' commitment to democracy.

The Big Flip, Great Replacement, and the Question of American Democracy

For many years, the mere exposure to the idea of the big flip has shifted senses of racial threat and caused more support for discriminatory ideas (Craig and Richeson 2014c; Craig, Rucker, and Richeson 2018). On a mass scale, throughout the Trump era, ideas of threat from the big flip have been prodded by political elites to Americans to such a degree that they cemented demographic determinism in the minds of Republicans. Far-right channels and outlets have advanced this idea, which now functionally exists as the "Great Replacement."

I described the gestation of demographic determinism as an idea. The functional role of conservative parties in the United States, amid their alignment with White-identity politics, provides the institutional framework for why demographic determinism can be threatening to so many Americans. To add, GOP elites have repeatedly signaled to their voters that Black Americans and other Americans of color are threats. Their messaging has also gone about connecting the Democratic Party, in their minds, even further with negative outcomes. Third, Republican elites have had ample opportunities to bring in more voters of color, which would have worked to vitiate *some* degree of association of the Republican Party with Whiteness. These three dynamics set up the simple, dangerous scenario regarding the future of American democracy: Demographic determinism leads to a reduction in confidence in the democratic system.

What I am describing here is a public-wide level of erosion of the current American system of government. One of the two major parties in American politics has hitched its wagon to the bunk idea of demographic determinism that questions commitment to democracy. As a conservative party, the GOP is already less likely to uphold democratic ideals unless they benefit the party. And as elites advance demographic-deterministic ideas that threaten Republicans' confidence in winning elections, it erodes their voters' support for democracy.

Republicans come to believe that their party will be unable to win by sheer numbers because they are a shrinking majority of the American public. Yet they want to win because they see their party as one of the only bulwarks in place to maintain their sense of normalcy in the changing American landscape. So, in their minds, one of the only viable and successful ways of keeping this power is to play dirty—to use political tactics that question the legitimacy of elections, promote violence, elect strongman and -woman leaders, and ultimately become less supportive of conventional American democratic practices. Demographic determinism causes these Americans to want flip democracy in order to maintain their power.

5

Demographic Determinism and Prediction

Politically Predicting the Big Flip?

The 2010 Census cemented the big flip narrative. It gave insight into the current demographics of the United States at the time, and some data-minded demographers began crafting models about what the data points demonstrated about the future of America. One particular model stuck in the public coverage of the 2010 Census: the majority-minority flip. This same coverage helped to advance demographic determinism in the mass American public and put forth the notion that White Americans, for the first time, were going to become a numerical minority, while Americans of color would surmount them as the emergent numerical majority.

> In the wake of a presidential election that underscored the rising political clout of fast growing minority groups, the Census Bureau's new population projections reiterate the trend. These projections, the first to take account of the 2010 Census results, paint a picture of a nation that will become increasingly diverse, beginning at the bottom of the age distribution.
>
> (Frey 2012)

The information was new, which left it ripe for research. Scholars took up investigating the ways that Americans reacted to this information, giving special attention to White Americans because of their position of power in American society and how their political views have been historically affected by local shifts in racial compositions. Racial demographic change had happened on smaller scales throughout the country prior to the twenty-first century; as a theory, it came to be known as *group threat theory* or *racial threat theory*. Racial threat theory describes how changing group sizes

The Big Flip. Andrew Ifedapo Thompson, Oxford University Press. © Oxford University Press (2026).
DOI: 10.1093/9780197822173.003.0005

can lead to a sense of threat expressed by the dominant group because group members feel an encroachment on their relative status through those changes (Blumer 1958).

These reactions gave insight into a set of expectations of what could happen within politics in light of the developing narrative about the big flip. The flip worried a great deal of White Americans. The information was expected to cause a sense of racial threat, on a national scale, for the first time in American history. Around the time of the release of these census projections, social scientists began investigating how the projections of the big flip were altering Americans' views of one another. Within these studies they gave overwhelming attention to White Americans, in part because of the perceived threat to their relative status (Sohoni 2022). Some of the most prominent research that was put forth in this time was conducted by Maureen Craig and Jennifer Richeson (2014a; 2014b). Across a series of studies, these scholars find that simply providing information about the majority-minority flip led to grand shifts within their views of politics and of minority racial groups. Craig and Richeson show that when White Americans are shown the majority-minority flip information, they express more conservative ideological views and more support for conservative policies that are both race-specific and race-neutral. Moreover, they also express even more support for restrictive immigration, less support for affirmative action, and less support for funding healthcare. The fact that Craig and Richeson find a conservative shift across all of these policy measures indicates that the racial threat elicited from the big flip is *not* limited to attitudes about racial groups. Importantly, this is one of the first indicators that racial threat could motivate ideas outside of a race-exclusive context. In short, this is a precursor finding for the way attitudes toward democracy are affected by sentiments of racial threat. It is the central, normative outcome in question about the big flip. I spell out this line of reasoning later on in this book.

In the conclusion of their work, they write the following:

> The present research provides a detailed examination of how the perceived loss of majority status by Whites in an increasingly diverse country affects the expression of racial bias. This research provides insight into how Whites may react to the impending demographic shift and highlights potential for perceived threat and intergroup hostility. In a nation on the precipice of arguably the greatest change in racial make-up since the Immigration and Nationality Act of 1965, it is vital to understand how both racial majority

> and minority group members react to this change and, in turn, the potential consequences of such reactions for intergroup relations.
>
> (Craig and Richeson 2014b)

Craig and Richeson also find a similar shift in attitudes toward racial tolerance in a separate study (Craig and Richeson 2014a). White Americans who read over the information about the majority-minority flip express significantly more negative attitudes toward a variety of racial groups—namely Black Americans, Asian Americans, and Hispanic Americans. They also find that this same information on the majority-minority flip alters White Americans' implicit attitudes toward their racial group and Americans of color. They become more implicitly pro-White and anti-minority.

> This framing suggests that the White population is losing its majority status, despite the fact that it will remain the largest single racial group in the nation, compared to any other group individually. Although the authors of such reports may simply be trying to reflect the growing diversity of our nation, the present work suggests that they may also be evoking group status threat in White Americans that can result in heightened racial bias.
>
> (Craig and Richeson 2014a)

This piece effectively validates racial threat's centrality to the story of the majority-minority flip. Within another related study this research team conducted around the same time, they found that this same majority-minority flip information about increases in the Hispanic American population led to a conservative shift among non-Hispanic racial minorities (Craig and Richeson 2018). Although these findings are significantly more limited in scope—because the racial group samples in this study are much smaller than those in their former studies—they still are able to identify that threat seems to operate in a similar fashion for racial minority groups. Therefore, they assert that racial demographic change for outgroups is crucial to how we ought to think about racial threat. Racial minorities express a similar level of threat when they learn that their groups are *not* increasing in size.

Throughout these studies, the central implication is that Americans have some ability to understand and predict how racial demographic changes will look within the country. The very existence of a sense of threat and increasingly negative attitudes toward Americans of color is direct evidence of the idea of prediction as a part of the big flip. I bring to bear the efficacy of the majority-minority flip, as Craig and Richeson claim it, by bringing their study into the contemporary political context.

Bringing Craig and Richeson to Bear

I first conduct a study utilizing the same experimental design that Craig and Richeson used in their earlier research agenda. In this extension and replication of their research, I expand on the outcome questions they ask Americans to accommodate some vital contextual changes in American politics.

Within this study, I give close attention to American political discourse about the changing demographics of the country. I field this study in the fall of 2020, which is done for a variety of reasons that are contextually important to investigating demographic determinism. My first reason is to replicate the same study within a radically different political moment. Craig and Richeson conducted their previous two studies in the later years of the Obama administration, and, as I have demonstrated and advanced in earlier chapters, many Americans then were making inferences about the future of the country through the lens of Obama. Beyond his tenure in office, Obama's legacy still can motivate how Americans think about the future of the country, but in the fall of 2020, the participants of my study are surveyed after three years of Donald Trump's presidency. Moreover, these ideas of threat could have shifted because of how they became mainstream in American politics through the rise of Trumpism. Political scientists have given further evidence and credence to the idea that Obama was a chief motivator of some voting for Donald Trump in the 2016 election. To this, political scientist Diana Mutz writes the following:

> Racial status threat makes perfect sense occurring immediately after 8 years of leadership by America's first African American president. It is not racism of the kind suggesting that whites view minorities as morally or intellectually inferior, but rather, one that regards minorities as sufficiently powerful to be a threat to the status quo. When members of a dominant group experience a sense of threat to their group's position, whether it is the status of Americans in the world at large or the status of whites in a multiethnic America, change in people's sense of their group's relative position produces insecurity.
>
> (Mutz 2018)

Filtering this understanding through the context in which Craig and Richeson conducted their study, we can see that Americans made inferences about the future of the country and its politics during the Obama era.

White Americans could have been feeling a greater sense of racial threat because they saw a changing country in which their power could be usurped by growing, apt racial minorities, but also, at that time, they were lacking certain narratives that became mainstream during Trump's term in office. So, by replicating Craig and Richeson's same study in 2020, I investigated how this same information worked to affect White Americans' views of racial politics within Trump's administration. The year 2020 was plagued by the COVID-19 pandemic and worldwide protests about the killing of George Floyd, so these added dimensions likely worked to shift the way Americans think about racial politics. Another reason I conduct this study in the fall of 2020 is to use the context of the 2020 presidential election and thereby add another vital political dimension to this study. The salience of politics at the time of the study adds further magnitude to the stakes of racial demographic change, particularly among the most threatened Americans. Moreover, there were a variety of concerns about the anti-democratic behavior of elites and the public in the midst of the election. So, for this reason, I include a set of anti-democratic measures.[1]

In terms of the specific details of this study, I use the exact same treatment Craig and Richeson (2014b) utilize in study 3. This treatment articulates that there will be a majority-minority flip, while also providing data about the changes. Importantly, it describes a host of racial groups changing in size, emphasizing that Hispanic Americans and Asian Americans are projected to grow largely (figure 5.1).

I ultimately expect to replicate their same set of findings along the lines of racial threat, as well as expand on previous findings they uncovered along the lines of rightward turns. My first hypothesis coheres with the central idea of the big flip about senses of threat expressed and projected by White Americans. This expectation is as follows:

> Priming racial demographic changes (using the same treatment as Craig and Richeson 2014a) will cause White Americans to express greater levels of racial threat, H1.

This hypothesis works both as good social science, replicating the same findings to provide further legitimacy to the theoretical concept, and as an

[1] These latter two contextual factors are crucial to describing the political moment in which I conduct this study. I will describe my findings among the outcome variables for attitudes toward Black Lives Matter (BLM) in chapter 7 and anti-democratic attitudes in chapter 8.

In a Generation, Racial Minorities May Be the U.S. Majority

By: S. Roberts

A new analysis of 2010 U.S. Census Bureau data suggests that America might become a White-minority nation faster than once predicted. The nation's racial minority population is steadily rising and currently makes up 35 percent of the United States. This advances an unmistakable trend that could make racial minorities the new American majority by midcentury, a transformation that is occurring much faster than anticipated just a few years ago.

Demographers calculate that by 2042, Americans who identify themselves as Hispanic, Black, Asian, American Indian, Native Hawaiian, or Pacific Islander will together outnumber non-Hispanic Whites. Four years ago, officials had projected the shift would come in 2050. This shift can already be seen in several U.S. states; currently, four states as well as the District of Columbia have minority populations that exceed 50 percent.

The main reasons for the accelerating change are rapid immigration growth and significantly higher birthrates among racial and ethnic minorities. As White baby boomers age past their childbearing years, younger Hispanic parents are having children – and driving U.S. population growth. New estimates show minorities increased to 107.2 million people in 2009, largely boosted by a surge in Hispanic births. During this time, the White population remained flat, making up roughly 199.9 million, or 65 percent, of the country. The group predicted to post the most dramatic gain, Hispanics, is projected to nearly triple in size by 2050. There are now roughly 9 births for every 1 death among Hispanics, compared to a roughly one-to-one ratio for Whites.

The Census Bureau projects that ethnic and racial minorities will constitute a majority of the nation's children under 18 by 2023 and of working-age Americans by 2039. Indeed, about 49.6 percent of babies born in 2011 were White, compared to about 50.4 percent who were racial minorities.

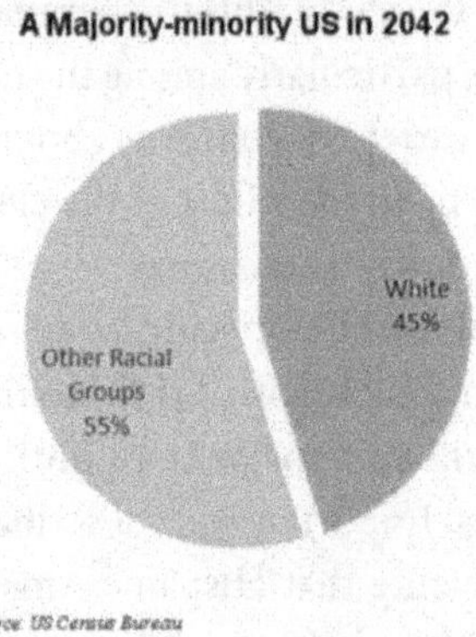

The latest figures are predicated on current and historical trends, which demographers say can be reasonably expected to continue.

Figure 5.1 Article describing that, as of the 2010 Census, racial minorities might become the numerical majority group. Details include increasing immigration and higher birthrates among racial minorities. Pie chart displaying racial minorities at 55% and Whites at 45%.

affirmation that their results were not limited to the context in which they conducted the studies.

After this initial test, I will evaluate a second hypothesis that will serve as an initial affirmation of the partisan element of demographic determinism. This is to affirm that priming racial demographic changes with the same treatment will have partisan-specific impacts on future projections of American society, affecting Democratic and Republican White Americans in drastically different ways. Specifically, I expect that Republicans will become more pessimistic about the future of the country (H2a), while Democrats will become more optimistic (H2b) upon being exposed to the same information. This hypothesis feeds directly into my last on the individual-level ideology expressed by both Democrats and Republicans. Following from the expectations on the future of the country, I also expect that both partisans will become significantly more polarized among their expressions of ideology. In effect, Democrats will become more expressively liberal (H3a) and Republicans will become more expressively conservative (H3b).

Study Design

I conduct this study with White Americans only (N = 717), which again adheres to the structure of Craig and Richeson's design, serving as a replication and extension years later. Upon exposure to this same information they present about the big flip, I then assessed White Americans' attitudes on two sets of feelings about the future of the country. The first outcome measures sentiments of threat specific to the big flip. The question posed asked to what extent they agreed with the following statement: "If they increase in size, racial minorities are likely to reduce the influence of White Americans in society." Overall, this measure captures the perceived social place of White Americans—and the extent to which they anticipate they will lose it as Americans of color increase in population.

The second measure I used assesses feelings about how American society is developing. The question is framed as "What is your view of American society?" Answers ranged from "American society is getting much worse every year" to "American society is getting much better every year." The idea captured here is the predicted threat the big flip presents to American society on the whole, which functions in a different place relative to, simply, White Americans' status.

Shown below, I ultimately find that White Americans *are* again threatened by the information about the big flip, thereby replicating Craig and Richeson's results. These Americans feel that White Americans, on the whole, will lose their influence to Americans of color as the big flip occurs ($p = 0.0062$; figure 5.2).[2]

[2] I control for demographic characteristics in my analysis, including education, gender, party identification, age, income, and media consumption.

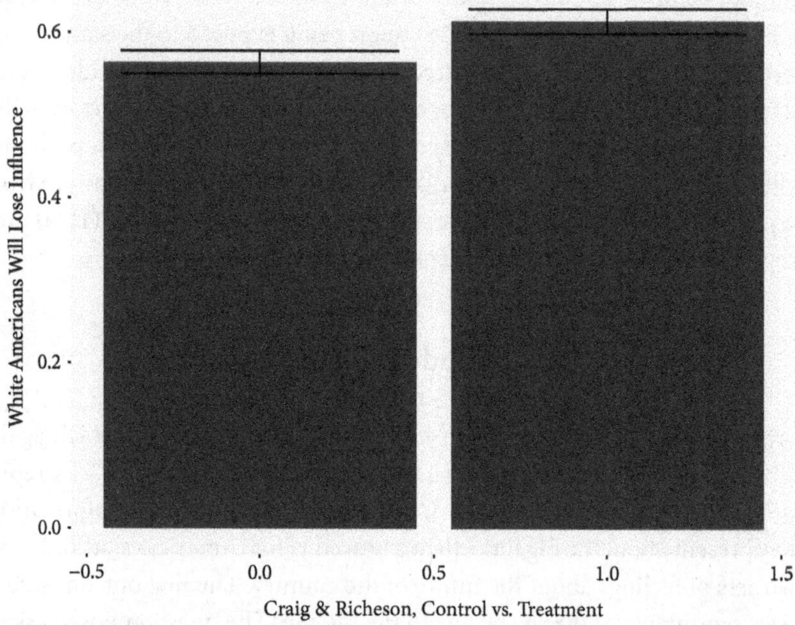

Figure 5.2 Bar plot comparison between control and treatment measuring support for the idea that White Americans will lose influence if racial minorities increase in size. Depicts that the treatment significantly increase support for this idea.

In terms of the second measure that I use, White Americans do *not* collectively feel concerned about the future of American society. This is to say, an overall sentiment of racial threat in the future does not emerge. Importantly, this story immediately changes the moment I assess how White Democrats and White Republicans react to this same narrative about the big flip (figure 5.3). To test how these Americans, respectively, react to this information, I use an interaction between the treatment and party identification. This test seeks to uncover how Democrats and Republicans exposed to this treatment think about the future of American society, compared to those in the control group.

When I investigate White partisan heterogeneity among reactions to the big flip along party lines, I detect massive differences in perceptions of the future of society. In figure 5.3, the Y-axis captures the positive or negative feeling Americans express about the future of the country. These are on a 0–1 scale, with 0 representing the perception of the United States getting

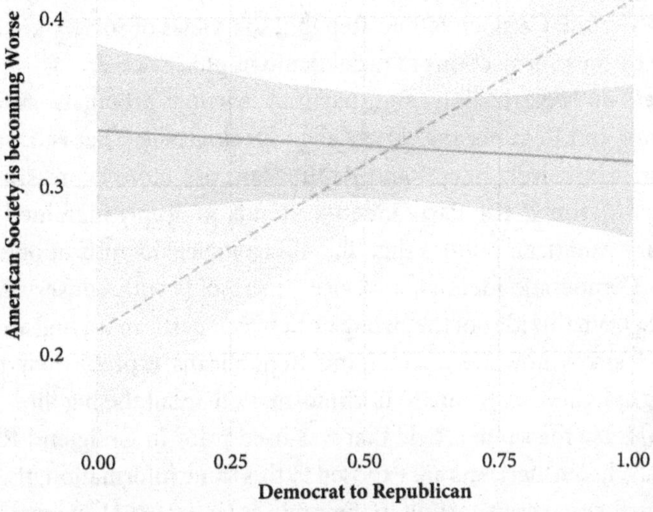

Figure 5.3 Interaction plot depicting the effect of the Craig and Richeson treatment on the perception of the American way of life becoming better or worse across Democrats to Republicans. Upon receiving the treatment, Democrats become significantly more supportive of the idea that the American way of life is becoming better and Republican become demonstrably more supportive that it is becoming worse.

significantly worse and 1 representing the perception of the United States getting significantly better. The control group shows the baseline for both Republicans and Democrats—Republicans are much more positive than Democrats about the future, which makes sense given that this study was conducted when Republicans controlled the government.

Additionally, recall that when I conducted this study, the 2020 presidential election campaign was in full swing. Democrats were pessimistic about the future of the country, in part because Donald Trump was president, while Republicans were more hopeful for the same reason. This explains the control group, which is in the dotted line in figure 5.3. When both of these groups are exposed to information about the big flip, their perceptions about the future of American society shift drastically ($p = 7.48e{-}05$); Democrats become significantly more hopeful, while Republicans express that the country is getting worse. This inversion in perceptions of the future is stark, and it confirms the first of the three *P*'s representing misperceptions of the big flip. Despite the country's future being nearly impossible to predict, both White Democrats' and Republicans' views of society are affected strongly by these projections of racial demographic change.

Studies on polarization and partisan sorting articulate how both Democrats and Republicans closely align ideologically. That is, Democrats are more expressively liberal and Republicans are more expressively conservative (Mason 2018). Party identification is so deeply ingrained in contemporary American politics that liberal ideological identification strongly predicts Democratic identity, and vice versa holds with conservatives. So following from this idea of the strong tie between partisan sorting and polarization, I assess how Democrats and Republicans express their political ideology in light of exposure to this information about the big flip.

Again, I use the same article that was used prior in Craig and Richeson (2014b). When Americans are exposed to this same information, the big flip causes further partisan sorting in their minds ($p = 0.0893$), shown in figure 5.4. Importantly, as visualized within the figure, sorting happens on both ends of the spectrum; that is, Republicans identify more conservatively while Democrats identify more liberally.

The fact that I am only identifying racial demographic change in this study is crucial to thinking through how the information is being processed by Americans across hypotheses H2 and H3. Throughout the treatment, there is no mention of the American political system. Additionally, there is no mention of political parties, ideology, or how society might politically change. Simply put, politics are explicitly absent from the treatment. Despite this absence of mention, White Americans still infer political ideas when they think about the big flip. The innocuous demographic information in the treatment causes White Americans to fear more about their relative status in society. This sense of threat could stem from a variety of places—from the fear of losing their social influence, discrimination against them increasing, or stories about White Americans being valued less in Hollywood. All of these sentiments of threat could be, and likely are, present, in this expression of a sense of threat.

The analyses I conduct after this initial test of racial threat help round out the story of how White Americans are processing this information. Perceptions about the future of society are indicators of how the big flip factors into politics, filtered through Americans' partisan identity.

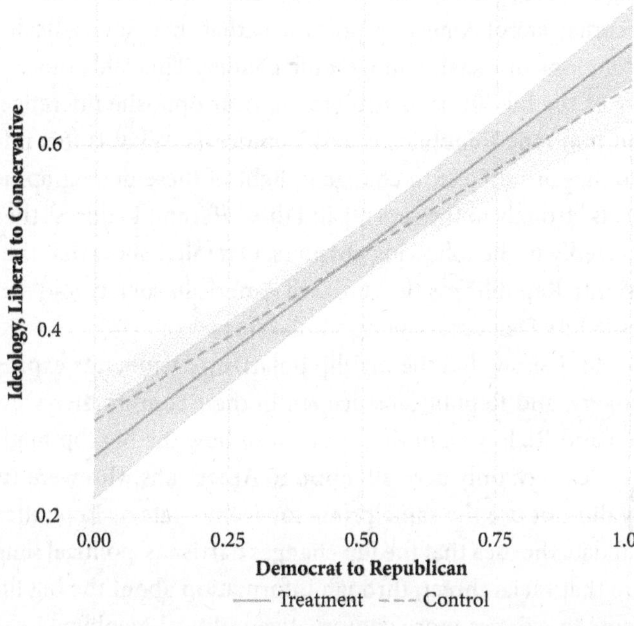

Figure 5.4 Interaction plot depicting the effect of the Craig and Richeson treatment on ideology measured posttreatment across Democrats to Republicans. Upon receiving the treatment, Democrats become significantly more liberal and Republicans become more conservative.

The measure of perceptions about perceptions of the future of American society is one of the best indicators within this study on how political values and perceptions are factored into predictions of the big flip. When thinking about the future of American society, Republican and Democratic White Americans are led to have widely different perspectives after mere exposure to information about the big flip. Democrats, who at the time of the study in September 2020 were quite pessimistic about the future of American society, become significantly more optimistic about the future. They shift roughly 10 age points. Moreover, I find an exactly similar yet opposite shift among Republicans, who were quite optimistic about the future of American society, which is evidenced by the control group. But reading over the information about the big flip leads them to become just about 10 points *more* pessimistic about the future prospects of the country.

Prediction about demographic change leads to radically different perceptions about the same information. What I show, which is not present within Craig and Richeson's initial studies because their work was conducted during an earlier era of American politics, is that there are radically different interpretations of racial demographic change. This adds more tapestry to the story of the big flip in that there are near opposite inferences being made about it among Republicans and Democrats. What is this inference? Partisan politics are subject to change in light of these demographic shifts. This connects strongly to the second and third *P*'s, and I address these ideas more concertedly in the following chapters. Overall, I show that the big flip frightens White Republicans the future of American society and somewhat encourages White Democrats along similar lines.

In figure 5.4, I show that the big flip polarizes: Democrats express more liberal ideology, and Republicans deepen in their conservative views, generally. Craig and Richeson, in their pursuit of how the big flip might move Americans' ideology, only gave attention to Americans who were Independent. They did not use the same prime for Democrats or Republicans. My findings validate the idea that the flip changes partisans' political senses. The findings are that racial threat, through information about the big flip, leads Independents to express more conservative political ideology. I show that this dynamic is not limited to political Independents, who do not function as the "middle" of the political spectrum (Klar 2014; Klar and Krupnikov 2016; Klar, Krupnikov, and Ryan 2022), which makes the explanation of their conservative ideological movement more difficult. My test of Democrats' and Republicans' ideology is therefore a more grounded test of the influence of racial threat on these views. Threat causes further polarization on the tail ends of the political spectrum. The big flip strengthens Democrats' and Republicans' views—without any mention of how the country might change because of it.

All of these findings, taken together, provide a series of important indicators. First, the predictions of the flip were still potent when Craig and Richeson conducted their study in the early 2010s. I go on to show that these sentiments might, in fact, be *more* potent among White Americans. The same prime shifts senses of threat among White Americans generally, and even more crucial to the function of the big flip, I find significant heterogeneity along partisanship. Democrats and Republicans have widely variant perceptions of the big flip. These perceptions lay the groundwork for the attention I pay to partisanship throughout this book. Racial threat from the big flip mostly remains for White Republicans, while for White Democrats the big flip represents hope about the political future of the United States. These two groups are inferring the same future from the big flip, but their divergent emotional responses stem from different outcomes for their parties. For this reason, I pay close attention to how partisans react to *all* information related to the big flip. Partisanship is important to the inferences Americans make about the big flip because it is a key misperception, but misperceptions held across the American public lead to different emotional reactions among partisans. Democrats and Republicans agree on demographic determinism; they both agree that the flip will change the country. They even agree on its effect on the future of the country's political landscape. They agree on the predictions. They diverge, however, when they start thinking about how they themselves and their party will be affected. These partisan emotional reactions to the changing country are deeply contingent on the groups that are perceived to be growing in size. Next, I show that altering information about the predictions radically shifts how Americans feel about the future of the country.

The Flip Side of Big Flip

The processes of the big flip come from a variety of places—that is, there are mechanisms at work regarding threat. One of the distinct places from which threat operates is the subject of immigration. It is a central process of diversification and key to the inferences Americans make about racial demographic change. A variety of Americans' presumptions are coming from stereotypes that are made about immigrants—many of which are non-White, but even more particularly come from Latin America.

There is a long history of views about immigration being closely connected to sentiments of threat. Feelings about immigration, on the whole, are closely tied to prejudicial racial attitudes Americans hold (Burns and Gimpel 2000; Citrin et al. 1997) and how Americans think about policies connected to immigration, such as welfare (Garand, Xu, and Davis 2017). Popular messages in media have often framed immigration as threatening to native-born Americans. In recent years, however, these messages and reactions to them have changed. Again, similar to my findings about general views of racial demographic change, these ideas have shifted along partisan lines (figure 5.5).

Republicans view immigration as more threatening than they have in the past, while there has been a steady decline in threat among Democrats and Independents. One of the most potent motivators of these sentiments is the emotions they attach to immigrants. Among those Americans that feel the

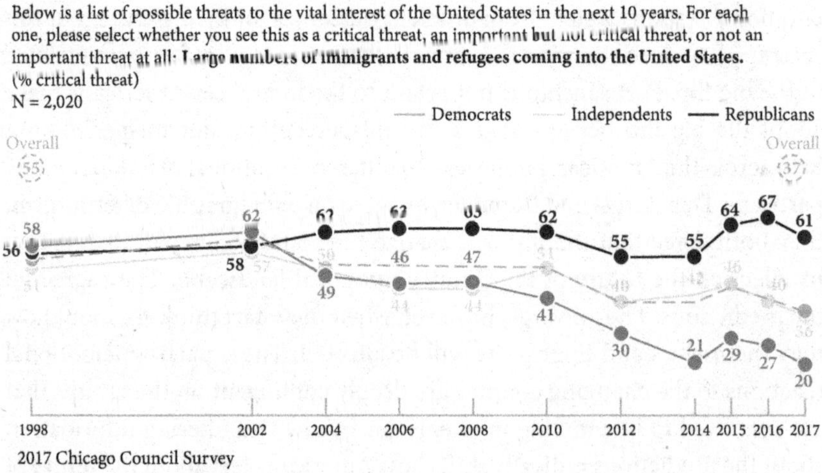

Figure 5.5 Plot of Americans' perceptions of immigration as a threat from 1998 to 2017.

most threatened, anger is the most potent emotion that drives their attitudes about immigration (Banks 2016; Phoenix 2019).

I seek to alter these sentiments by altering how Americans think about immigration's tie to the big flip. More specifically, I engage in priming another type of immigrant group, one that sits outside of the bounds of stereotypical perceptions of immigration. In this study, I conduct another experiment that involves a different prime about immigration. I tell participants that the big flip is actually being driven by European immigration and that Europeans are slated to be the largest immigration group in years to come. My main intention behind this study is to assess how this reframing of immigration shifts emotions, attitudes, and expressed ideology about the big flip—similar to how I conducted the previous study extension from Craig and Richeson.

I simply tell White Americans that Europeans are the fastest-growing immigrant group and that this group is projected to become the largest by the mid-century. This is the typical narrative about Latin American and Asian immigrants, the latter of which has recently been shown to be the fastest-growing group (Budiman and Ruiz 2021). The control group is not exposed to this information; they simply move on to the outcome variables.

Upon exposing White Americans to this information, I then assess how this affects their sense of anger. This measure simply asks, "How angry do you feel about the diversification of the United States?" Below, in my analyses, I investigate two ways of measuring this outcome: First, the main effect of the treatment, where I compare the average anger level of the treatment directly to the control. Second, I assess the interaction of party identification with the treatment. Following recent findings, Republicans should be more affected by the information because their attitudes toward immigration have recently grown more oppositional, and immigration that will effectively make the country Whiter should assuage their sense of threat. In other words, I expect that Republicans' baseline level of anger about immigration is in part based on their projections that the number of people of color will increase. The information about Europeans will mitigate those concerns, thereby reducing their sense of anger. I do not expect this same dynamic among Democrats because these partisans have been far less concerned about immigration in recent years.

Below are my results. White Americans *on the whole* become less angry when they learn that Europeans are rapidly increasing in size. Their anger reduces by nearly 5 age points (p = 0.06; figure 5.6).

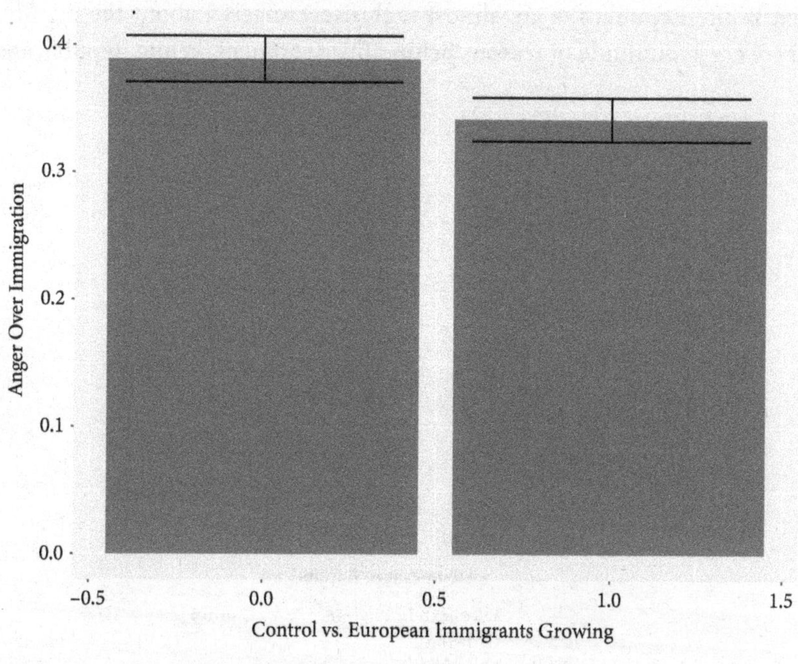

Figure 5.6 Bar plot comparison between control and treatment measuring support for the idea that White Americans will lose influence if racial minorities increase in size. Depicts that the treatment significantly increases support for this idea.

This is a clear demonstration of how the presumptions of immigration shape how White Americans think about the future of the country. Reframing immigration as something that leads to more Europeans clearly comes across as less threatening to White Americans.

Next, I conduct regressions using interactive effects, with party identification as the moderator. This allows me to compare how both Democrats and Republicans react relative to one another. I also include controls in this analysis for education, media usage, age, gender, region, and ideology (figure 5.7).

The left end of the graph represents strong Democrats, and the right end consists of strong Republicans. Importantly, there is heterogeneity among party members. Increasing the European population decreases anger almost exclusively for Republicans, as Democrats exposed to this same treatment express nearly equally low levels of anger about the diversification of the United States.

This finding also confirms my expectation that anger about the diversification of the United States is unidirectional among Republicans. This means that White Republicans are almost exclusively angered about the big flip. There are a multitude of reasons behind this sentiment. White Republicans

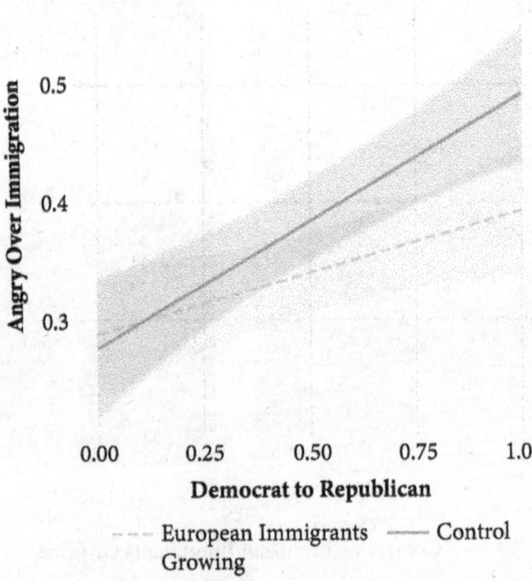

Figure 5.7 Interaction plot depicting the effect of the treatment on anger over demographic change posttreatment across Democrats to Republicans. Upon receiving the treatment, Republicans become less angry.

perceive that these changes will affect their status in society and their party's position. As I mentioned in my explanation of demographic determinism, Republicans are inferring a political future from simple information about how race could change within the United States. They are engaging in a type of prediction about the future state of society.

These predictions are unfounded because they exist within the social world, but in their minds, they nonetheless exist. As a result, they are politically relevant and ought to be taken seriously. I show that when the presumptions about demographic change are questioned and White Republicans are told that Europeans are slated to be the largest growing immigrant group, they then become more emotionally positive about the future of the country. Their anger is assuaged when stereotypes do not mesh with predictions about immigration.

Priming the idea of a European influx, in a roundabout way, assures that the White majority of the country will be maintained over time. In effect, the European immigration information assures White Republicans that the big flip will *not* happen. So, by extension, they infer that their party will not be as affected by Americans of color increasing in size.

Following this idea, I also find evidence in this same study that Republicans' political views also shift in light of this same information. Along with their ideology ($p = 0.030$) and support for immigration ($p = 0.075$), their attitudes move in a liberal direction. Believing Europeans are the fastest-growing immigrant group leads Republicans to identify as more liberal, while Democrats stay nearly the same; White Republicans also become more supportive of increasing immigration into the United States (figures 5.8 and 5.9).

Within this experiment, I show that Republicans' predictions about the country's demographic change motivate their feelings about the future. From my replication of Craig and Richeson's study, we know that Republicans are already angry about the big flip, and when they are primed to think about it, they become angrier. Conversely, I show that when they are told that European immigrant populations will increase, they become less angry and, on a surprising level, more liberal and supportive of immigration.

My findings speak to the way that conservative ideology and immigration attitudes are partly driven by perceptions surrounding the big flip. Threat clearly drives these attitudes, so much so that its absence leads to moderate views among White Republicans.

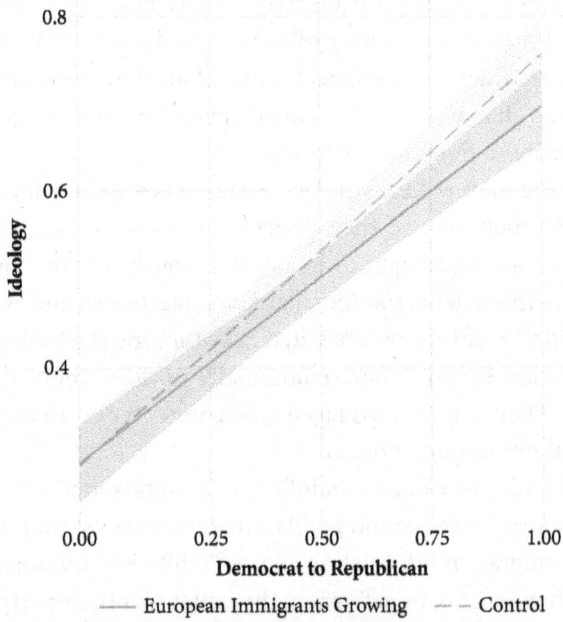

Figure 5.8 Interaction plot depicting the effect of the treatment on support for increased immigration measured posttreatment across Democrats to Republicans. Upon receiving the treatment, Republicans become more supportive of increased immigration.

Predictions about America's Future

Within this set of studies, I show how predictions about the future racial structure in the United States lead to changes in how White Americans think about their future. The abstract nature of these projections is crucial to the story that is told through their priming. In opposite directions, I show that priming the big flip leads to sizable changes in emotions and political attitudes.

First, on emotions, I do not intentionally use inflammatory language in these experiments. There is a series of works that intentionally prime emotions, like anger, in order to assess its effect on how Americans consider politics (Marcus 2000; Brader and Marcus 2013; Valentino, Wayne, and Oceno 2018). Some find that priming extreme ideas can even trigger bodily responses, which shift people's attitudes (Bakker, Schumacher, and Rooduijn 2021). Most of these studies will describe politics in more extreme

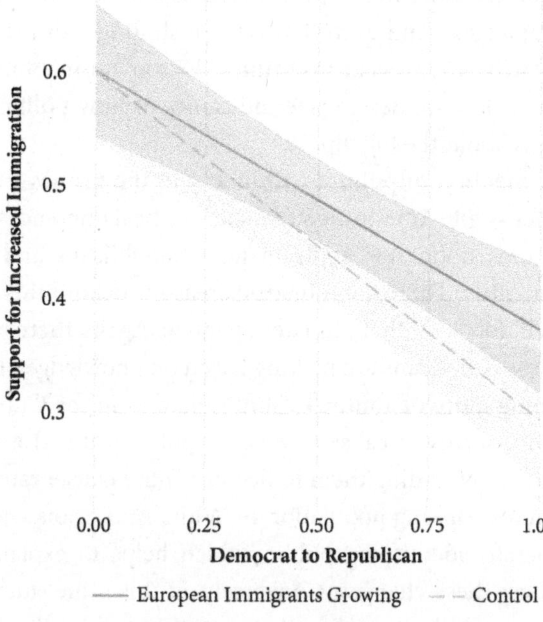

Figure 5.9 Wording and structure of treatment.

ways or encourage participants to consider how they are feeling, say, along angry or anxious lines. I first replicate a previous study from Craig and Richeson (2014b) that describes racial demographic change in simply descriptive ways. The information provided in the article causes feelings of threat among White Americans, but in no place does it describe the future of the country as threatening or say that society will change. Similarly, in the second study, which describes European immigration, I do not mention whether American society will or will not change. I only provide a few sentences to Americans that Europeans are projected to be the largest growing immigrant group. Any and all emotional responses that emerge from these treatments are done by additional inferential work among the participants. More specifically, I mean that White Americans in these studies are extrapolating how they think the future of the country might look and how they are affected by the information I provide. This type of assumption is what shapes the misperception of prediction I initially described in this chapter. Americans learn about the projections of the big flip and predict significantly more about the future of the country than demography would allow for. Changing racial demographics does not mean anything about the future of American society other than how Americans adjust their sense of self in light of these changes—and even that type of shifting attitude is unknowable because it will simply occur over time. More to our inability to predict, within these first few studies we see indicators of how political ideas are affected by ideas about the big flip.

There is no mention of politics within any of the primes I use in these experiments. Yet White Americans still make political inferences from them. For one, it causes noticeable shifts in how Republicans and Democrats ideologically identify. There are numerous reasons behind this shift in ideology, and I will focus on them in later chapters. Again, there are apparent predictions these Americans are making based on knowledge of the big flip. Whites becoming more of a numerical minority, as in the Craig and Richeson replication, seems to cause a sense of political threat among White Republicans, thereby leading them to become more conservative. They are predicting that a shrinking population of White Americans will likely lead to a more liberally identifying public, which helps to explain the anger they express over these changes. Conversely, in this same study, it appears that Democrats could be assuming the same thing about the future of the country, which would make them more optimistic about the future and also more expressively liberal. Regarding immigration, I also show suggestive evidence that White Republicans could be more concerned about the future of the country than Democrats. The European immigration prediction leads Republicans to express less anger over future US demographic changes. It also causes them to express slightly less conservative ideology and become more supportive of immigration, relative to Republicans who are not exposed to this information. I find no shift in these political attitudes on the side of White Democrats.

These findings help to paint the picture of what is going on in Americans' minds when they express their ideas about how the big flip could affect them. My experiments offer insight into how priming this information could affect their ideas en masse.

The Big Flip in Their Own Words

A thicker description, particularly what is happening in Americans' shifting views, is not possible in these first few studies. We are simply able to evaluate how Americans read over the articles and primes provided to them. We can assess how they react to this information, but we are unaware of how they think about the changing country.

To gather a more robust sense of how Americans are inferring and predicting from their knowledge of the big flip, I turn to qualitative methods and investigate specifically, in a longer, open-ended response format, how information about the big flip causes Americans to think about the future of the country. The data gathered from these interviews came from both individuals and a focus group directly reacting to ideas of the changing country. I focus on which ideas jump immediately to mind when Americans read and think about the big flip. In this study, I provide Americans with an article I designed that describes the big flip in a politically innocuous way (figure 5.10).

The article does not prime ideas about politics or emotions; this is to substantively follow the previous studies and to gather a clearer picture of what is emerging in Americans' minds. In this study, I provide the article in figure 5.10, then ask participants to describe their reactions at length in an open-ended format. Within the following descriptions, I detail the age, race, gender, political identity, and state each participant lives in, using pseudonyms to protect their identity.[3]

There are a series of major themes that emerge in reaction to the big flip. Many of the Americans who express concern and anger about the coming changes tend to identify more closely with the Republican party and are more conservative. Take Jarrod, for example: Jarrod is a fifty-seven-year-old White man who identifies as a moderate Republican. He lives in Montana, and after reading over the big flip article, he reacted in the following concerned way:

> This is very depressing because I don't need to hear that my race is dying out because our current president and vice president couldn't get their act together and stop the border crossing. They didn't even care and were actually letting them fly in secretively. This is an outrage. We already have enough poor people that aren't being taken care of why bring in more?

To Jarrod, the future of the country generates a strong sense of worry, and he even is able to identify where he thinks the threat to the country's future is coming from. First, his emphasis on "my race" is significant.

[3] I conducted this study in partnership with More in Common in March 2022 with a diverse sample of 274 Americans.

U.S.

U.S. Census Bureau Sees White Americans Falling to Minority in a More Racially Diverse America

10-20-2022

Washington, D.C. – Detailed new projections from the U.S. Census Bureau find that the U.S. population will become more racially diverse in coming decades.

The largest increase in racial diversity will be seen among younger generations while older Americans remain predominantly non-Hispanic white. Altogether, between 2016 and 2045, the country's Hispanic and Asian populations will rise 74% and 82% respectively, accounting for most of U.S. population growth during that period.

Over the same period, the older white population will stop growing altogether. Already, for the first time, whites are in the minority among children under the age of 5 and will be a minority of all young people under the age of 18 before the end of the decade. By 2044, whites will be a minority of the entire population.

According to Dr. Robert Manning, a sociologist at the University of Kansas' Center for the Study of Demography, "This is without historical precedent. Whites are becoming a minority in the U.S. as a whole, and the former minorities are going to be the new majority, as they are in some parts of the country already."

Figure 5.10 Mock article, used as treatment, describing how the United States will soon be a majority-minority country.

Some contemporary discussions about the big flip go as far as describing it as a "replacement" (Miller 2020), but the idea of White Americans "dying out" is even more visceral than the idea of replacement because it evokes the extinguishment of White Americans' existence. The start of this line of reasoning is arguably a place from which extreme political ideas can extend. If certain Americans agree that Whites are dying out because of racial demographic change, and they agree with Jarrod that this is very depressing, then they might be more willing to defend White Americans from the otherwise certain death.

Another important aspect of Jarrod's reaction in invoking "my race" is the fear that White Americans' decreasing numbers could work to activate a type of White identity (Jardina 2019), especially among Americans like Jarrod. That is, it seems as though White identity is not universally supported among all White Americans, but those whose political identities are more closely connected to protecting their White identity. I confirm this to be a common thread in reactions to the big flip, and it lends further support to the stakes of the flip for democracy. White Americans' sense of White identity is activated by their sense of threat, which can reinforce their need to protect this identity. So to echo Jarrod's ideas about his race dying out, protecting White identity might require these Americans to take drastic actions. They might feel the need to take violent or discriminatory actions against the people they view to be the most threatening to their senses of self and identity. Extending this idea further to perceptions of American democracy, self-protection from this threatening future would mean turning their anger onto the entire system. I address all of these dynamics in later chapters. The main misperceptions of the big flip lead these Americans to turn their anger toward certain Americans of color and, among the most angered and threatened, toward the entire system of democracy.

With Jarrod's reaction, we see that the depressing ideas of the big flip are attributed to the Biden administration. There is a throughline between this sentiment and what I find in experiments 1 and 2. Again, I do not mention the Biden administration or politics in any of the articles provided to respondents in my study. Jarrod is not told to think about politics, yet he does. This is crucial to the overall story of the big flip: It is implicitly political to many who view it *because* it is about race in the United States. Threatened Americans like Jarrod do not compartmentalize these predictions to only demographics. At their core, they describe a future political landscape. Biden and his administration are attributable despite the fact that the article describes these predictions as long-standing trends. Jarrod goes so far as to assert conspiratorial ideas by saying, "They didn't even care and were actually letting them fly in secretively." Not only is this sentiment unsubstantiated, but it is also not detailed within the article at all. It is clear that

Jarrod is connecting these dynamics to the media content he consumes (Kistner 2022). From this statement, it is clear that he is familiar with the idea of the big flip, and his threatened sentiments are linked to some other sets of misperceptions he has.

Jarrod goes even further to describe his emotions about the big flip. He says, "This is an outrage." He is angered that White Americans are going to become a numerical minority, just as White Republicans are in my first two experiments. Undoubtedly, he has a sense of how the future of the country will look. Part of this idea connects to how he thinks about the future Americans of color, whom he considers to be "poor people who aren't being taken care of." This assertion could either be a dog whistle (Mendelberg 2001; Thompson and Busby 2021), or a further inference he makes about Americans of color, or it could be both. Jarrod essentially predicts that the American government will be overburdened by more people of color. This does not logically connect to White Americans becoming a minority—unless he considers Americans of color to also be poorer than White Americans. This affirms research other political scientists have conducted showing that welfare is race-coded (Gilens 1995; 1996). Jarrod's reflection here shows that this race-coding runs so deep that the increasing number of Americans of color extends in the opposite direction—that is, more people of color equal more welfare recipients. Jarrod's detailed reaction here elicits a great deal of themes surrounding the big flip and ideas of race in the United States generally.

Arnold, a thirty-three-year-old White man who lives in North Carolina and identifies as a traditional conservative Republican, reacted to the same information in a more moderated way than Jarrod. Yet his reaction evokes another set of themes that are crucial to the political story of the big flip and misperceptions about these demographic predictions. He says the following:

> I didn't really feel any type of way other than that this change will be a slow transition over many years. I think this concept is incredibly charged and many people will have differing opinions on it. I feel like it will not be a good thing but I could not really give a reason as to why.

Differently from Jarrod, Arnold explicitly expects the big flip to happen at a slower pace. This prediction of US racial demographics is a more grounded and realistic expectation of the process of change. The big flip is not something that will happen in one fell swoop; it will instead occur incrementally.

Despite expecting the big flip to be gradual, Arnold is still concerned. He says he feels like the changes will not be good, presumably for the country. Yet he does not articulate these proclivities. Arnold here is expressing an implicit sense of threat. He is unable to identify the origin of the threat but knows it is there somehow. This sentiment might partially come from the information environment Arnold is in. He may get a series of messages about the future demographics of the country through social and mainstream media channels. So when he is primed with this information to think about these changes, he does not have a full sense of where the threat is coming from, but he *knows* to feel concerned. The messages, in effect, are working to generate a threat. And while this could be where the threat is motivated, it is likely not the only source for Arnold.

Arnold is a younger Republican White man who is still expressing threatened ideas that mimic Jarrod's perspective. Their similar party, ideological orientation, race, and gender identity are telling of their ideas. Despite being in different generations, they have similar views about the big flip. They both make similar predictions, which I find are filtered through their views of their own racial group (White Americans) and the future of their party (the Republican Party). So, with their two sets of identities, Arnold and Jarrod affirm the importance of the second and third of the three *P*'s: people of color and partisanship.

Through a series of a few other responses to this same question, I find that threat also takes some slightly different forms—especially for people who do not identify as Republican. Bill, a forty-two-year-old White man from suburban Ohio who identifies as an Independent with conservative values, says the following in his response to the big flip:

> I don't think that "whites" becoming a minority as a whole is necessarily bad except that it will do nothing to eliminate the racial grievance industry who will continue to be racist and claim victim status to maintain power.

First, Bill acknowledges that there might not be anything inherently bad with White Americans becoming a numerical minority. However, the statements he makes following this assertion call his initial statement into question. He references the "racial grievance industry," which is a common right-wing talking point and speculation that assumes that there is a cottage industry on the Left for discussing racial politics (Starkes 2016). The common accusation of this industry is that it overblows race politics issues for the sake of monetization. Bill is concerned that the demographic changes would not alter how people working in this industry profit, nor would it affect their claims to victim status to "maintain power." With a slightly different stance from theories of racial threat, Bill here is claiming that people in the racial grievance industry are already in positions of power—which also implies that changing group sizes would not alter this current racial structure. Through the use of dog whistles, Bill seems to be saying that people of color are already in positions of power.

This assertion adds an important new dimension to our study and understanding of the big flip. Some Americans who are threatened by the United States' multiracial future already perceive that the flip has happened, and they view it as a part of a sea change in the country's cultural dynamics. Bill's presumption connects closely with Claire's response to the big flip, in both of their expected changes to the country.

Claire is a forty-five-year-old Hispanic woman from urban Arkansas who identifies as an Independent. She expressed a different type of emotion that motivates her sense of threat:

> I am surprised to read that whites were a minority in the following years and yet they would be proud to be but at the same time it is sad to know that with the passage of the years the traditions will be lost to . . . so much mixture of cultures.

Claire's response mirrors others. She expresses both surprise and sadness about the changing country. Her response is about a type of cultural loss she anticipates, which negatively affects her sense of the cohesive culture she sees in the United States.

The responses I gather display important contextual differences in how Americans—specifically right-leaning Americans—think about the big flip. Bill's, Claire's, and Jarrod's responses show how expansive sentiments of threat can be, but importantly there are a number of throughlines weaving the overall tapestry of how the big flip operates in Americans' minds. Predictions about the country's future racial structure cause Americans to make inferences and predictions in a host of other areas.

First, the big flip is overtly political in nature. Recall that the article featured in this study does not describe anything about American politics; yet despite this absence, Americans like Bill grow concerned and depressed about what the flip might do to the political cohesiveness of the country. This is a crucial aspect of the longer story of the big flip and the ultimate conclusion of demographic determinism. This deterministic view causes the most politically worried Americans to lose faith in the democratic system. That the mere mention of the majority-minority flip elicits political ideas shows the extent to which racial demographics have become politically charged across the public.

On the political nature of the flip, I take the empirical test of racial threat from demographic change another step even further. A key limitation in the experiment above and the subsequent interviews that are conducted is that I utilize a prime that activates ideas about the big flip. It works to draw the reader into the idea of racial demographic change, which could cloud and shape their views about *how* the country is changing simply because it instructs them to think about these changes in specific ways. As a result, it makes it slightly more difficult to make scientific inferences about what participants specifically think of the article. Is it the headline of the article, the tone of the big flip, or how it is being articulated? These are questions that go unanswered through the use of this medium to test the idea of the flip.

An even stronger evaluation of how Americans process the flip is in the ideas that come to the top of their minds when they are prompted. As a question, it is this: What ideas come to mind when Americans think of the big flip? Even more to the question of the future of American democracy, the question that follows is this: Are ideas about the big flip causally linked to demographic determinism and democratic erosion? This investigation extends beyond ideas of priming the idea through curated content. In terms of hypothesis testing, social scientists describe this as a "hard test" of the question. It is more difficult to uncover or address because it is put through even more theoretical and empirical scrutiny through the test. Next, informed by the responses above, as well as the political idea of the big flip, I qualitatively and quantitively test the function of the big flip across Americans through a research design that captures top-of-mind ideas about racial demographic change, which I evaluate in descriptively rich and causally identifiable ways. This design represents an empirical throughline in this project that touches on all three *P*'s in demographic determinism and allows me to identify a variety of specific dynamics of fears of the big flip in direct and comparative ways.

A Hard Test of the Big Flip

I use a single simple question to prompt ideas of the big flip. The exact wording of this question is this: "You may have heard of the diversification of the United States. Tell us what immediately comes to mind when you think about racial demographic change within the US. (Please tell us in at least two sentences.)" Upon their responses, I then measure a series of attitudes that directly connect to demographic determinism. Following from the theorizing and initial empirical testing, the main expectation is that Black Americans will be among the top-of-mind groups when Americans think about racial demographic change (H1). This will help to confirm the first of the three *P*'s of demographic determinism. The element of prediction about the country's future will not cohere across the public in ways that have been previously described by the census, among other sources. Beyond this, I seek to further validate my findings from the studies I conducted previously in this chapter. Specifically, I will assess the extent to which anger is generated from the simple question of diversification. Lastly, in a direct point of comparison across variant groups that are top of mind across racial groups, I will use a technique to link the groups mentioned in the open-ended responses to expressed anger over racial demographic change. This is, in effect, a mixed-method technique, combining quantitative and qualitative data for the sake of best assessing which groups directly elicit anger comparatively with others. I begin with the responses to this open-ended prime.

Top-of-Mind Responses

Americans, in a variety of ways, import ideas of how they envision society to change, but in categorically different ways, emphasis on Black Americans often comes in the form of describing a power shift. One example is the following block quote. It comes from one respondent who, when thinking of the diversification of the United States, says:

> Whites are becoming more and more discriminated against. Blacks are using the slave excuse that has long been repaid back to them. Every person should be judged as a person irregardless of skin color. There are just as many bad whites as bad blacks and bad brown, red, yellow, etc. skinned people.
>
> (White woman, age forty-seven, moderate Republican, Dauphine County, PA)

Importantly, deep sentiments about racial groups and discrimination against White Americans immediately come to mind for this American. This response directly connects to the findings that replicate Craig and Richeson (2014b). It concerns the zero-sum evaluation of power per anticipations of what will come from the big flip—by Whites becoming a minority, the coextensive expectation is that they will lose power and influence. Moreover, for this respondent, Black Americans come to mind after her considerations of White status, specifically the ways she thinks Black people use slavery as an excuse. The ideas expressed in this response highlight the role of prediction and the perception of people of color (which will be discussed at length in chapter 6). This White woman holds negative views about the future of the country, links those views to White status, and attributes this declining status to Black Americans. In kind, I find this thematically among a series of other responses in this same study.

**

> I think about the recent movement of Black Lives Matter. I think that all lives matter not just Blacks. As a minority I feel that we should be focused on the overall picture of society instead of just small minority groups.
> (White and Native man, age forty, Independent-leaning Republican, Knickerbocker, TX)

**

> I think of black lives matter causing much racial tension. I think out-of-touch crazy liberals wanted to make everything about race. I think of liberals who greatly exaggerated racial issues in order to play the victim or to sympathize with the "victims" in order to obtain power. They see racial tension as a means to an end. I also see them mostly as morally weak people who like to create problems that don't exist, or minimally exist in order to make themselves seem morally superior, in which they claim to be so anti-racist, but really they just use race and use minorities in order to feel good about themselves because they are morally weak and pathetic.
> (White woman, age thirty-five, Independent, Columbus, OH)

**

> I think that racial demographics have changed a lot since I was a kid. I think that now it's so sad but blacks feel like they are of higher power than any other race. It's so sad but that's the way it is.
> (White woman, age fifty-nine, strong Republican, Allen, TX)

The themes, sentiments, and feelings among respondents within this study are consistent. Despite the fact that they come from various places across the country, we do not see that their senses of threat or concern are limited to any one region of the United States. When gently encouraged to think about the diversification of the country, White Americans express (1) fears of the loss of power of Whites, (2) frustrations and anger over Black Americans seemingly gaining power as a result of demographic changes, and (3) the view that points 1 and 2 are deepening.

A key follow-up question to these responses, which speaks to the efficacy of the big flip, is, How much these are one-off responses? That is, is there consistency in the respondents' anger? While a useful point of inquiry, I do not want to understate the importance of the above responses. White Americans from thousands of miles apart are concerned about the same racial question of the big flip and willingly express these ideas after an unintrusive question about the diversification of the country. Already, this consistency connects to the above studies and shows the pervasiveness of the threat from the big flip.

Notwithstanding the importance of the qualitative responses, to the point of consistency across the entire sample of 1,511 White Americans, I am still empirically able to validate the role of anger that is tied to predictions about the big flip. The diversification prime is randomly assigned, and I measure anger about racial demographic change posttreatment, which provides me the ability to assess the impact of the question of anger. The measure I use for anger is the same as the measure I use within experiment 1 in this chapter. Recall that when White Republicans believe that Europeans are the increasing immigrant group, they express less anger about demographic change.

In figure 5.11, I use the same model as in the aforementioned experiment and uncover a flipped response in expressed anger among White Republicans in light of the prime.

Using linear regression, I show above that White Republicans primed about racial demographic change are expressively angrier than those who are not ($p = 0.004$). The first takeaway from these results is that I affirm the converse role of anger toward racial demographic change to the assuaged anger. Crucially, this emotion is limited to White Republicans. These respondents become 8 age points angrier ($p = 0.003$), while the White Democrats primed are statistically indistinguishable from those in the control group ($p = 0.42$). Here, Republicans are already expressively angrier about demographic

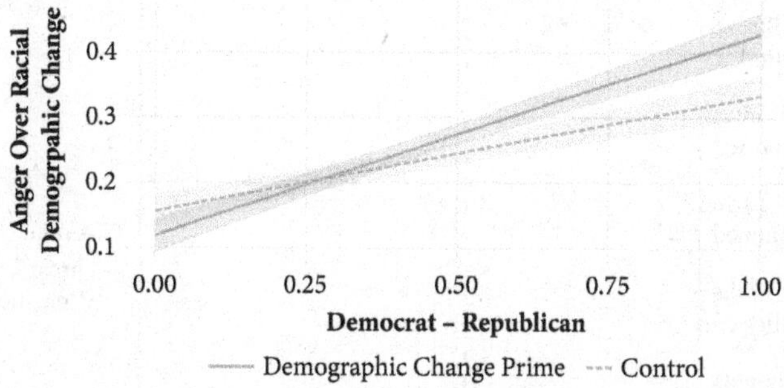

Figure 5.11 Coefficient plot identifying the relationship between groups mentioned in response to the prime and anger over racial demographic change.

change relative to Democrats (15 age points higher in the control group), but within-party group comparisons reveal that the already high Republican anger can still rise further.

My findings here on anger do well to demonstrate the partisan nature of anger over the big flip (I will focus on the third *P*, partisanship, in chapter 7) as well as the notion that it is not limited to the select qualitative responses I identify. Merging these two approaches, I look next to anger and its connection to the specific groups referenced by respondents. To do this, I use a previously validated Boolean coding schema to capture all mentions of racial and ethnic groups.[4] Across the variant mentions, Black Americans are a sizable group mentioned in the responses, but they are nearly equivalent to Latinx Americans.[5] The group mentions do well to give a global assessment of the frequency of each group, but do not do well to articulate how the group mention is tied to other political attitudes. To do this, I code each mention of a racial or ethnic group as a dummy variable, then include all in a single regression model. This method allows me to identify how the mention of a group corresponds with a quantitative measure—particularly in this case, anger about racial demographic change.

As I find within this comparative model, White respondents who talk about Black Americans when they think about the diversification of the

[4] I test for mentions of each group with the following coding schema: Black Americans ("blac|afric"), Latino Americans ("latin|hisp|mexl"), Asian Americans ("asia|china|chinese|korea"), immigrants ("immigra").

[5] Regarding percentages of group mentions, Black Americans are mentioned 13% of the time, Latinx Americans are mentioned 15%, White Americans are mentioned 32%, Asian Americans are mentioned 5%, immigrants are mentioned 12%, and minorities are mentioned 21%.

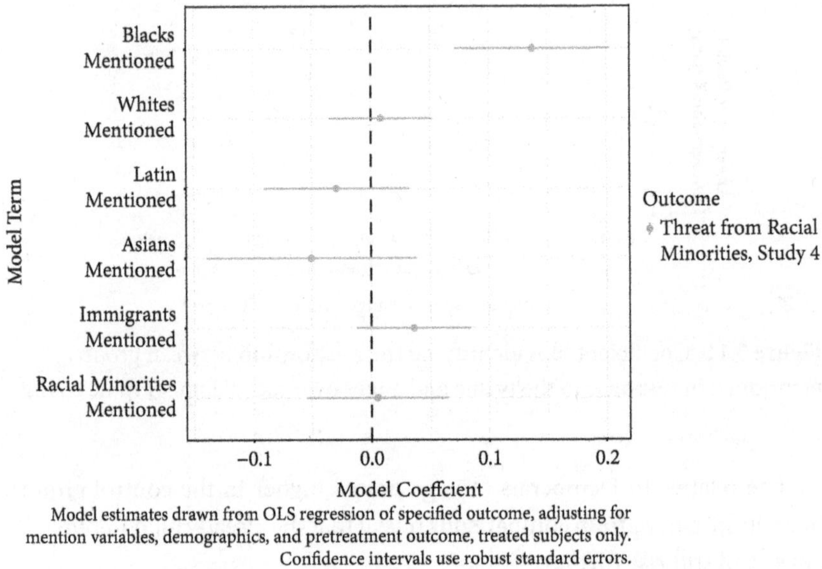

Figure 5.12 Coefficient plot identifying the relationship between groups mentioned in response to the prime and expressed threat from racial minorities.

United States are significantly angrier about racial demographic change ($p = 0.004$, figure 5.12).

Comparatively and importantly, mentions of other groups also generate reactions of anger, but in the opposite direction. White Americans who mention Latin Americans ($p = 0.04$) or Asian Americans ($p = 0.01$) appear significantly less angry. This direct point of comparison is indicative of the role Black Americans have on the racial threat from demographic change. The study shows that it is functionally different from other racial groups; thoughts of Black Americans alone are tied to increasing anger. Also noteworthy is that racial minorities *and* immigrant mentions do not affect anger.

One last empirical point that is vital and connects to the second *P*, people of color, in demographic determinism comes from a measure of threat included in this same study. I use a closed-ended measure that asks, "How threatened do you think racial minorities will be by the year 2060?" using a 1–7 Likert scale, where 1 is Not Threatening and 7 is Very Threatening. Ultimately, I find another strong connection between a sense of threat and views of Black Americans (figure 5.13).

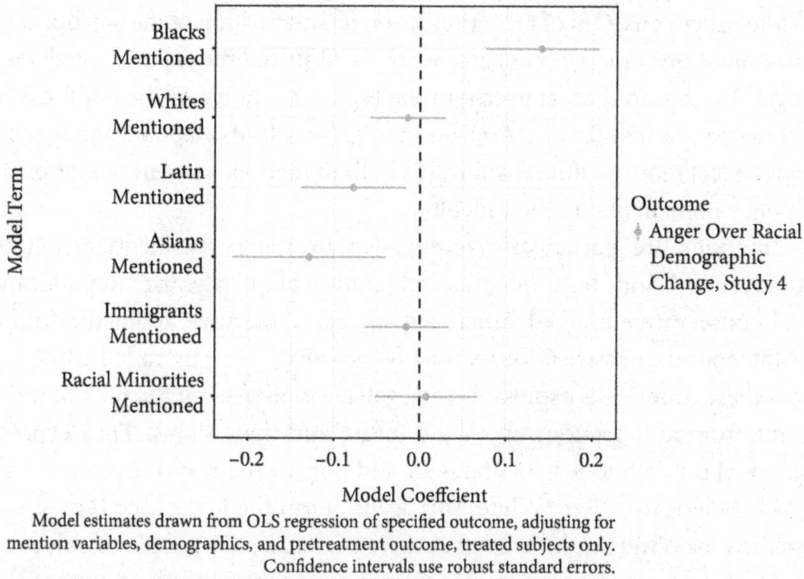

Figure 5.13 Predicting support for threat from racial minorities.

Exclusively among the White Americans who mention Black Americans in their responses, I find a significantly stronger sense of threat from *all* racial minorities ($p = 0.0003$). The measure I use captures ideas about the entire group. As such, I am able to much more definitively say that Black Americans play an important role in the perceptions of racial minorities on the whole. I find that all other groups *do not* increase a sense of threat from racial minorities despite near equal mentions among Latin Americans and immigrants, which helps further validate the role of Black threat in the interpretation of racial minorities. The two models using the mentioned groups show clear evidence of the fundamental role of Black Americans in how White Americans process the future demographics of the United States. I explore this even further in chapter 6.

Conclusion

In this chapter, I have charted out the first of the three *P*'s in demographic determinism. Prediction, which is nearly impossible in the context of racial dynamics and dimensions, lends itself to negative reactions among a broad swath of Americans. As I consistently show, it is most strongly felt among

White Americans. Out of mere prediction or anticipation of the big flip, negative emotions emerge: concern, worry, and in the most punctuated way, anger. I also find that, converse to the typical narrative of the big flip, the alternative discussion of European immigration leads Republicans specifically to feel more positive. I show this both in their views of immigration as a policy domain and in their ideology.

Emotions are particularly accentuated by the party identification of Americans. I find, both quantitatively and qualitatively, that Republicans and conservative-minded Americans are more negative about the future of the country. A variety of reasons is provided, in open-ended ways, for why these Americans express these negative emotions, but the bulk of them come from anticipations about the future and their status. They express worry about White loss of status in addition to the status ascendence of Black Americans. Here, White Americans affirm the first of the three *P*'s—prediction. White, right-leaning Americans know that people of color are increasing in number, yet they incorrectly conceptualize the future of the country. Racial minorities or people of color, to many Americans, are deeply enmeshed with ideas of Black Americans. This is the second of the three *P*'s, people of color. In the next chapter, I show how this second *P* further builds the overarching idea of demographic determinism.

6
POC = Black

The second *P* of the three misperceptions that motivate demographic determinism is people of color (hereafter POC). Particularly, this idea concerns how POC are considered and how minoritized Americans think of themselves. When Americans conceptualize the big flip, their ideas about the country changing are deeply contingent on who they think about when they think of the diversification of the United States. As an element of the big flip, the second *P* of the three *P*'s largely concerns *who* leaps to mind when Americans think about the changing demography of the county.

In this chapter, I detail how there are strong, historically grounded ideas in American society of who POC are, and that they are overwhelmingly presumed to be Black Americans. I describe this as the result of the long arc of the racial binary system in American racial politics. I show that POC are often deeply conflated with Black Americans. This dynamic also cuts in multiple directions: for how non–Black Americans think of POC in the context of the big flip as well as Black Americans' ideas about who POC are.

I start by reviewing the history of the racial binary, then test the current efficacy of how the idea of the binary motivates perceptions of racial minorities—in terms of identification among Black Americans, Asian Americans, and Latinx Americans. Overall, these empirical tests show that minoritized racial groups, considered in terms such as *people of color* or *racial minorities*, often strongly evoke ideas of Black Americans that particularly sit in tandem with Hispanic/Latino Americans in the minds of many in the American public. The historical legacy of Black Americans' minoritized status in the United States overdetermines mass public ideas of the big flip. When Americans, by and large, think about the particular groups making societal gains and the actual expected group size, Black Americans are actively present in the envisioning of the future. This helps to explain how the threat from demographic determinism operates, with deeply anti-Black sentiments in tandem with anti-Latino and anti-immigrant ideas.

The Big Flip. Andrew Ifedapo Thompson, Oxford University Press. © Oxford University Press (2026).
DOI: 10.1093/9780197822173.003.0006

The History of the Binary

The Black-White binary, or paradigm, sits at the core of American racial politics. It is a simple, powerful, and sometimes controversial conceptualization of how race functions in the United States. Juan Perea succinctly articulates how it functions:

> [The Black-White binary is] the conception that race in America consists, either exclusively or primarily, of only two constituent racial groups, the Black and white. . . . In addition, the paradigm dictates that all other racial identities and groups in the United States are best understood through the Black/white binary paradigm.
>
> (Delgado and Stefancic 1998)

It necessitates a core idea: Black at the bottom and White at the top of the racial hierarchy. Every other racial group exists in a middling space between these two polarities. While many dynamics in American racial politics reinforce these core ideas of the binary, when it is evoked in popular discourse it often comes with an added criticism that it is too simplistic, marginalizing, and reductive of the experiences of all other racial groups. Critics articulate that race in the United States is a far more complex system that necessitates the overt inclusion of other racial groups into the discussion—namely Asian Americans, Latinx Americans, and especially Indigenous Americans. Importantly, this reductive nature of the Black-White paradigm is exactly how it operates. It *is* reductive and limiting, which is both the practical function of paradigms in general (Kuhn 1996) and also an important role in structuring racial politics in the United States. Crucially, the Black-White paradigm orients how Americans think about racial groups, which, deeply relevant to the big flip, thereby governs the process of how racial groups can change. In short, the binary sets the boundaries by which racial groups can shift over time.

Within this chapter, I show that the paradigm has led to a set of unique racial identification circumstances for various marginalized racial groups. As a term, *people of color* is considered to be a catch-all idea in American politics that represents all racial minorities. This term is often evoked to describe minority groups as a collective. While conceptually helpful, it bears out differently when operating in real racial politics. Catch-all ideas of

POC or racial minorities do not capture the predominant ideas that drive how Americans think of this group term. When minoritized Americans are thought about en masse, Black Americans are often top of mind because of historical, cultural, and social legacies. In this chapter, I empirically show that the Black-White paradigm in American politics racializes the term *people of color* and brings Black Americans to its fore. This ultimately makes racial minorities difficult to call to mind without implicitly evoking Black Americans.

I then show that the Black-White racial paradigm extends beyond the pictures in non–Black Americans' minds. It has also led Black Americans to identify more closely as POC than Asian Americans and Latinx Americans. I also show the same relationship within the context of POC—Black Americans express greater levels of linked fate toward the term *people of color* than do Latinx or Asian Americans. Regarding levels of ingroup-specific identity and POC identity, I find some evidence that Black Americans identify more closely as POC than as Black Americans; most importantly, however, is that both POC and ingroup identity is significantly more important for Black Americans than it is for Asian and Latinx Americans. In short, POC identity is a far more salient idea for Black Americans than any other group. I attribute this to the positionality of Black Americans at the bottom of the racial hierarchy in the United States and the frequent focus on Black people in racial politics.

I then show the deep relevance of POC as the second *P* in demographic determinism. Americans' association of Blackness with POC also determines how Americans consider future changes to the racial composition of the United States. Simply put, non-Black Americans infer ideas about Black Americans when they come across information about POC—echoing the same ideas I show at the end of chapter 5. A major set of ideas that comes to mind for Americans when they consider the big flip is the Black American population increasing in size, gaining political power, or both. I show this dynamic through another series of studies. Specifically, priming ideas about POC population growth leads Americans to infer that Black Americans are overwhelmingly increasing in number—when they are, in fact, not, per census reporting. Extending beyond simple priming of racial demographic change generally, I show this inference to be at work even in data interpretation. I randomly assign respondents to read about simple trend lines: one that describes a growing POC population and another that presents more specificity of the individual groups growing. Through both qualitative and quantitative means, the data visualization of POC increasing in size leads Americans in large orders to project that Black Americans are increasing in population.

The inference that POC are mostly Black Americans then greatly heightens racial threat, thereby affecting views at large about American democracy. The second *P* in demographic determinism directly leads threatened Americans to worry about the future of the country and express more support for anti-Black, anti-democratic attitudes—namely political violence and election denial. I conclude this chapter with a set of implications for the study of race and racial demographic change. Conceptually, I assert that Black Americans and ideas about Black Americans ought to be considered in discussions about POC.

Black Americans and the Color Line

The function of race in the United States has adhered to the binary in uniquely strong ways. Theoretically, this has been described as the "color line." The essence of the color line helps to describe the separation between White and Black America—politically, economically, and culturally. At one point, the line was defined through the institution of slavery. Subsequently, it was Jim Crow and segregation. Despite the different institutions, the color line has always been in reference to racial inequality.

Since the passing of the Fifteenth Amendment, ideas of race and color in US politics have been intimately tied to Black Americans' rights. The explicit language of the amendment affords that "the right of citizens of the United States to vote shall not be denied or abridged by the United States or by any State on account of race, color, or previous condition of servitude" ("U.S. Constitution: Fifteenth Amendment, Resources, Constitution Annotated, Congress.Gov, Library of Congress," n.d.). The intention of the amendment was to provide voting rights and protection for Black Americans, who had been previously denied these rights, yet the language vaguely describes the groups who are being protected.

In another example of the implicit mention of Black Americans in racial politics, Langston Hughes describes how the color line functioned even amid the excitement and jubilation of the end of World War I on Armistice Day:

> Everybody poured into the streets to celebrate . . . Negroes, too, although Negroes were increasingly beginning to wonder where, for them, was that democracy they had fought to preserve. In Cleveland, a liberal city, the color line began to be drawn tighter and tighter. Theaters and restaurants in the downtown area began to refuse to accommodate colored people.
>
> (Hughes and Rampersad 1993)

The perpetual White domination and Black subordination are at the core of the color line in the United States. Due to the clear and persistent delineation of American society, the binary in the color line was implied.

Black historian Kelly Miller, in his recount of the centrality of race in the early twentieth century, describes the centrality of the color line in the article "Negroes or Colored People":

> If a street car or automobile should maim or kill an individual in any of our cities, the first query that springs to the lips is not whether the victim be Jew or Gentile, Christian or heathen, native or alien, but is he white or colored? . . . In everyday procedure one's racial cognomen, expressed or inferred, is as essential as his surname.
>
> (K. Miller 1937)

He goes on later to describe how *colored* has a more wide-ranging definition, yet it operates differently in practice: "In the broadest sense, the term 'colored' includes all non-Europeans, without regard to nationality or degree of inter-mixture of blood. Colloquially speaking, in the United States, the terms 'Negro' and 'Colored' are used synonymously, and denote a non-White person of African descent, without reference to blood composition."

Ultimately, he says that the consideration of *colored people*, as an expansive term, fails to capture how the idea is used in practice. He writes that there are context-specific functions of Blackness across the country, but that, on the whole, the delineation of *colored* was directly equivalent to *Black*.

> It would be utterly meaningless to ascertain the number of colored farmers in California or the number of colored land owners in Oklahoma if Japanese, Chinese and Indians are to be placed in the same category. In several of the states, colored people of Negro, Indian, Mongolian and Mexican varieties have different legal status among themselves as respects intermarriage, attendance upon the public schools and traveling in common carriers.

> Separate cars and waiting rooms provided for the races in the South are usually marked "For White" and "For Colored," but in the states of Texas and Oklahoma these separate facilities are designated "For Whites" and "For Negroes," the reason being that in Texas, especially the Southern portion of the state, there is a great number of Mexicans and in Oklahoma a large number of Indians, who are legally classified with the whites. I have ridden in the rear section of a street car in El Paso, Texas, set aside for Negroes. The front section, reserved for whites, was occupied, in the main, by Mexicans whose average color was darker than that of the rear seat occupants.
>
> (K. Miller 1937)

Through Jim Crow, discriminatory policies, and popular discourse, as Hughes and Miller describe, *colored* was a term synonymous with *Black*. It has functionally been the central idea of the color line, branching out into policy. Housing policy, for example, explicitly, implicitly, and systematically barred Black Americans from becoming homeowners, often using the language of "colored" residents (Thurston 2018). Public facilities denied access with signs, policies, and staff to "colored people," all the while the main implication was that Black Americans were at the center of these denials.

For as long as race has existed in American politics, the color line and the terminology that defines it have been front and center. *Colored*, *colored people*, and other ostensibly more wide-ranging terms have colloquially referred to Black Americans. Importantly, historically we see that, because of the racial binary or color line, *Black* functions as a metonym for *non-White*, which historians have consistently articulated: "For many white women, 'racially different from white' meant simply 'Black'" (Frankenberg 1993). Warren and Twine advance this idea further, saying that "Blacks, at least at the national level, serve as the anchor for Whiteness" (1997).

The strong, hard-and-fast separation between White and Black America has left an indelible imprint on how Americans think about race and politics. Racial discussion over the span of time has consistently implied or reinforced this line. This has led scholars to anticipate that the color line would continue to restrict Black Americans: "African Americans continue to be surrounded by an often impermeable color line, defining political and social life primarily in terms of their race" (Sears and Savalei 2006). But despite this expected persistence, the political language of race changed over time. Many times, these changes have implied a movement away from the color line or that its nature has changed, when in reality it has immense staying power in how race operates in American life.

Changing Terms, Same Blackness

In a brief history of the evolution of Black American identification, Martin writes, "After the Civil War, freedman came into use, succeeded by Afro-American, even Afra-American, tan, colored, negro, and Negro" (B. L. Martin 1991). Over decades, terms that have described Black Americans have shifted because of the changing societal lexicon about race, ideas surrounding the accuracy of terms, and criticisms of previous terms.

In recent years, one such critique and inflection point in the racial description of Black Americans came with the assertion by Jesse Jackson that "just as we were called colored, but were not that, and then Negro, but not that, to be called Black is just as baseless," though he led in establishing the term *Black* two decades earlier ("Leaders Say Blacks Want To Be Called 'African-Americans,'" n.d.). This was part of a greater public conversation in the late 1980s and early 1990s of whether *Black* or *African American* was a proper term. Earlier in the same century, the term *Negro* was strongly argued against, thereby moving national discourse toward *Black*. This criticism was leveled on a national level particularly by Stokely Carmichael in his book *Black Power: The Politics of Liberation in America* (Hamilton and Ture 1992).

The terms under which Blackness has been considered have arisen within the confluence of Black leaders and the Black mass public, as well as the changing societal norms. The United States has racially diversified, and with dynamics of racial demographic change, that diversification will continue to occur. With these racial shifts, ideas about the terminology used to describe Black Americans and other racial minority groups have evolved.

The most recent iteration of the discussion of race and color has come to describe POC. Popular discourse, conversation, and critique within political science have led to the burgeoning idea of the political consequences of POC as a group and identity (Pérez 2021; Eidgahy and Pérez 2022; Pérez et al. 2022; Pérez, Robertson, and Vicuña 2022). Functionally, the idea is meant to capture racial minorities, and scholars have shown that it has an emergent importance to racial identity. Specifically, scholars find that, among those who most closely identify as POC, events in politics that affect one racial minority group can work to shift the political positions of these group members.

Some within this same discussion have used *BIPOC* (Black, Indigenous, and People of Color) as an amended version of this concept, which is meant to more fully represent Black and Indigenous Americans alongside other racial minorities (Clarke 2020; Davidson 2022). This shift in political focus, I argue, has occurred in tandem with expectations about racial demographic change and recent movements in the United States in hopes of building solidarity across racial minority groups.

I show that POC as an idea is often implicitly associated with Black Americans—at times the same amount as other racial minoritized groups, and other times significantly more than other groups. Moreover, in comparative ways on individual identification, Black Americans identify far more closely with POC identity and senses of POC-linked fate than do Asian Americans or Latinx Americans. This historical legacy of *POC* equaling *Black* motivates a different set of expectations we can have about perceptions of racial demographic change.

Expectations

Accounting for the historical pertinence of Blackness to perceptions of minoritized groups in the United States, I expect that this legacy still strongly influences how POC are considered en masse. By this, I do not mean to say that when Americans think of POC they will think solely of Black Americans. Rather, that ideas of Black Americans instead overdetermine how POC are considered together. As a result of this association, when the changing country is considered, Black Americans will then be among the most referred-to groups. This, ironically, molds ideas of the big flip despite Black Americans not growing in size in any capacity (Crowder and South 2008; Alba 2018b). Forecasted models of the shifting demographics, discussion of birth rates, and other forms of empirical evidence about group-size change in the United States all *do not* describe Black Americans as a group growing in size. In some cases, anticipations of the big flip do concern the misunderstanding of Black Americans' increasing size, while others concern a large increase in Black Americans' societalinfluence in American society and politics.

Across variant racial groups, when POC are considered Black Americans are top of mind. This expectation is born out of the historical function of race within the United States, and it works as an affirmation of the historical legacy and function of the color line. Empirically, this sentiment is that Black Americans are strongly associated with POC across the American public. My major hypothesis is that this view pervades a broad swath of Americans. I surmise that it cuts in ingroup and outgroup directions. By this assumption, I expect that Black Americans will identify more closely as POC than other racial minority groups (H1). I additionally expect that White Americans will view POC or racial minorities as mostly consisting of Black Americans (H2a). This anticipation, along with inferences about Black Americans, will activate a sense of racial threat from Black Americans and alter their ideas about the future of the country (H2b).

My full anticipation is that the association of Blackness as the antithesis of Whiteness has shaded Americans' expectations of racial demographic change. Black Americans' status in the racial hierarchy and their historical centrality to racial politics and the advancement of civil rights all color this expectation. As I will reiterate throughout this chapter, I do not describe and theorize the centrality of Black Americans to POC as a means to ignore other minoritized groups, such as Asian, Latinx, and Native Americans. I simply intend to show that when Americans conceptualize these ideas of the changing country, they are *not* using empirical projections that have been put forth, nor are they holding the aforementioned groups in a cohesive, evenly distributed manner. Next, I describe the studies I conduct to investigate these expectations.

Testing the Association of POC among Minoritized Groups

Within my first set of studies, I go about investigating the extent that there is a connection between POC identity and Black Americans' political identities relative to other large minoritized groups. To do this, I conduct a series of nationally surveys, with oversamples of Black Americans, Asian Americans, and Latinx Americans on their ingroup racial attitudes. I then conduct a series of descriptive tests on their respective POC identities (N = ~1,200, totaling roughly 3,600, table 6.1).[1]

[1] This study design is the first of its kind, investigating how these prominent racial minority groups, en masse, react to narratives about racial demographic change.

Table 6.1 Sample composition[a]

Gender	Black Americans	Latino/a Americans	Asian Americans
Male	43.4%	46.2%	48.7%
Female	56.2%	52.3%	50.3%
Nonbinary	0.4%	1.5%	1.0%
Sample size	1,204	1,203	1,211

[a] See appendix 1 for a full demographic composition.

Turning to my hypotheses, first to test H1, I use a set of measures that capture the importance of POC identity and the strength of respondents' sense of linked fate as POC. Further, as a check on these measures of POC identity, I utilize specific racial group measures of racial group identity and linked fate points of comparison across each group. That is, the importance of Black/Latinx/Asian identity is measured in relation to identification with POC. These measures work as additional tests of the validity of H1. These checks allow me to differentiate if the specific racial group identity of Asians, Latinx, and Black Americans is a more or less potent sentiment among each respective group, relative to their POC identity.

Identification among Minoritized Groups as People of Color

To test H1, I first measure the importance of being a person of color and the sense of linked fate to POC across Black, Asian, and Latinx Americans. This measure reads as follows: "How important is being a person of color to your identity?" Below, I use the average score of POC importance for each respective group. On the importance of being POC, I find sizable differences in identification on a 0–1 scale, where 0 is not important at all and 1 is very important (figure 6.1).

Black Americans on average identify very strongly as POC, with an average rating across the entire sample of 0.83. To put the scaling of this variable into context, I code "Very Important" responses as 0.75 on the 0–1 scale. As such, Black Americans on average view being POC as very important to their expressions of identity. This level of identification sits in contrast to

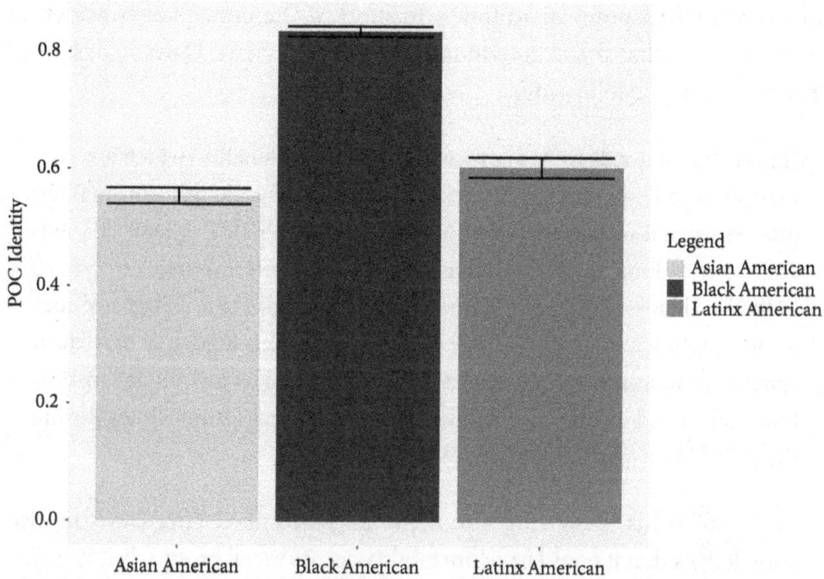

Figure 6.1 Bar plot, identifying expressed POC identity across Asian, Black, and Latinx Americans.

Latinx Americans and Asian Americans as shown in the graph above. Asian Americans (0.55) and Latinx Americans (0.60) are significantly lower in their POC identity, which roughly corresponds with POC identity being "Somewhat Important" among both Asian Americans' and Latinx Americans' views of their identity. Comparatively, Asian Americans' and Latinx Americans' attachment to POC identity is significantly lower than that of Black Americans (the difference in means tests yield $p < 2.2e{-}16$ for both comparisons). This works as my first confirmation of my H1 expectation. By orders of magnitude, Black Americans identify more closely as POC than do Latinx and Asian Americans.

In a second test of H1, I assess the senses of POC linked fate across Black, Asian, and Latinx Americans. I operationalize linked fate as the idea that what happens to other POC will affect what happens in people's own lives, extending this idea directly from Dawson (1995). The wording of this question is "How much do you think that what happens generally to people of color in this country will affect what happens in your life?" As an idea, linked fate describes a collective consideration that Black Americans have and express their political attitudes. In short, it is a process of considering group interests that shape individual-level political views. Dawson describes this process as the following:

> [Linked fate extends from a] procedural view of rationality (which is somewhat akin to Downs's [1957] views on economizing the decision-making process when less than perfect information is available). This heuristic suggests that as long as race remains dominant in determining the lives of individual blacks, it is "rational" for African Americans to follow group cues in interpreting and acting in the political world. This tendency of African Americans to follow racial cues has been reinforced historically by institutions developed during the forced separation of blacks from whites during the post-Reconstruction period. (1995, 71)

Early on in his theorizing about the idea of linked fate, Dawson also acknowledges that it could have portability across racial groups, but its function would be idiosyncratically contingent on the historical context of the specific group. In footnote 3, he adds this:

> This heuristic should in principle be applicable to other groups; the particular way it is manifest would depend on the historical context. For example, in many periods and places, a Jewish person's religious identity might well have dominated all other social identities; in the France of the 1980s, North Africans' identity and political struggles with other French were tied to the North Africans' belief in Islam. For African Americans, I shall argue, identity has been tied to subordinate economic status. (1995, 23)

The dynamic historical function of linked fate for non-Black groups here is crucial for the next analyses. Given the importance of history to Black ingroup linked fate, when we consider the extent to which Black Americans and other minoritized groups think of themselves as POC, their group-contingent historical relationship with the idea will be visible. So if Black Americans identify more with POC than other groups, this will indicate stronger historical connections than among Latinx or Asian Americans. Again, in the analyses below, I show the same relationship across racial minority groups (figure 6.2). This expectation from H1 is exactly what I find.

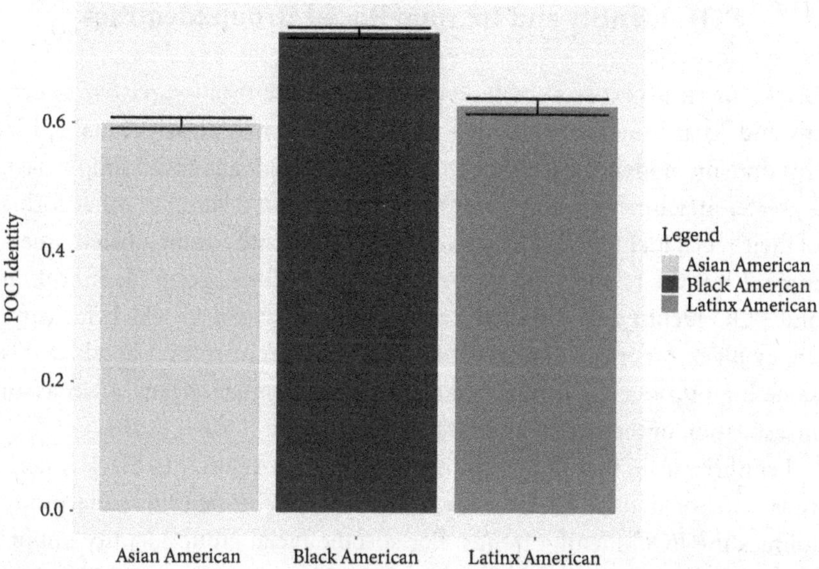

Figure 6.2 Bar plot, identifying expressed POC-linked fate across Asian, Black, and Latinx Americans.

Black Americans feel a significantly greater sense of POC-linked fate than both Latinx Americans (11 age points greater, $p = 2.654e{-}14$) and Asian Americans (14 age points greater, $p < 2.2e{-}16$). This difference further validates the idea that POC identity connects to Black Americans more than other racial minorities (H1). Importantly, I show that Black Americans feel a greater ingroup connectedness with POC identity than *either* Latinx or Asian Americans do. On its own, this idea of POC-linked fate matters for Black Americans' attachment to POC identity because it concerns a collective sense of identity, thereby capturing a different dimension of identity than the evaluation of POC identity importance (figure 6.1). The POC racial identity measure captures the individual importance of POC identity, while linked fate is about a greater connection to POC as a group. So the fact that I find identical consistency and magnitude among both of these measures shows that POC identity matters on both an individual and collective level for Black Americans, while it remains at similar levels for Asian Americans and Latinx Americans. To summarize, there is a uniquely Black historical relationship in individual identification as POC.

POC Identity and Ingroup Racial Group Identities

Black Americans express greater levels of POC identification relative to Latinx and Asian Americans, though this dynamic could be self-contained in this domain of identity. In other words, Black Americans could simply have a greater attachment to POC identity that bears no relation to other forms of their racial identity. To further validate POC identity among Black Americans, I test the relationship between expressed Black group identification and POC identity. Specifically, I am testing the extent to which identifying as Black American connects to being a person of color. I conduct this same ingroup test for Latinx Americans and Asian Americans again as an investigation of their comparability or lack thereof.

I confirm again that POC identity connects more closely to Black Americans' sense of identity. First, the identification with their specific racial group mimics the POC identity trends. For specific racial group identity importance, Black Americans rate significantly higher on a 0–1 scale (0.78)[2] than Asian Americans (0.64) and Latinx Americans (0.65). (See appendices 2 and 3 for a visual comparison.) Across groups, Black Americans are significantly greater than both groups ($p < 2.2e{-16}$), and importantly, Asian Americans and Latinx Americans are statistically insignificant in comparison ($p = 0.17$).

I find this same statistical relationship between specific racial group linked fate. That is, Black Americans express a significantly greater sense of specific group linked fate ($p < 2.2e{-16}$) than both Asian and Latinx Americans, while these groups express similar, indistinguishable levels of linked fate ($p = 0.70$). (See appendix 3).

In terms of within-group comparisons, I also find that POC and specific racial group identity are more closely correlated for Black Americans than for other racial groups. This relationship is most stark in identity importance. POC identity importance and Black identity importance are highly correlated (0.79 correlation coefficient). Latinx-POC identity (0.59) and Asian American–POC identity (0.58) are not as strongly correlated. This is the best internal validity test of the relationship between Black identity and POC identity. Black Americans think of themselves more as POC than Asian Americans and Latinx Americans do. I find this exact same relationship with linked fate (appendix 3).

[2] Interestingly, POC identity's importance sits a few points higher than Black identity's importance. This is not to imply that it is stronger, as the difference between POC identity and Black identity is negligible.

Distinct POC Identification

The tests of general reporting and correlation tests between specific racial group identity and POC identity confirm H1. Black Americans identify far more closely with being POC than other racial groups. Moreover, within additional validation tests, I find that Black identity is closely tethered to POC identity, again more closely than for Latinx and Asian Americans. While there is still a connection among these other groups, the difference across groups is noteworthy. The reasons for the connection between POC identity and Black identity are manifold. As Dawson articulates in his theorizing of linked fate, historical context is the key determinator of the efficacy of linked fate for Black Americans. The legacy of the color line and the orientation of the racial binary affirm and reaffirm the idea that *POC* implicitly refers to Black Americans. Additionally, Black Americans have one of the longest, most storied legacies of race within the United States due to the country being built off of the institution of slavery. As such, I argue that Blackness exists in the background of a variety of ideas of race, even when it is not overtly mentioned.

Next, I test how strongly White Americans associate *people of color* with *Black Americans* within the context of the big flip. To do this, I conduct a large experiment that taps into the racial group or groups at the top of Americans' minds when the idea of racial demographic change is primed. I use closed- and open-ended means to learn which groups jump to respondents' minds and the downstream effects of these associations on their feelings about race and democracy.

Priming the Implicit POC Assumption

I aim to prime ideas about the changing demographics in the United States, conducting this experiment using CloudResearch (N = 2078). (See appendix 5 for sample demographics.) Through multiple checks on top-of-mind ideas, this study is designed to identify who comes to mind when Americans think about POC increasing in size. Following my previous studies in chapter 5, this study helps to clarify the pictures in White Americans' minds of who they consider to be changing in the country. This project also builds on the work that other scholars have done on the question of the future demography of the country (Craig and Richeson 2014a, 2014b, 2017; Mutz 2018; Abascal 2020; Krosch et al. 2022).

Many of these studies have utilized primes that address POC on the whole. That is, they refer to demographic change as the growth of POC and the shrinking of White Americans, using text or figures, often in the context of mock articles (Craig and Richeson 2014a, 2014b; Major, Blodorn, and Blascovich 2018; Levy and Myers 2021).

I assert that, because of the historic prominence of Black Americans in American racial politics, among many of these studies there has been a hidden dimension of Black racial threat in their primes. As a means of testing this assertion, I design two conditions in this study that help to better identify the POC inference being made about racial demographic change. I utilize two trend lines that describe racial demographic change in the same way, but with different contexts. Both conditions present data visualization scenarios to participants that by mid-century (roughly the year 2046) POC will become the numerical majority. The only difference in the conditions is the way they visualize the demographic projections. The first condition shows that POC will overtake the numerical majority of White Americans (figure 6.3a). The second condition presents the same information, but it shows the specific groups and how they are growing in size (figure 6.3b).

I randomly assign respondents to conditions 1, 2, or a pure control group (3) that does not receive any prime.[3] Upon receiving this prime, I then present respondents with my main outcome variables, testing for H2. Specifically, I expect that a large portion of the growth of POC is being inferred to be Black Americans—this, as I mention earlier in this chapter, will likely occur alongside ideas that Hispanic/Latino Americans are increasing.

To capture this dimension, I utilize one closed-ended measure, which asks, "Which demographic group will grow the most between now and 2060? (You may select more than 1)," then offers the following groups as response items: "Black Americans, White Americans, Asian Americans, Hispanic Americans, and Other (please specify)." Respondents could mark as many groups as they wanted.

The other measure is an open-ended one, which asks respondents to answer in their own words, "What groups come to mind in the previous graphs?"[4] Confirmation of H2 would consist of the POC increase

[3] I have no issues of statistical power within this study, as I have roughly seven hundred respondents in each condition, which is well over the threshold of identifying small effects (appendix 5).

[4] This measure is condition-contingent, so analyses will only include conditions 1 and 2, not the control condition.

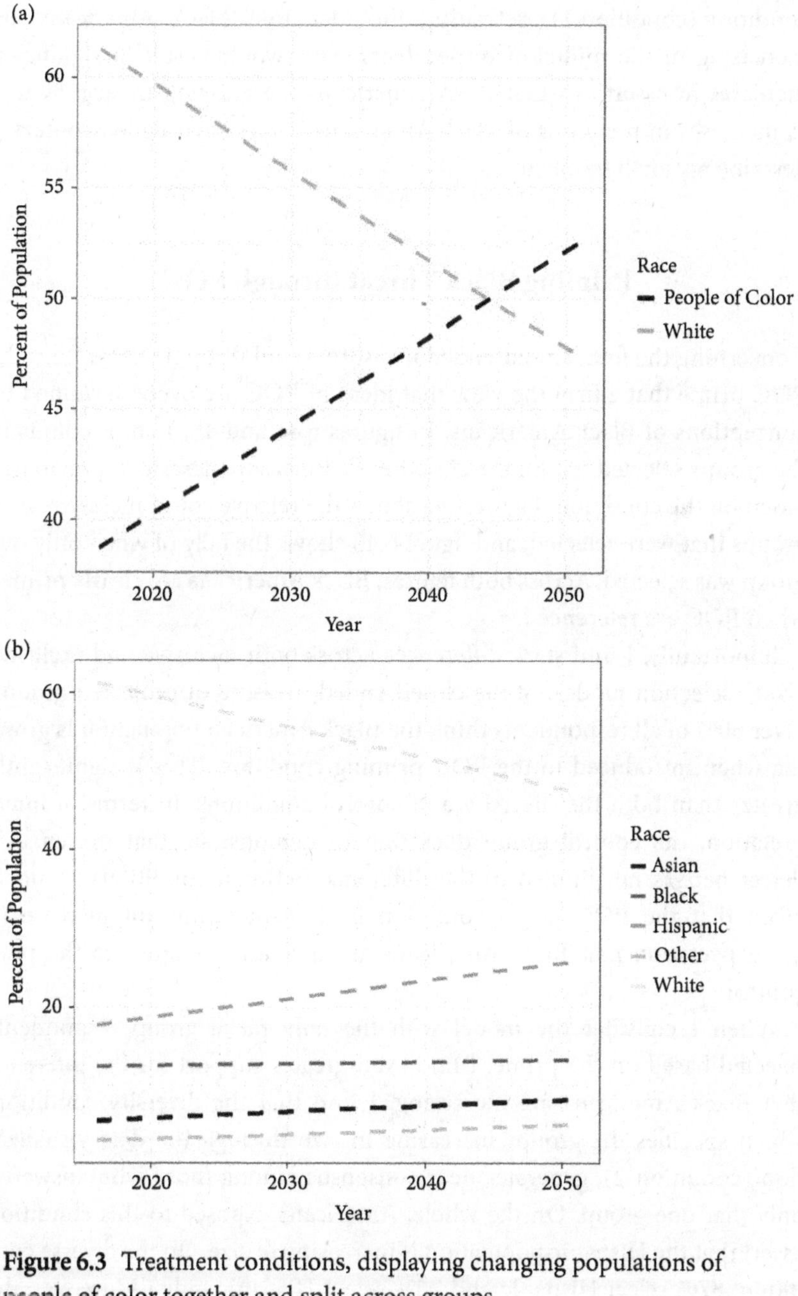

Figure 6.3 Treatment conditions, displaying changing populations of people of color together and split across groups.

condition (condition 1), activating the idea that Black Americans are increasing in the minds of respondents. This would result in significant increases in assertions that Black Americans are growing in size, as well as increases in mentions of Black Americans in the open-ended context. I describe my analyses next.

Priming Black Threat through POC

Concerning the first, closed-ended measure, I find distinct effects from the POC prime that affirm the view that ideas of POC are overdetermined by conceptions of Black Americans. In figures 6.4a and 4b, I show counts of the groups selected within the closed-ended measure described previously, based on the condition. Figure 6.4a shows the relative count inclusive of all groups that were selected, and figure 6.4b shows the tally of when only one group was selected. Across both figures, Black Americans are clearly primed when POC are referenced.

Importantly, I find stark differences across both inclusive and exclusive group selection models of the closed-ended measure of projected groups. Over 60% of all respondents think the Black American population is growing when introduced to the POC priming condition. This is significantly greater than both the diversity and control conditions. In terms of interpretation, the control group does well to demonstrate that the effect I detect here is not limited to the difference between conditions 1 and 2, given that the POC graph condition leads to a significant increase in the expectation that Black Americans are increasing relative to the pure control.

When I consider the model with the *only* racial group respondents selected based on the prime, I find even greater support for the inference that Black Americans are increasing. I find that the diversity condition, which specifies the groups increasing in size through the data visualization (condition 2), generates near consensus among those who answered only that one group. On the whole, Americans exposed to this condition assert that the Hispanic population is increasing in size. (In the diverse condition, 87% select Hispanic and 78% select Hispanic only.) Moreover, the control shows this to essentially be the baseline of consideration among Americans—they are aware that the Hispanic population is increasing. (See appendix 1 for detailed descriptive statistics for the entire sample and subset

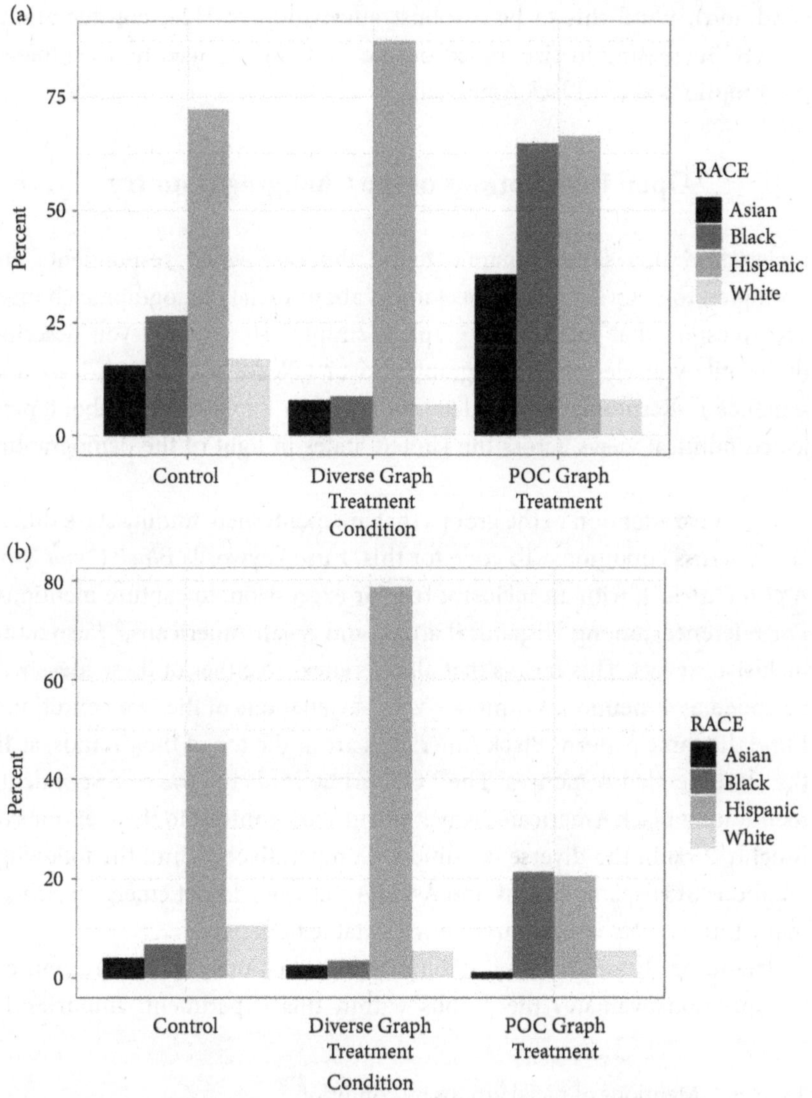

Figure 6.4 Bar plot, identifying expected groups increasing in size.

of various racial groups.) Yet when the POC priming condition is presented, it greatly increases the sense that the Black American population is growing (64% inclusive and 21% exclusive) and greatly decreases the number of people who solely think the Hispanic population is growing (decreases by over 20 percentage points, relative to both the control and the diverse condition). I find this to be a robust affirmation of H2a; considerations of POC increasing in size, based on the POC prime, lead to accentuated presumptions about Black Americans.

Open Descriptions of the Changing Country

I also find this same dynamic to be the case when respondents are prompted to describe their expectations about racial demographic change. The question that follows the graph is simply "How would you describe the results you viewed in the graph above? (Please tell us in at least one sentence.)" Respondents use details that often explain more about projected political views across the United States in light of the demographic changes.

I first give attention to the groups that are mentioned, finding stark differences across conditions. To code for this, I use keywords *Black* ("*blac*") or *Africa* ("*afric*"), with an inclusive regular expression, to capture mentions. For reference, among Hispanic/Latino[5] and Asian Americans,[6] I use more inclusive strings. This means that all references to either of these ideas will be coded as a mention. Within keyword evaluations of the two conditions, I find the same pattern: Black Americans are at the top of their minds, as in the closed-ended responses. The POC prime leads to 76% of respondents mentioning Black Americans, which sits in stark contrast to the mentions of roughly 25% in the diverse condition. Comparatively, I find the following mentions of Hispanic/Latinx and Asian Americans do not emerge nearly as many times across conditions (shown in table 6.2).

Extending beyond these descriptive evaluations of the responses, the question evaluates the graphs within this experiment. Importantly,

Table 6.2 Mentions of racial groups by condition

Condition	Black/African American mentions	Hispanic/Latinx American mentions	Asian American mentions
POC	**76.3%**	**0.03%**	**23.6%**
Diverse	**24.6%**	**57.8%**	**17.6%**

[5] Hispanic/Latino = "hispani|mexic|latin|spanish|venezu|salvado".
[6] Asian = "asia|chines|korea|japan|vietna|cambodi".

below I show, through a series of responses, that simple mentions of Black Americans do not fully articulate the tone of White Americans who are making these inferences about the future of the country. Many go further to give normative evaluations of how they perceive the country to be going, even emphasizing extremist, anti-Black views. The following are a few examples of these responses (table 6.3).

These respondents describe the graph as an indicator of Black Americans increasing in size despite it describing POC on the whole. Beyond this, they articulate feelings of threat, some reaching into explicit anti-Black racism. One respondent intimates that the time ahead for the country is scary, not articulating anything beyond this idea. Of the select responses, the comment on Black Americans "overbreeding" is by far the most extreme, as it animalizes Black Americans and clearly articulates that they ought not to grow in size as a group. Importantly, as I also show, with other data points wherein White Americans are better able to articulate their feelings,

Table 6.3 Responses to prime

	Response examples	Demographics
1	"The white population was decreasing while the black population was increasing."	White woman, age 49, moderate Democrat, Atlanta, Georgia
2	"The overbreeding blacks are experiencing a population growth that is outpacing whites, putting them as the majority by 2050."	White woman, age 43, strong Republican, Rutledge, Tennessee
3	"I am hopeful that I will not be negatively impacted by this. Scary time ahead for certain!"	White man, age 38, moderate Democrat, Henrico, Virginia
4	"The population of white Americans is steeply declining while the population of black Americans is just as sharply increasing."	White woman, age 57, Independent-leaning Republican, East Haven, Connecticut
5	"There was a decrease in white people. There was an increase in black people."	White woman, age 34, strong Democrat, Bronx, New York
6	"That white people were at an all-time high but coming down. The trend for black people is on the rise and will intercept the white race by 2040."	White man, age 45, Independent-leaning Democrat, Herculaneum, Missouri

many are not concerned about censoring their extreme beliefs. Although the open-ended questionnaire did not request the respondents' general feelings about the conditions, respondents still articulated ideas similar to response 3 above. The POC treatment caused strong, unprompted expressions of threat, relative to the control and diverse prime provided.

The qualitative dimension of this project is crucial for getting even more deeply at the question of the pervasiveness of anti-Blackness across the public. I surprisingly also find that this sentiment is *still* prompted in response to the diversity treatment. Bear in mind that this graph shows Black Americans, relative to other racial minority groups, are not projected to increase in size. I find that even among clear interpretations of the diverse condition, explicit expressions of anti-Blackness emerge. The following respondent, a thirty-eight-year-old Independent-leaning Republican White woman from St. Louis, Missouri, interprets the diverse condition first as something that cannot be empirically validated, yet she still paradoxically emphasizes her views about the empirics shown of what she thinks about Black Americans:

> Imaginary, nobody knows what they will really look like. It's funny the blacks kill each other so much it never rises.

The open-ended and closed-ended measures of perceptions of diversification empirically show the same idea—Black Americans are *strongly* associated with the idea of POC increasing within this study. The coherence of both the closed-ended and open-ended responses helps to strongly confirm the idea of overt associations of Black Americans and POC across the White public. It demonstrates that this idea is a culturally relevant idea, despite the dearth of discourse about Black Americans increasing in size. This ultimately confirms H2a.

These attitudes and ideas expressed do not fully encompass all views and attitudes expressed along other racial groups. Others mention the role of immigration and call to the nature of US racial demography as a melting pot (table 6.4).

Importantly, ideas of the big flip are connected to ideas that Americans have about Black Americans *amidst* other racial minority groups, particularly Hispanic and Latino Americans. As I assert in H2a, I expect as much when I prime these anti-Black sentiments through an increased level of support for anti-democratic ideas, which I describe in detail next.

Table 6.4 Responses to prime

	Response examples	Demographics
1	"That the legal and illegal immigrants are breeding at a rate enough to take the population majority by 2040."	White male, age 45, moderate Republican, Spokane, Washington
2	"I think its just more of a melting pot. To me, it means we are experiencing a wider range of politics, religions and just lifestyle choices."	White female, age 36, Independent, Kelly Ridge, California
3	"I have read that Whites will become the minority over the next view years. Blacks and Hispanics will continue to grow over time. Interracial couples will increase as well, as society has become more accepting of them."	White woman, age 47, strong Democrat, Dublin, California
4	"What immediately comes to mind are more Latinos, Black and Asian people in any given neighborhood. Right now, there are plenty of neighborhoods composed entirely of white people."	Latina woman, age 36, strong Democrat, Twin Falls, Idaho

Political Projections and Democratic Erosion from the Ideas about POC

Associations of Black Americans with the changing demographics of the country are not at all limited to immediately racialized views of anti-Blackness. They translate directly into attitudes about the political system and the future of American politics, amid ideas of political collusion across racial minority groups (Knowles, Tropp, and Mogami 2022). In effect, the second *P* in the three *P*'s of demographic determinism, POC, has a political potency in and of itself. Here, I am describing how it namely motivates ideas about POC voting for the Democratic Party. The diversifying country leads Americans to infer that Democrats will be advantaged by these changes, and here I *specifically* mean that it emerges from inferences about Black Americans.

Next, using the same study above, I show that the POC prime leads White Americans to infer that the country is becoming more Democratic. This is a direct test of demographic determinism. It is framed as follows: "How will the politics of the United States change between now and 2060? It will become [much more Republican or much more Democratic, 1–7 on the Likert scale]." As I find, the POC graph leads to a significant uptick in ideas of the Democratic Party being advantaged ($p = 0.0001$) in the coming years.[7] Shown in figure 6.5 is the direct comparison between the diverse and POC graphs on these demographic determinism lines.

Beyond the main effects, I find a series of additional dimensions to the operation of the POC graph that does more to describe the intimate

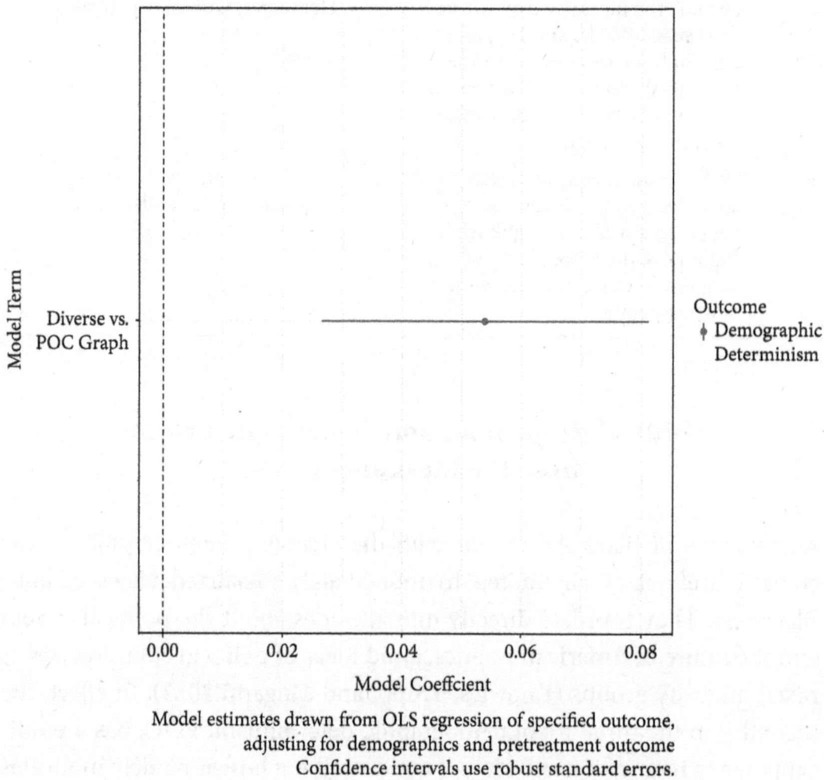

Figure 6.5 Coefficient plot of effect of POC graph on demographic determinism.

[7] I find significant effects of the POC graph relative to the pure control (the group that received no prime), which does well to validate the idea that the diverse graph has no clear floor effects ($p = 0.035$).

relationship between Black Americans and presumptions of the Democratic Party being advantaged. When I interact party identification with the primes, I detect null differences between Republican and Democratic inferences about who they presume to be advantaged (p = 0.93). Shown in figure 6.6 are displays of the interactions, which reveal that there are consistent increases in inferences of the Democratic Party being advantaged upon review of the POC graph, relative to the diverse graph.

Altogether, these results confirm that when White Americans think about the number of POC increasing, they first infer that the number of Black Americans is increasing. Across partisan lines, this is not a normative, uniform judgment of the future of the country; this will be made apparent in chapter 7. I find that in a unidirectional way, White Republicans become significantly more anti-democratic in reaction to presumptions about demographic determinism.

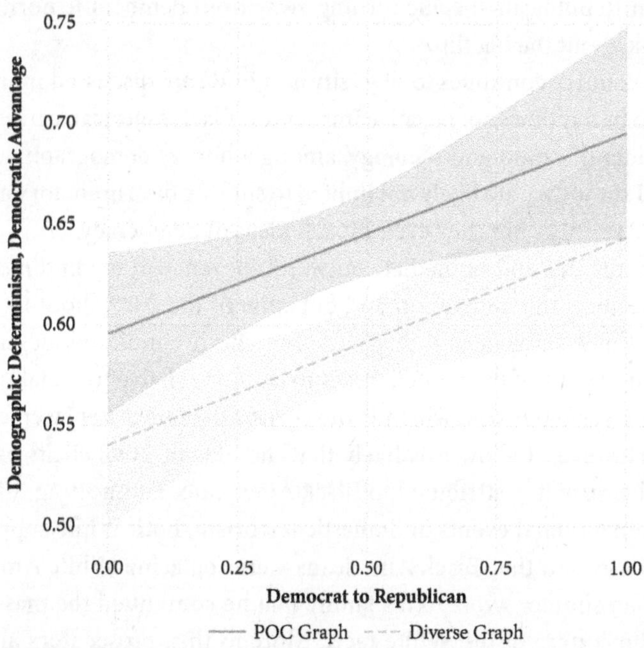

Figure 6.6 Interaction plot depicting the effect of POC graph vs. diverse graph on demographic determinism measured posttreatment across Democrats to Republicans. Uniform effect of POC graph increasing demographic determinism expectation of Democrats having advantage.

The Second *P* of the Three *P*'s: The Democratic Legacy of Black Americans

In the previously mentioned studies, I show that priming the idea that POC populations are increasing taps intothe historical legacy of the second of the three P'sand its contemporary function. So when POC are discussed and referred to within politics, they are strongly associated with Black Americans. *POC* is not a catch-all term for racial minorities due to the cultural rootedness of Black Americans in racial politics. This second *P* also directly affects ideas about the future US politics, even as it relates to the diversification of the country. When Americans are shown a simple graph that says the POC population is increasing, they are more likely to think that the population of Black Americans is increasing, which then further pushes the notion that the United States is going to become even more supportive of the Democratic Party. This sets up the last of the three *P*'s, partisanship, and ultimately helps to explain Republican-specific turning away from democratic norms when they think about the big flip.

As the country continues to diversify and POC are discussed more, there is likely to be a spillover of negative impacts on Black Americans, irrespective of party identification and ideology, among a host of demographic characteristics. I show they are likely not limited to shifting discriminatory attitudes or general feelings, but they even broach ideas of democracy.

The pertinence and immediate outward relevance of my findings in this chapter capture the motivation and outcome of the 2022 shooting in Buffalo and the 2015 shooting in Charleston. Both conditions describe the White population of the United States in decline relative to racial minority groups increasing in size, which is the core of the Great Replacement conspiracy. However, I show it is likely that the idea of POC elicits extremist support because it is attributed to Black Americans. Connecting this to the two aforementioned events of domestic terrorism, both White supremacist terrorists asserted that Black Americans were replacing White Americans. The Buffalo shooter wrote to his family that he committed the mass shooting for the "future of the White race." More to this, prosecutors articulate that "Gendron's motive for the mass shooting was to prevent Black people from replacing White people and eliminating the White race, and to inspire others to commit similar attacks" (Ly 2022). He also cited the domestic terrorist who committed the Charleston church shooting in 2015 in his manifesto (Beals 2022). It is clear from the language White supremacists use about the Great Replacement conspiracy that Black Americans are front and center in *who* they think are replacing: White Americans. The key irony is that the population of Black Americans is *not* increasing compared to that of Latinx and Asian Americans. Moreover, when I prime these groups correctly in accordance with census projections, ideas of Democratic advantage decrease. For the big flip, Black Americans are therefore central to the political story.

Discussion

Throughout this chapter, I confirm that the long history of the racial binary is still relevant to contemporary American public views and especially to the big flip. Legacies of anti-Blackness and the role of Black Americans in racial politics overdetermine, even future, ideas of the country changing. This happens without the information environment in discussion of the big flip incorporating ideas of Black Americans increasing in size. In other words, when Americans think of POC, Black Americans jump to mind often in tandem with Hispanic and Latino Americans particularly. I show that this holds both for senses of identity among Black Americans and outward perceptions of POC within the context of the big flip. The association of *Black* and *POC* is woven intricately in the minds of Americans across racial groups. Across the board, Americans think the changing country will lead to a more liberal turn, giving Democrats an advantage over Republicans. This sets the stage for my evaluation and of the third and final *P*: partisanship. I show next how this dynamic alters Republicans' very sentiments about the entire system of American democracy.

7
Demographic Determinism and the Partisan Inference of the Big Flip

The third and final *P* that motivates demographic determinism is partisanship. This extends directly from the presumptions that motivate second *P*, POC. Because Americans infer POC are predominately Black, they take this idea further. They then incorporate the historical political relationship Black Americans have with the Democratic Party onto *all* POC—in effect assuming that the Democratic Party will receive overwhelming support as POC increase in size. Of course, they do this all while presuming that the population of Black Americans is greatly increasing.

In this chapter, I show that this idea of an overwhelming Democrat electoral advantage in the big flip is the baseline assumption in how both Democrats and Republicans think about it. I then go further to show just how intimately Republicans' views of democracy are tied to their big flip presumptions. On a causal level, when Republicans are primed with information claiming that the Republican Party will be at an advantage as a result of the big flip, they express less racially threatened views and more pro-democratic views. This same concern does not extend to Democrats—they are not any more racially threatened or anti-democratic when primed to think that Republicans will be at an advantage. Ultimately, I define the dynamic that I detail as the partisan inference of the big flip—the assumption that the majority-minority flip will be a Democratic advantage. On the whole, I show Republicans' views of democracy to be contingent on who they presume will be able to win in electoral politics. I begin by detailing the recent dynamics of the big flip, the racial threat from it, and its contribution to democratic backsliding in the United States.

The Big Flip. Andrew Ifedapo Thompson, Oxford University Press. © Oxford University Press (2026).
DOI: 10.1093/9780197822173.003.0007

The Big Flip and Democratic Backsliding

Over the past several years, the United States has undergone democratic backsliding (McCoy, Rahman, and Somer 2018; Levitsky and Ziblatt 2018; Carey et al. 2019; Norris and Inglehart 2019; Graham and Svolik 2020). This shift has included the erosion of democratic norms, increased support for political violence, and institutional means of preventing democratic participation (Gandhi 2019; Kalmoe and Mason 2022; Bartels 2022). Among the public, these anti-democratic views reached a fever pitch in early 2021 with the January 6 insurrection at the US Capitol building—one of the only times in American history when citizens have assertively contested the results of a democratic election.

Racial threat has been shown to strongly motivate these shifting attitudes in the public and in the January 6 insurrectionists (Bartels 2020a; Pape 2021). The racial diversification of the United States is a strong driver of this sentiment of threat. A great deal of Americans feel threatened by the country's future racial demographic landscape, the prospect of losing power, and the idea of their way of life fundamentally changing. These senses of threat emerge from anxiety and fear about these changes, which then manifest in changes to political support (Brader, Valentino, and Suhay 2008). A few examples of how these threatened attitudes are emerging in politics come in the ongoing debate about critical race theory in high schools (Ray and Gibbons 2021), as well as backlash over pushes for the representation of POC in media (B. Anderson 2021).

I argue that there is a fuller story behind the connection between racial threat and anti-democratic views. It concerns relative power gains and losses for *partisans*: Republicans perceive a loss for themselves and their party through racial demographic change. They anticipate that the increasing size of racial minority groups and diminishing number of White Americans will result in the Republican Party being less able to win elections across the country. Perceptions of this partisan disadvantage then feed directly into racial threat among Republicans, which ultimately changes how they think about democracy. They become less supportive of it because they think their party will be unable to win.

The conclusion of this story is that these fearful Americans become more willing to support the rollback of American democratic institutions and engage in anti-democratic behavior. In this chapter, I show that Republicans' concerns about racial demographic change stem from inferences that they make about racial minorities' party identification. Their racial attitudes are intertwined with their partisan ones. I call this the "partisan inference of racial demographic change."

Republican partisans feel a racial threat from racial diversification because they project it to be harmful to their party. Following this, their attitudes toward democracy are then tied to their perceptions of demographic change. If this idea holds, then threat and anti-democratic support should decrease among Republicans when they learn that these demographic changes will benefit their party. This is exactly what I find.

I causally test the utility of the concept through a set of preregistered experiments. Within these studies, I explicitly frame racial demographic change as a phenomenon that will benefit either Democrats or Republicans. This framing tests the partisan inference in demographic change for both party members. When Republicans are told that their party will benefit from racial demographic change, their perceptions of racial threat are assuaged. Most significantly, their support for anti-democratic ideas decreases.

Within my first experiment, I show that reframing the partisan inference leads Republicans to express more positive feelings about racial demographic change and become warmer toward racial minorities and immigrants as a whole. I also show wide-ranging effects, in that this narrative leads Republicans to express warmer feelings toward the Black Lives Matter (BLM) movement. In a second experiment using the same design, I show that this same framing shifts Republicans' attitudes toward democracy. When the Republican Party is framed to gain an advantage from demographic change, it causes party members to express *less* anti-democratic support in both abstract and policy-oriented domains.

As a third test to validate the causal connection between racial threat and anti-democratic attitudes, I prime the idea of racial demographic change using a light-touch treatment that only involves one open-ended question. In this study, I determine that this simple prime leads Republicans to express significantly more anti-democratic attitudes. This study provides further qualitative evidence of how threat operates in the minds of Republicans.

Ultimately, I show that Republicans' racially threatened attitudes and anti-democratic sentiments are closely tied to their inferences about racial demographic change. I make direct comparisons throughout these experiments and demonstrate that the partisan inference of demographic change holds specifically for Republicans.

My findings lead to two major implications. The first is that racial demographic concerns among Republicans are contingent on their party's perceived likelihood of winning. Secondly, I demonstrate that concerns for the Republican Party's position motivate ideas about racial threat, which suggests that racially prejudiced views may rest at the core of Republicans' anti-democratic support. This causal connection between racial threat and anti-democratic support leads to the consideration of race and democracy as deeply intertwined in the United States—so much so that racial priming could sway public support for democratic norms and institutions. Works in political science have shown some policy issues to be superficially race-neutral (Gilens 1995, 1996). Here I submit that we must also consider that ideas about democracy itself have reached a similar point: that attitudes toward American democracy have become contingent on Americans' racial views. In summary, contemporary views of American democracy appear directly related to and *motivated by* the interplay between race and partisanship. Thus, American democratic values might shift with perceptions and inferences made about racial demographics.

Racial Threat Reconsidered

Racial threat has a long history in the study of American politics. It has been identified in two distinct empirical ways: when the number of racial minorities *actually* grows (real demographic change), or when it is *projected* to grow (perceived demographic change). When either of these dynamics happen, White Americans express a sense of fear about their status (Blumer 1958; Blalock 1967; Key and Heard 1984; Fossett and Kiecolt 1989; Quillian 1995, 1996; Craig and Richeson 2014b). Throughout this area of study, the size of racial minority groups is a proxy for their influence and Whites' influence. It is zero-sum. The more racial minority groups grow in size or are perceived to grow, the more they can influence American politics, culture, and society. Scholars have shown that racial threat from these real and perceived changes leads to more prejudiced views toward minorities (Quillian 1995), more punitive attitudes (Dixon 2006), and a host of other political attitudes. More recent work shows that local, real changes to demographics are less potent in driving conservative shifts in political support (Hill, Hopkins, and Huber 2019). On a broader level, the phenomenon of racial threat from demographic change has contributed to the emergence of far-right politics throughout many Western democracies (Bonikowski 2017; Hanley and Vachudova 2018; Eatwell and Goodwin 2018; Vachudova 2020; Lührmann and Lindberg 2019; Marinov and Popova 2021).

The United States is undergoing a unique experience relative to these other contexts. A majority-minority flip is occurring on a national level for the first time in the history of the country—a near-unprecedented moment among Western democracies too. Within this flip, racial minorities will overtake Whites as the new majority group for the first time in American history. At this point, these projections are salient among the public, though they are not limited to perceptions of racial dynamics. I show that Americans, both Republicans and Democrats, have made an implicit partisan inference about this coming flip: that Democrats are slated to gain more political advantage over time because of their perceived appeal to racial minorities.

This Democratic-advantage inference has been considered in a variety of ways over the past few decades. A recent example fueling far-right support is the Great Replacement conspiracy. White nationalists have long advocated the idea that elites are attempting to subvert the power of Whites through immigration and declining birth rates. In short, politicians have weaponized demographic change. The Great Replacement conspiracy has recently caught fire within contemporary American politics. In 2017, Unite the Right protestors in Charlottesville evoked this notion when they chanted "Jews will not replace us" (Katz 2017; Wildman 2017).

Over the past decade, portions of the Republican Party incorporated these ideas of racial threat into their messaging. Earlier iterations of the Great Replacement were advocated by the Tea Party, and once the faction captured the Republican Party, the idea took root in mainstream GOP rhetoric (Blum 2020). The elite messaging has borne out in political attitudes (Hopkins 2021). Recent work has found strong correlations between Republican voters' animosity toward Democratic-linked social groups, many of which are racial minorities, and support for Donald Trump (Mason, Wronski, and Kane 2021).

Another historical and punctuated example of the Democratic-advantage inference of racial demographic change came in the GOP Autopsy report following the electoral loss to Barack Obama in 2012, described in chapter 3.

So, this idea of racial demographic change advantaging the Democratic Party has functionally existed in both extreme and moderate wings of the party. I argue that this overarching concern for the future of the GOP taps into potent aspects of American political culture—namely, the tyranny of the majority and the function of conservative parties. I connect these ideas next to racial threat and then to why Republicans' partisan inferences about racial demographic change are crucial to understanding democratic backsliding in the United States.

The Tyranny of the (Racial) Majority

The Madisonian and Tocquevillian conceptions of the tyranny of the majority are closely linked to Republicans' feelings of racial threat. For one, Madison's idea of the structure of American government works to assuage ideas that the will of the majority can overtake that of minorities:

> [I]n the federal republic of the United States . . . all authority in it will be derived from and dependent on the society, the society itself will be broken into so many parts, interests, and classes of citizens, that the rights of individuals, or of the minority, will be in little danger from interested combinations of the majority.
>
> (Hamilton, Madison, and Jay 2008)

In short, the American federalist system will work to prevent the majority from using their numbers to subsume the interests or the rights of the minority. Tocqueville writes similarly:

> In the United States the majority has an immense power in fact and a power of opinion almost as great; and once the majority has formed on a question, there is, so to speak, no obstacle that can, I will not say stop, but even slow its course and leave time for the majority to hear the cries of those whom it crushes as it goes. The consequences of this state of affairs are harmful and dangerous for the future.
>
> (Tocqueville 2003)

In reflections on Tocqueville's interpretation of the will of the majority, Maletz writes, "Majority rule is characteristically populist, to be sure, and enforces its egalitarianism through an adamant repudiation of all forms of 'aristocracy'" (2002). In the tyranny of the majority, there is an active fear that the majority will run roughshod over the interests of the minority because of their sheer numbers. Both theorists offer up institutional reasons why federalism will work to prevent these issues, but they do not correct for these sentiments among the public.

Concerns of the tyranny of the majority are embedded within early ideas of American political culture. They shape how Americans consider ideal forms of democratic governance, which calls for an equitable representation of public interests regardless of numbers. Despite this American tradition emphasizing egalitarianism and protection of the interests of minorities, the cultural view does not exist within a vacuum. Multiple American traditions function at once, often in direct contrast to one another (Smith 1993, 1997). Specifically, support for protections against the tyranny of the majority mesh with ascriptive hierarchies and inegalitarian ideology. Under ideas of the ascriptive racial hierarchy in the United States, White Americans can reasonably and legitimately hold the numerical majority. When Americans of color acquire this position, it becomes illegitimate. The interplay between the multiple cultural American traditions then helps to explain Republican anxiety about changing racial demographics *and* the ultimate conclusion that is drawn from it—a movement away from democracy in response to threat.

Republicans perceive that racial minorities will exercise a tyranny of majority when they become a numerical majority. Why is this a Republican-centric concern? They infer that racial minorities identify more closely with Democrats. And what is their response to this perceived tyranny? A turn toward anti-democratic means to secure their power. What I am describing here is the defense of egalitarian ideas through inegalitarian means, an idea that connects the multiple traditions thesis to the historical emergence of conservative parties in Western democracies.

The overarching argument is that conservative parties have used democratic means to secure power because it was advantageous. The Democratic-advantage inference of racial demographic change makes democratic elections a less viable option because the GOP appears to have tethered itself to a shrinking constituency. What happens when perceptions of the ability to win through democratic means break down? Under this same theory of conservative parties, ideas about democracy also break down, which Przeworski describes: "If some important political forces have no chance to win, those who expect to suffer continued deprivation under democratic institutions will turn against them" (Przeworski 1991, 32). Stemming from this concept, I argue that racial threat from demographic change offers a challenge to democratic institutions because Republicans perceive they will not be able to consistently win office. Take, for example, Lindsay Graham's assertion about the Republican Party in light of Mitt Romney's 2012 loss: "The demographics race we're losing badly. We're not generating enough angry white guys to stay in business for the long term" (Helderman and Cohen 2012). Additionally, Donald Trump articulated a similar idea about the functional ability of the GOP before the 2016 election when he said, "I think this will be the last election if I don't win" (Neidig 2016). Republicans' inference from the growing numbers of racial minorities and decreasing White population is that they cannot win elections through democratic means. As such, democracy loses favor in the eyes of Republican supporters.

The Ostensible Partisan Threat of Racial Demographic Change

Republicans want to maintain their numbers against what they view to be a tyranny of the majority brought about by the political threat of Americans of color, which they assume will benefit their political opposition. This is an incorrect assumption about the future of the country that is based on racial stereotypes and has been primed consistently through elite messaging. There is mounting evidence that different racial minority groups do not overwhelmingly support the Democratic Party (Lopez et al. 2016; Domínguez 2022; Mutnik and Ferris 2022; Caputo 2022; Stewart et al. 2022). Moreover, demographers consider that racial demographics are unlikely to change in the way that some have previously predicted (Alba 2018a; Alba, Beck, and Basaran Sahin 2018). Despite the empirical ambivalence about the future of the country, these misperceptions still exist in the public.

The misperceived, deterministic threat from demographic change moves beyond considerations of party competition. It then affects attitudes toward democratic politics for reasons that directly point to the big flip. There is mounting evidence that Republican voters are becoming increasingly supportive of authoritarian practices—for example, political violence and limiting Democrats' participation (Yokley 2021; PRRI 2021; Kalmoe and Mason 2022). These views are deeply tied to the partisan orientation of racial threat.

Empirically, I test a series of ideas central to the development of antidemocratic attitudes around racial demographic change: (1) the partisan inference made about racial demographic change, (2) what reframing that inference should do to perceptions of racial threat, and (3) how the changes

Table 7.1 Hypotheses

Motivation	Description	Hypothesis
Clarifying the partisan inference about racial demographic change	Racial minorities increasing in size is advantageous for **Democrats**. Making this explicit will not affect racial threat attitudes among either Republicans or Democrats because it fits the norm.	H1
Reframing the partisan inference about demographic change	Racial minorities increasing in size is advantageous for **Republicans**. Making this explicit will decrease racial threat among Republicans because it will diminish anxieties and concerns about the future of the party.	H2
Causally connecting racial threat to anti-democratic attitudes	The reduction in threat from reframing the partisan inference about racial demographic change will lead to a reduction in anti-democratic support among **Republicans**. This frame will assuage concerns about the party's ability to win elections in light of racial demographic change.	H3

to threat affect partisans' support for anti-democratic actions. I describe each of these motivations and assign hypotheses to each in table 7.1.

Clarifying Anti-Democratic Concepts

Before I describe my research design, I will first clarify the anti-democratic concepts I am measuring. This is to explicate the bounds and constraints under which these empirical tests are being conducted. Ahmed (2022) provides a useful structure and framework for approaching the analysis of democratic backsliding in the public. There are categorical and contextual differences across each of the measures I use. On the categorical differences in anti-democratic attitudes, I investigate *violations of laws* and *violations of ideals*. Violations of laws capture public support for actions that undermine formal institutions that manage democratic competition. Violations of ideals capture aspirational views on how democratic politics ought to be conducted.

Regarding contextual differences, the following experiments are conducted with cross-sectional studies, which prevents an assessment of attitudes over time. I am primarily concerned with the internal validity of the experiment, which involves direct comparisons across partisans. I compare Democrats' and Republicans' shifting anti-democratic attitudes. As I will describe in the procedure section, I use two partisan frames of racial demographic change for my treatments, and I compare these to a frame on racial demographic change that does not include the partisan frame. This allows me to isolate the partisan effect of the treatment, then compare the effect of each partisan frame (Democratic or Republican advantage) on each partisan group. The stakes for these comparisons are that Republicans' anti-democratic support will be the same as Democrats in response to the Democratic-advantage frame or significantly lower than Democrats in response to the Republican-advantage frame.

Orientation of Experiments

I use a set of preregistered vignette experiments to test my hypotheses. In these experiments, I explicitly indicate which party is projected to benefit from demographic change. The baseline condition I use describes the racial majority-minority flip generally, which allows me to isolate the effects of each partisan frame. Then, within my outcome measures, I assess the extent to which these frames affect racial threat (experiment 1 and 2) and support for anti-democratic ideas (experiment 2) among Republicans and Democrats.

More specifically, in experiment 1, I test how partisan frames about changing demographics affect how Republicans and Democrats feel about these changes and their feelings toward POC and immigrants (H1, H2). This allows me to capture emotions about demographic change and feelings toward racial minority groups, which are two crucial components of racial threat (Brader, Valentino, and Suhay 2008; Mutz 2018; Reichelmann and Hunt 2021; Sohoni 2022). Within experiment 2, I test how these same partisan frames affect Republicans' and Democrats' anti-democratic support (H3) and racial threat (H1, H2).

Experiment 1 was conducted, and all respondents were compensated through online vendor Lucid Fulcrum in April 2021 (N = 1,087; for full sample demographics, see appendix 1). Experiment 2 was conducted with a representative sample through Forthright (formerly Bovitz, Inc.)[1] and is census-matched on gender, race, and region (N = 1,274). Next, I detail the experimental procedure.

Experimental Procedure

Respondents provided consent, completed an attention check, which filtered out inattentive participants, then answered demographic items at the beginning of this survey.[2] Upon completing these pretreatment items, respondents were randomly assigned to one of the three conditions. (See table 7.2.)[3]

Conditions 2 and 3 address the partisan inference of racial demographic change. Condition 1 is a baseline condition that simply describes the racial majority-minority flip. I administer the treatment in two steps. First, all respondents are provided with the following question: "Which of the following events is projected to occur in the United States by mid-century?"

Upon completing the question, all three treatments then tell respondents that the correct answer to the question is that "racial minorities will overtake Whites as the majority group." Conditions 2 and 3 further articulate that the Republican Party or Democratic Party, respectively, is projected to gain more supporters from the majority-minority flip (appendix 1). All respondents then complete a series of posttreatment items that correspond

Table 7.2 Conditions in order

Conditions	Description
1	Majority-minority flip
2	Majority-minority flip + Republican frame
3	Majority-minority flip + Democratic frame

[1] This survey platform has been utilized in a series of previous works (Druckman, Peterson, and Slothuus 2013; Rothschild 2020; Bakker, Lelkes, and Malka 2020).

[2] As a second quality check, respondents also completed an open-ended question asking them to describe their community. Those who did not answer the prompt or provided an indecipherable response were excluded from the sample.

[3] I use block randomization on party identification to provide sufficient statistical power across conditions (appendix 8).

with racial threat (experiment 1 and 2) and support for anti-democratic ideas (experiment 2).

Next, I present my analyses for experiment 1. I use linear regression with interactions between the treatment and partisan identification to test my hypotheses.

Reframing the Partisan Inference of Racial Demographic Change

I start with hypotheses 1 and 2. H1 expects that the Democratic-advantage frame will wield no effect on the sense of racial threat across partisans. H2 expects that the Republican-advantage frame will cause Republicans to express less racially threatened views. To start, I use two measures of worry and concern about racial demographic change.[4] I use linear regression with interactions, testing for the treatment moderated by party identification.[5]

I find consistent effects across both expressed emotions. First, the Democratic-advantage frame has no statistically significant effect on either Republicans' or Democrats' concerns or worries (figures 7.1–7.2; appendix 2). Regarding the Republican-advantage frame, Republicans express significantly less worry ($p = 0.014$) and concern ($p = 0.036$) about racial demographic change when they are told their party will benefit. Within all of the following figures, the bold line represents the partisan-advantage treatment, and the dashed line represents the control. Party identification is scaled from 0 to 1, where 0 is strong Democrat and 1 is strong Republican.

These two sets of findings confirm H1 and H2. I identify null effects for the Democratic frame, which provides evidence for the idea that a Democratic advantage is implied in the general discussion of the majority-minority flip (the control). Conversely, I find that the Republican frame assuages concern and anxiety among Republicans specifically.This is evidenced by the near flat line across partisans exposed to the Republican-advantage treatment (figure 7.2). Strong Republicans and strong Democrats express nearly identical levels of concern and worry about demographic change when they learn that racial demographic change will advantage the Republican Party.

[4] The question is "How do you feel about a diversifying United States?" Both of these feelings are tested on a scale of 1 to 7, with 1 as Strongly Disagree and 7 as Strongly Agree. I rescale these variables 0 to 1, where 0 is Strongly Disagree and 1 is Strongly Agree.

[5] I control for ideology, education, media consumption, gender, race, and age.

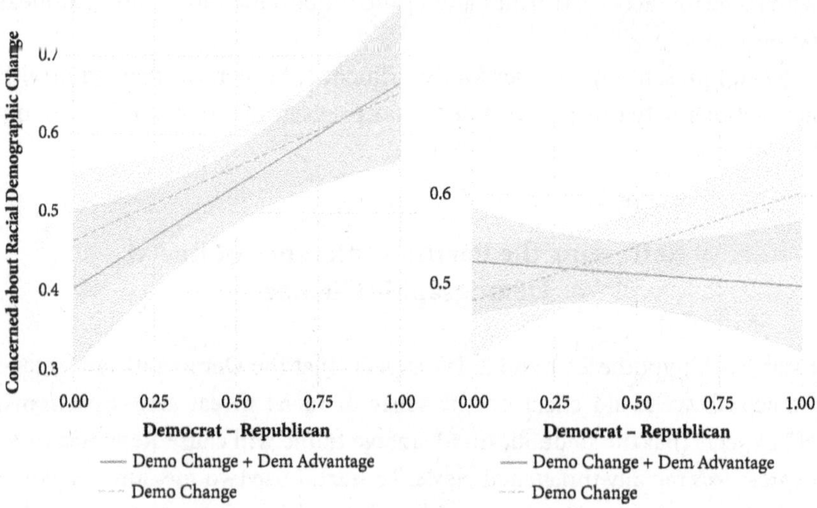

Figures 7.1–7.2 Interaction plot depicting the effect of partisan advantage concern over demographic change posttreatment across Democrats to Republicans. Republicans become less concerned upon receiving the Republican advantage treatment.

Next, I test the effects of the partisan-advantage frames on group-related feelings as a second evaluation of racial threat. To rehash my hypotheses, I expect that the Republican-advantage framing of demographic change will increase Republicans' warmth toward Black Americans and racial minorities overall, following from chapter 6 (H1 and H2). I use the same linear models with feeling thermometers about racial minorities (Black, Asian, and Latinx Americans), immigrants, and the BLM movement (figures 7.3–7.5). First, I test H1 again across all three feeling thermometers. (See appendix 3 for full tables.)

Testing for H1 across group-based feeling thermometers, I again find that the Democratic-advantage frame has no significant impact on these views for either Democrats or Republicans. This confirms the idea that a Democratic advantage is implicit within ideas of racial demographic change. Figures 7.6–7.8 below show the same linear models, testing the impact of the Republican-advantage frame.

The Republican-advantage frame causes Republicans to express *warmer* attitudes toward racial minorities ($p = 0.032$), immigrants ($p = 0.032$), and BLM ($p = 0.0581$). This signifies the strength of Republicans' perceptions of

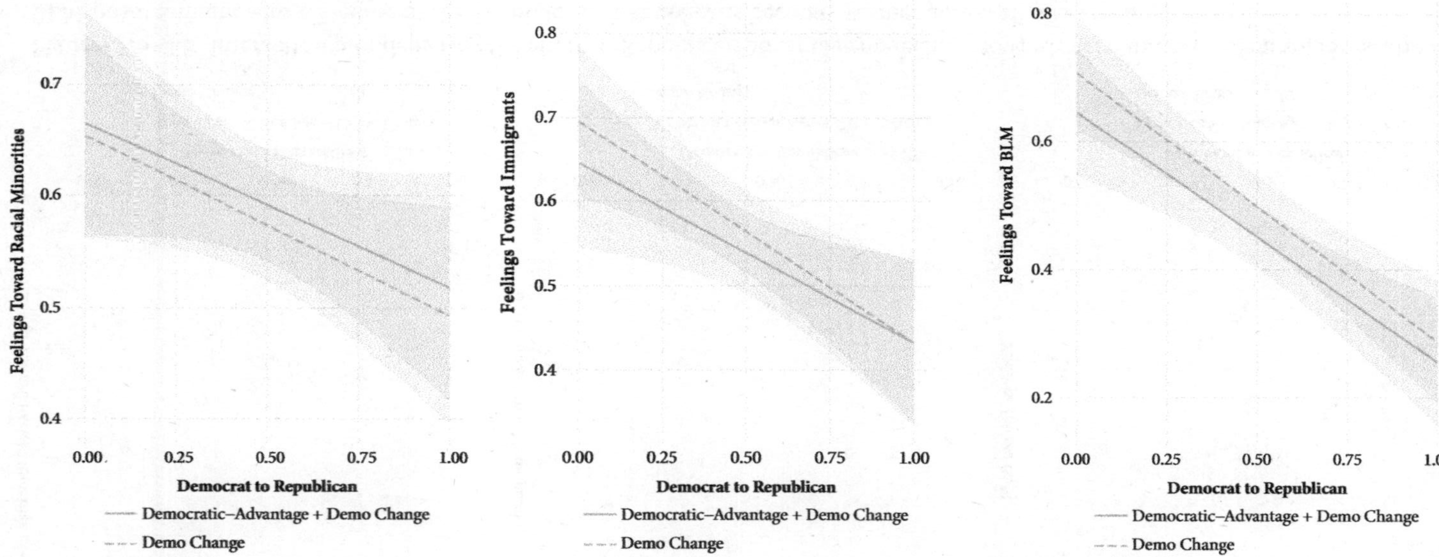

Figures 7.3–7.5 Interaction plot depicting the effect of Democratic advantage on feelings toward racial minorities, immigrants, and BLM posttreatment across Democrats to Republicans. Null differences across partisans.

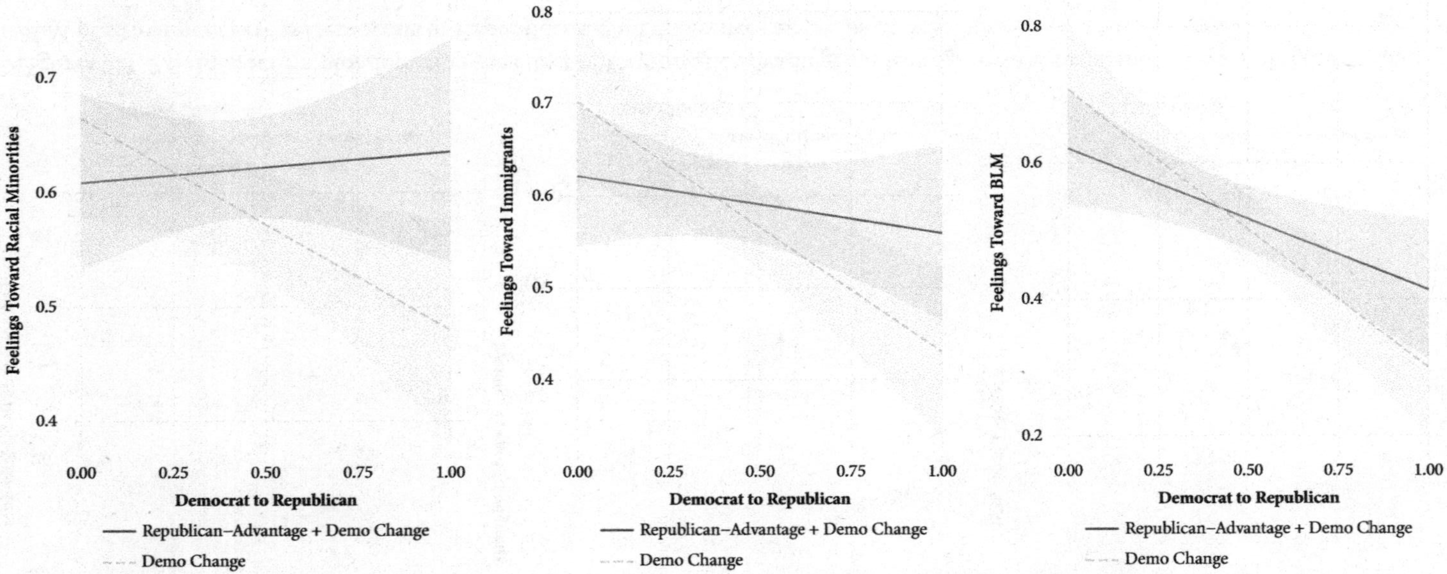

Figures 7.6–7.8 Interaction plot depicting the effect of Republican advantage on feelings toward racial minorities, immigrants, and BLM posttreatment across Democrats to Republicans. Republicans become warmer across all measures.

racial demographic change, while also showing that a similar concern does not exist among Democrats.

Connecting these emotions and group-based feelings together, I identify that these different dimensions of racial threat are connected to Republicans' partisan inferences about racial demographic change. Republicans' senses of racial threat appear motivated by their perception of which party will benefit from the diversification of the United States. As the country becomes more racially mixed and less White, they presume their party will be at a disadvantage. Moreover, Republicans particularly are susceptible to this framing relative to Democrats, who are unmoved by either party-favoring or opposing ideas of demographic change. Reframing the same majority-minority flip as a GOP advantage vitiates these ideas of threat. It makes Republicans more emotionally positive and warmer toward POC, immigrants, and even the BLM movement, which receives little support among Republicans generally (Horowitz, Hurst, and Braga 2023).

This first experiment validates the idea that threat among these partisans is motivated by who they perceive to win from racial demographic change. However, I also theoretically connect these partisan sentiments to views of democracy. I expect they are importantly tied to anti-democratic support among Republicans (H3). Next, I turn to a second experiment, which uses the same design and tests the effect of the partisan-advantage frame on anti-democratic attitudes. I also replicate H1 and H2 as a further display of the validity of the partisan inferences in racial demographic change.

Reframing Racial Demographic Change, Reducing Anti-Democratic Attitudes

I test the exact same frames from experiment 1 in a second experiment, using a representative, non-probability sample conducted through Bovitz, Inc. All respondents were compensated (N = 1,274; see appendix 2 for full demographics).[6] First, I retest the same outcome measures from experiment 1 that evaluate H1 and H2. Using the same linear model that tests the treatment effect moderated by party identification, I confirm again that the Republican partisan frame decreases Republicans' worry ($p = 0.032$) and concern ($p = 0.028$) about racial demographic change. Additionally, I create a composite scale, which collapses feeling thermometers on racial

[6] I block randomize thetreatment on party identification.

minorities, immigrants, and BLM, and I find that the Republican-advantage frame on racial demographic change increases warmth on all three measures ($p = 0.078$). These results replicate experiment 1 and confirm H1 and H2. (See appendix 4 for these analyses.) Validating these sentiments over multiple studies demonstrates that the primes function as expected in vitiating Republicans' racially threatened feelings. This is a precondition of what I expect along anti-democratic lines.

Next, I test the role that partisan perceptions of racial demographic change have on anti-democratic attitudes. I use two sets of measures of these views. The first is a scale that measures violations of laws and ideals, which I created and pretested. Secondly, I use a set of adapted measures from Graham and Svolik (2020). The first is a composite measure I designed and validated in a separate study conducted using a diverse sample of Americans[7] in September 2020 through Lucid Fulcrum. All respondents were compensated ($N = 518$). The measures I test here intend to capture zero-sum ideas about the function of democracy and partisanship. These measures are shown in table 7.3, along with their corresponding anti-democratic categorization.

These items load well together in a single scale ($\alpha = 0.91$). Using a simple difference-in-means test, I find a large difference between Republicans and Democrats' anti-democratic attitudes ($p < 0.01$; Republicans are

Table 7.3 Description of outcome variables

Please share to what extent you agree with the following statements:	**Anti-democratic categorization**
1) It is reasonable to use violence against people who are politically opposed to me.	Violation of law
2) I care more about my political party winning office more than I care about democracy functioning well.	Violation of ideals
3) I support institutions and practices that prevent people I dislike from participating in politics.	Violation of law
4) The point of politics is to win at all costs.	Violation of ideals
5) I am comfortable with less democracy if it also means my political opposition losing.	Violation of ideals

[7] This sample is primarily White (70%) and is nearly evenly spread along gender lines (52% women). On party identification, there are slightly more Republicans (40%) than Democrats (33%). For full sample demographics, see appendix 2.2.

11 percentage points more supportive). This shows there to be important partisan views that correspond with anti-democratic views.

I test these same measures in experiment 2 and collapse them into a single scale ($\alpha = 0.86$). Using the same linear model that I used to analyze experiment 1, I then test the effect of the partisan-advantage treatments with this anti-democratic scale using the same linear models from experiment 1 (figures 7.9 and 7.10; see appendix 5).[8]

Across these measures, when Republicans learn that racial demographic change will benefit their party, they express *less* anti-democratic sentiments ($p = 0.027$), confirming H3. In comparison, the Democratic-advantage frame does not significantly move partisans' anti-democratic support ($p = 0.526$), which confirms H3. The Republican-advantage frame clearly reduces Republicans' larger support for anti-democratic ideas.

As another test of H3, I use party-contingent items adapted from Graham and Svolik (2020).[9] I list the adapted measures below:

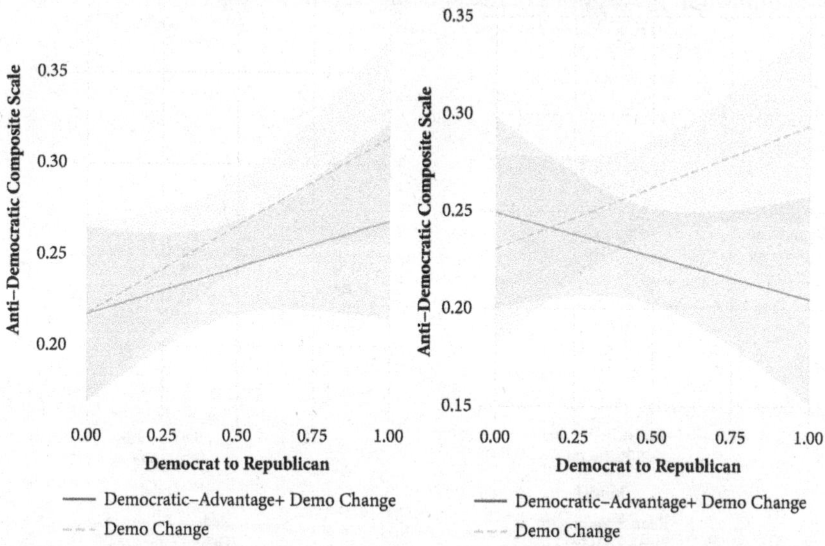

Figures 7.9–7.10 Interaction plot depicting the effect of partisan advantage on anti-democratic support posttreatment across Democrats to Republicans. Republicans become less anti-democratic in response to Republican advantage frame.

[8] I control for ideology, region, age, gender, race, and media consumption.

[9] By party-contingent, I mean that respondents viewed a particular wording of the measure based upon their party identification.

1) A proposal to reduce the number of polling stations in areas that support [Republicans/Democrats].
2) [Republican/Democratic] governors should prosecute journalists who accuse them of misconduct without revealing sources.
3) [Republican/Democratic] governors should ban far-right group rallies in state capitols.
4) [Republican/Democratic] governors should ban far-left group rallies in state capitols.

In my analysis of the effect of the partisan-advantage frames on these views, I use linear regression to analyze the effect of the Republican-advantage and Democrat-advantage treatments. Due to the party-contingent nature of the outcome measures, I subset on party identification. As shown in figures 7.11 and 7.12, the idea of partisan utility holds across three of the four measures. I also find null effects for the Democratic-advantage frame, again confirming my expectation that this advantage frame is the baseline assumption in perceptions of racial demographic change.

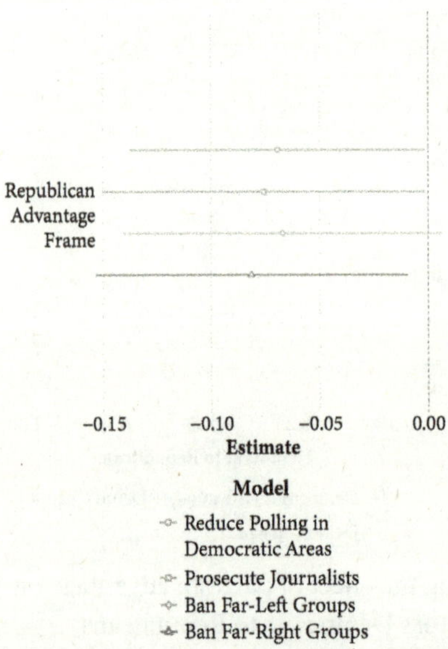

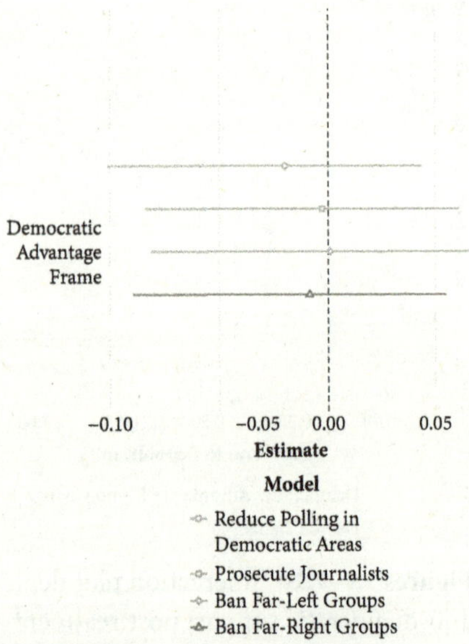

Figures 7.11–7.12 Coefficient plots of partisan advantage frame effects on support for anti-democratic policy, Republicans only.

Note: The baseline in each of these graphs is the general racial demographic change (condition 1). This figure shows the results of these comparisons along with corresponding 95% confidence intervals.

The Republican-advantage frame decreases Republicans' support for reducing polls in Democratic areas by 7 percentage points ($p = 0.046$); decreases their support for Republican governors prosecuting journalists who accuse them of misconduct by 7 percentage points ($p = 0.046$); and decreases their support for Republican governors banning far-right groups (8 percentage points; $p = 0.026$) and far-left groups (7 percentage points; $p = 0.073$) from holding rallies at state capitols. Republicans who receive the Democrat-advantage frame express no greater or lesser anti-democratic support. Moreover, Democrats are no more or less anti-democratic upon receiving either the Republican or Democrat advantage frames (appendix 5).

Further Validating the Partisan-Advantage Theory

As an additional validation check on the connection between racial threat and anti-democratic attitudes, I include another measure that describes an anti-democratic action directed toward racial minorities: "preventing racial minorities from participating in politics." Here again, the partisan-advantage frame for Republicans greatly decreases support for this idea ($p = 0.0003$; appendix 6), while the Democratic-advantage frame wields no effect. I also show some evidence of these frames decreasing affective polarization (appendix 6).

Discussion

Across these two experiments, I show that racial threat and ideas of democracy, among Republicans specifically, are intimately connected to their perceptions and inferences about racial demographic change. First, I show evidence that Republicans infer a Democratic Party advantage from the majority-minority flip. This meshes with some conventional understanding of racial demographic change and narratives that have persisted over the past decade. When I contest these questionable inferences by reframing demographic change as advantageous to Republicans, it reduces negative feelings that are connected to racial threat.

Following from this point is my most important finding in the study of anti-democratic attitudes in the American public: This same reframing decreases Republicans' anti-democratic support. I provide direct evidence that ideas of racial demographic change are wrapped up with partisan considerations among Republicans. I also am able to determine that these same racial concerns do not influence anti-democratic views among Democrats, which helps to isolate the development of these partisan attitudes. Here I directly connect racial threat to democratic backsliding attitudes in the public in a negative direction—that is, when the threat is reduced, so too is support for anti-democratic ideas. As a final confirmation of this causal connection and further validation of my theory on racial threat and democratic backsliding, I conduct a brief experiment that tests how increasing threat affects views of democracy. Without this test, I am unable to substantively confirm that the relationship between racial threat and anti-democratic views is causal in a multidirectional way for Republicans.[10]

Validating the Causal Connection between Threat and Anti-Democratic Attitudes for Republicans

I seek to validate the causal connection between racial threat and anti-democratic attitudes using a smaller experiment. In the second experiment, I identify that decreasing racial threat for Republicans using the partisan-advantage frames leads to a decrease in support for anti-democratic ideas. This is a unidirectional test of racial threat and anti-democratic views. To clarify the causal link between these concepts, I conduct a brief priming experiment through CloudResearch. All respondents were compensated (N = 2,161; appendix 7).

Respondents are randomly assigned to the following open-ended question, splitting the sample in half:[11]

> You may have heard about the diversification of the United States. Tell us what immediately comes to mind when you think about racial demographic change within the US. (Please tell us in at least three sentences.)

Upon answering this question, I measure support for the previous, pretested anti-democratic measure from experiment 2. It measures support for violence against political opposition, which is the most inflammatory

[10] Racial threat increasing = anti-democratic support increasing; racial threat decreasing = anti-democratic support decreasing.

[11] This is the same prime that is used in chapters 5 and 6.

anti-democratic measure on the entire scale. I also test for the same emotions about racial threat that I previously tested for—worry and concern about racial demographic change.

This design provides greater context to the prevailing narrative about racial demographic change—specifically, the ideas that exist in people's minds when they consider the majority-minority flip, and whether these ideas are explicitly connected to anti-democratic ideas. I seek to identify whether there are significant differences in how partisans primed by demographic change support violence toward political opposition.

For my analysis, I again conduct a linear regression, interacting the treatment with party identification as a moderator. I use a pre/post design, measuring support for violence pretreatment and posttreatment, and then I include a control for the pretreatment measure within analyses (Clifford, Sheagley, and Piston 2021). This technique increases the precision of detecting the effect of the treatment.

Increasing Racial Threat Leads to Increasing Support for Violence

Ultimately, I find that the demographic change prime strongly causes racial threat among Republicans. In measuring the same emotions toward racial demographic change, Republicans who receive the prime are significantly more concerned ($p = 0.0484$), worried ($p = 0.0963$), angry ($p = 0.0008$), and anxious ($p = 0.055$) about it. (See appendix 7 for results.) Additionally, when asked the simple open-ended question about racial demographic change, Republicans are significantly more supportive of political violence ($p = 0.0368$), as shown in figure 7.13.

Strong Republicans who are primed to think about racial demographic change are more supportive of violence than Democrats. This treatment is very light touch. It is a simple open-ended question. That it increases support for violence to such an extent clarifies the connection between racial threat and anti democratic attitudes among Republicans. To add further context and a thicker description to how this threat operates, I also will highlight Republicans' responses to the question. They indicate even more clearly the partisan orientation of racial demographic change in the minds of the public.

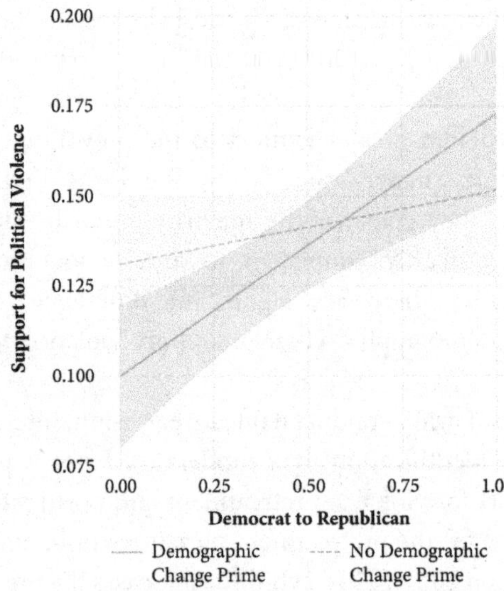

Figure 7.13 Interaction plot depicting the effect of demographic change prime on support for political violence posttreatment across Democrats to Republicans. Republicans become more violent in reaction to prime.

The following description expresses concern over the political power of Black Americans and undocumented immigrants. This respondent's answer is clearly racial *and* partisan in nature:

> It is my understanding that Whites will not remain the "majority." Blacks will gain more political power. Also more and more Latino people will gain power. I have no problem with either, as long as they are Legal American citizens. I do have a problem with Illegal immigrants and black democrats who support socialism.

The partisan connection between immigrants and Black Americans connects closely to the warmer feelings expressed in experiments 1 and 2, when Republicans learn that the GOP will be advantaged from racial demographic change. In short, the response adds further context to the inferred partisan orientation of these groups—they are assumed to identify more closely with Democrats. Below I display three additional responses to this same question, along with a brief categorization of the themes they address. The first response describes how the diversification of the United States is taking the country in the wrong direction. The second describes birth rates, the increasing number of Black Americans (which is incorrect), and the changing cultural politics in light of these changes (i.e., White Americans cannot say anything about Black Americans). The third response describes handouts and how the changing racial demographics could be used to sway voting in the direction of the Democratic Party. Lastly, the fourth response details what is essentially the idea of the Great Replacement being orchestrated through increasing illegal immigration, shown next in table 7.4.

These different responses detail multiple important dynamics to racial threat from racial demographic change. They discuss the changing cultural landscape and companies' hiring practices, and there are clear throughlines in their responses: (1) The Democratic Party is evoked in many responses, despite not being prompted in the question wording; (2) threat

Table 7.4 Responses to prime

Content	Themes
I believe that the diversification of the United States is turning the wrong direction. Many companies have [gone] this way of doing things, being more diverse [instead of] hiring those who are qualified for the job. In the coming years, we will see that this will not be a good idea.	General threat to the well-being the country
More black people are having children than white. White people can't seem to say anything negative about black people because they'll just say it's because we're racist. As years go by, recessive features like red hair and blue eyes will be less and less common and we'll eventually all look the same.	Increasing size of Black Americans, which is leading to changing cultural politics and political correctness
I try to stay away from anything that has to do with racial change and don't talk about it to anyone for any reason because it's getting way out of hand and way too many handouts are going on to try and sway the votes for the demarcates.	Handouts for seemingly undeserving Americans, which will benefit the Democratic Party
I think the country is purposefully being overrun by illegal immigrants. Democrats in power are willfully disregarding the law and order to change the makeup of our population. It's horrible.	The Great Replacement being orchestrated by Democratic Party

from immigrants and Black Americans is central; and (3) the effect of these changes on politics is made explicit by Republican respondents. All three of these themes add further validation to how racial threat from demographic change is tied closely to the Democratic Party. More substantively, regardless of the content of the responses, I show that this simple open-ended prime leads to more expressed threatened emotions and anti-democratic support among Republicans.

Conclusion

The implications of my findings are immense. In this chapter, I have presented a grand picture of Republicans' views of party and democracy. Their views of democracy are strongly motivated by a racialized partisan lens. They assume racial minorities are predominately Democrats, which shifts their support for democracy. Republicans assume they will not have the numbers to win nationally as POC increase in number, which is driven by the inferences that POC identify more closely with the Democratic Party.

In terms of values, Republicans engage in a utility-based evaluation of democracy—they will support it insofar as they can win. When they are told that the big flip will, in fact, *help* their party, Republicans become overwhelmingly less racially threatened and more pro-democratic.

In chapter 8, I detail how these associations with the future of the country no longer sit at the periphery of how Americans consider politics. They are front and center. Additionally, the conversation about the big flip has gone on to such an extent that variant narratives about the changes no longer exhibit different effects on the mass public. Elite messaging and general concern among the citizenry have led to a situation in which racial threat leads to democratic backsliding. Demographic determinism can perpetually erode support of democracy.

8

The Chronic Salience of Racial Threat in the American Public and the Future of American Democracy

The public plays a vital role in the process of democratic backsliding. As an institution, public opinion can legitimize ideas that bolster or erode the democratic process. In recent instances in US politics, we have seen how the public can even go so far as to give and take away the legitimacy of electoral results, with millions of Americans providing strong levels of support for the January 6 insurrection at the US Capitol. Crucially, in a democratic society, the mass of the public sets the tone for how the system functions. It can help to stymie elitist, anti-democratic behavior by dissenting when such ideas are put forth on a national stage—if these values and ideas are held and maintained. If the general public takes issue with anti-democratic actions expressed by elites or select interest groups, then it can declare these ideas to be extreme and outside of the bounds of normal political discourse. The public can say to representatives, "Your actions and words are not democratic. If you continue, you will no longer receive our support." They can vote the anti-democratic electorate out of office, push them to adjust their political platforms, cross them off the list of viable candidates, or even push them out of politics entirely.

For elected officials, this threat of sanctioning is crucial given that their key concern is reelection (Fenno and Hibbing 2002; Mayhew 2004). So, in effect, public opinion helps in maintaining what is politically reasonable or viable for political representatives to do while in office—it establishes accountability if they fail to adhere to expectations. Things that affect, shape, and shift the public's views about democracy are therefore central to whether pro- or anti-democratic ideas are advanced by elites.

A pro-democratic public would not elect an anti-democratic candidate; however, even as an institution, they can only do so much. On the other side, elites can still take advantage of burgeoning anti-democratic ideas across the

The Big Flip. Andrew Ifedapo Thompson, Oxford University Press. © Oxford University Press (2026).
DOI: 10.1093/9780197822173.003.0008

American polity—especially if they can use them in politically advantageous ways. Nudges toward further violent attitudes can greatly exacerbate these feelings. Charles Tilly describes this elite's elicitation of violent sentiments as "boiling a pot." Violent sentiments may exist out there in the public, but elites can help to heat things up even further by stoking anti-democratic rhetoric. Kalmoe and Mason write about political elites as catalysts for further violence:

> In many cases, the conditions for mass violence are present for quite some time, but a particular event and the immediate responses to it by leaders and citizens serve as the "spark" that rapidly shifts conflicted societies from high-tension peace to mass violence in short order. Individual acts of violence and other minor outrages involving hostile groups can spread violence like wildfire.
>
> (2022, p. 25)

The spread and maintenance of anti-democratic sentiment is the point of normative importance I focus on in this chapter. In my previous evaluation of the three *P*'s of demographic determinism, I ask how this unique form of racial threat connects to democratic erosion in the mass public. Through empirical tests, I show that each of the three *P*'s causally plays a pertinent role in demographic determinism and erosion. However, each of these evaluations is limited to being explanations of a given process. In this chapter, I look to see how they operate together in generating deterministic beliefs about the future of the country that are then connected to American democracy. Specifically, I ask, How embedded is demographic determinism in the White American public?

To evaluate this, I examine how persistently negative ideas about the function of American democracy work to create a political environment that drives the consistent erosion of democratic norms. Demographic determinism fuels this. As I consistently describe in previous chapters, since the turn of the century there has been increasing public attention to racial demographic change, which, through research, has been shown time and again to make Americans, specifically White Americans, feel threatened. They presume that they will lose power in society. It was not until recently that these threatened attitudes took shape on a wider scale beyond fringe extremist groups. The storming of the Capitol, the attempted assassination of Gretchen Whitmer, and other mobilizing events have displayed the fact that tens of thousands of Americans are willing to engage in anti-democratic actions; millions more in the mass public are willing to give their direct support.

Earlier scholarly work on racial threat from demographic changes across the United States articulated vaguely how these changes might affect politics. Craig and Richeson write, "[Our findings show] Whites may be increasingly likely and motivated to support conservative candidates and policies, in response to the changing racial demographics" (Craig and Richeson 2014b). Importantly, the implications Craig and Richeson engage with speculatively identify what politics could look like in response to the diversification of the country. At the time of their writing, many dynamics had not yet materialized. Other work articulates concern over the near future of politics: "The findings reported here underline the extent to which race—and, more broadly, ethnic conflict—has indeed become a principal line of political cleavage, not only in American electoral politics but also in America's broader, ongoing struggle to embrace and instantiate democracy" (2018). The connections Craig and Richeson drew between racial threat and support for American democracy yielded helpful ties, but predated their fuller materialization.

This is where we now stand. Demographic determinism is here and present in American politics. Racial threat and its pertinence to American democracy has now surfaced. In the previous chapters, I show the series of attitudinal changes along ideological and democratic lines that White Americans make from inferences about the future of the country and American democracy. They are driven by demographic determinism. These Americans predict (the first *P*) that they will lose their numerical majority to people of color (the second *P*), whom they consider to be mostly Black Americans, and they assume that people of color identify overwhelmingly with the Democratic Party (partisanship—the third *P*). The set of presumptions represents a future-oriented inference, and it leads White Americans to think they will lose their power in a democratic system. They lose faith in the system because they think it is becoming increasingly unfair to them. Ultimately, I consistently—and in real time—show that this large segment of threatened Americans has become more anti-democratic. In snapshots of different points in time, Americans' views about democracy change when they are primed.

This has manifold implications for how we think and theorize about democracy. Demographic determinism, at its core, is interpreted as a loss of White status folded into partisan politics. The major culprit in their minds is Black Americans overall and, by extension, the Democratic Party. White Americans, in the new political world that they are inferring, would have less of an ability to nationally dominate politics. Republicans will lose; Whites will lose. In short, there would no longer be supremacy through numbers required to win democratic elections. This does not mean they would be more discriminated against, suffer more issues, or face any other additional political problems. In terms of democratic politicking, even if there were a verifiable, predictable truth to demographic determinism, the Republican Party could build coalitions with other groups to secure victory, potentially tapering back their wants and needs in policy. The inclusive approach that the Republican Party could have taken in electoral politics, described in chapter 3, touches on exactly this. But because of internal pressure from the party, as well as a groundswell of public support for an exclusive, limiting approach to the White predominance in the GOP, the inclusive approach was beaten out. The outgrowth of this is the straightforward idea that many White Americans willingly support anti-democratic ideas and actions insofar as they protect the maintenance of their power. The *determinism* in *demographic determinism* calls to the inevitability of the racial and political changes of the United States, meaning any and all efforts to prevent it are available. Nothing is off the table.

Instead of reshaping the party and adhering to the rules of the game, the emergent party leadership pushed forth ideas of *changing the rules of the game*. So, on democratic theory, what follows from this is a grander question that extends beyond the contemporary moment: If this large portion of the White public is willing to thwart democracy for the sake of maintaining their sense of status, what does this tell us about democratic commitment? When we think about previous moments of a "functioning" American democracy, was it happening because of the masses' and elites' adherence to democratic principles? Or were their latent sentiments about maintaining power just simply not questioned at those earlier moments? Has democracy been maintained on a razor-thin edge for some time? Or conversely, were these moments of questioning the efficacy of the system just anti-democratic blips on the otherwise democratic radar? Looking to the future, is the erosion of democracy that comes from demographic determinism just the perfect storm of primers and indicators among a concerned segment of the American population? In this chapter, I ask how pervasive racial threat from demographic determinism really is.

Troublingly so, I find that the threat from this determinism has staying power. I test how much it maintains itself in the public by (1) priming it on a general level, (2) testing if a state-level variation alters ideas about it, (3) examining whether countervailing narratives shift attitudes more positively, (4) examining how efforts to correct the partisan uncertainty of the country's diversification alter support, and (5) looking to see if there is erosion over time as an effect of the threat generated. Within all five of these tests, I find that threat is generated consistently.

Theoretically, I conclude that threat is chronically salient. The condition of chronically salient racial threat gives elites fertile ground to sow the seeds of democratic discontent across larger segments of the public.

Fertile Ground: The Fungibility of Democracy among Elites

The set of inferences in demographic determinism has a uniquely American orientation, though the shift in perspective toward democracy has long been institutionally grounded in the function of conservative parties and their relationship to power. Aristocrats and the economic elite have viewed democracy as a system they could use to maintain their influence relative to previous governmental systems.

> Whether or not economic and political elites could overcome the enormous collective action problems of forging effective and strong political parties to defend their interests shaped democracy's long run evolution. Well-organized and highly institutionalized partisan defenders of old regime interests provided a way of "lowering the costs of toleration," and thus making democracy safe for key segments of old regime elites.
>
> (Ziblatt 2017)

On a collective level, elites have taken cues from others in the earliest processes of democratization in the West, and that, in turn, has led to them becoming more comfortable with democracy in its prospect and function. This came, namely, in the idea of ceding power to a system that would cater to more of the public. Over time, it also directly called for increasing suffrage, but this often came from pressure from below rather than the top.

This dynamic can also help to explain the elites' rationale for turning away from the system of democracy. In the same way elites grew comfortable with democracy, eventually supporting it out of ideas of self-preservation and interest, so too could they turn against it. Elites and aristocrats did not opt to support the system of democracy because it meshed with their moral principles; rather, they opted in because they saw it as the best means *at the time* for the sake of conserving their economic power. If they came to perceive the system as a less viable option for the maintenance of this power, they would discard it or move away from it.

To these elites, the system of democracy is seen as a tool that facilitates their power. Vitally, a tool is only as useful as its function. Under certain conditions, the system can be seen as less advantageous to the consolidation of power. And it is when democracy's usefulness erodes for conservative parties, I argue, that anti-democratic ideas emerge. Racial demographic change and the threat it generates is an event in which this erosion occurs. This dovetails with a similar dynamic among the mass public.

Historically in the American public, racial threat is already connected to democratic attitudes, such that those under threat tend to express more anti-democratic sentiments. The current nature of media and elite messaging in the United States has connected racial demographic change to the diminishing power of the Republican Party. I argue that this consistent beating of the racial threat drum has led to a situation in which threat is now chronically salient in large parts of the public. As an idea, I mean that there is a persistent and recurring anxiety at the top of many White Americans' minds. Racial threat can be generated irrespective of the content or discussion of racial demographic change, so long as the idea is present within that discussion. In tandem with the uniquely American function of demographic determinism, the racial threat is also existentially connected to democracy. I thus expect and confirm that when racial demographic change is primed, it will generate a sense of threat regardless of the direction of the information, which will then immediately lead directly to the erosion of democratic support.

I test for the chronic salience of threat through multiple means that capture public attitudes. One crucial test primes threat by using a light touch, simply asking Americans what comes to mind when they think of the diversification of the United States, intentionally using no language that could intimate threat. I have used this test in previous chapters to validate components of demographic determinism, but this test works to test all components and their residual impacts on feelings toward democracy. I randomly assign this question in an experimental context, allowing respondents to respond to it open-endedly. In this first test, I qualitatively confirm in the open-ended responses that the questions of diversification prompt strong senses of threat, and I quantitatively confirm that the respondents exposed to the prime express chronic senses of threat. I show that this simple prime not only generates a general sense of threat but also prompts extreme, anti-democratic ideas such as violence and eugenics.

I then go about testing variant narratives of racial demographic change in the United States. The standard narrative is that Whites will become the numerical minority by mid-century, yet it does not fully capture how demographics *could* change. I specifically go about testing two alternative narratives: (1) that Whites will *not* lose their numerical majority, and (2) even with the loss of majority, they will not lose their influence in society, which many scholars articulate. Both of these alternatives have been found to assuage feelings of threat in recent studies (Levy and Myers 2021). When I retest these ideas, I find that each one of these narratives nonetheless causes increased racial threat and greater expression of support for anti-democratic ideas, along with higher perceptions of Republican electoral legitimacy. I go further to show that these views do not erode over time among the same Americans introduced to these messages.

I validate the idea of chronically salient threats over the span of context, time, samples, and messages. My findings present a grand problem for American democracy: White Americans currently only need minimal messages about racial demographic change to turn against democracy, which even makes them more violent toward their fellow Americans. Messages that have previously worked to curb their fear now have similar effects of as messages that are intended to be more threatening. Well beyond this dynamic existing within one given instance, I also find evidence of the staying power of chronic threat. Once activated, it lasts weeks beyond its activation. I conclude by discussing mass-level implications for the system of American democracy.

The Increasing Political Salience of Racial Demographics

Racial demographic change has been a source of concern, intrigue, and anxiety for many Americans, and recently it has become more intimately tied to political concerns for the future (Mutz 2018; Craig, Rucker, and

Richeson 2018; Krosch et al. 2022; Reichelmann and Hunt 2021; Bartels 2020b, 2022). Most recently, through the increased salience of racially threatened messaging during the 2016–2020 Trump era, racial threat from the changing country gained even further prominence in the broader context of the American public. With the confluence of elite rhetoric, broadening media coverage, and growing public awareness (through the killing of George Floyd and subsequent protests, increased levels of hate crimes, and general discourse), ideas of racial demographic change have become more front and center in American politics (Peay and Camarillo 2021).

For especially progressively minded Americans, the developing public discussion of race has been a sign of progress. To many others, these same events indicate that the country moving "too fast" and the cultural ground shifting underneath their feet. Senate candidate Blake Masters asserted, "What the left really wants to do is change the demographics of this country. They want to consolidate power so they can never lose another election" (Blake Masters [@bgmasters] 2021). Similarly, Representative Matt Gaetz has consistently advanced these same ideas:

> "There is an attempted cultural genocide going on in America right now and it calls for patriots to stand up and say that America is a great country worthy of our pride and our defense. The left wants us to be ashamed of America so that they can replace America."
>
> (Rep. Matt Gaetz [@RepMattGaetz] 2020)

Demographic determinism now pervades American political discourse in such a way that Republican elites readily use the same language. Some extreme ideas about it and the threat it poses have moved from being niche to functioning in significantly more commonplace ways. Ideas like "White genocide" and the Great Replacement conspiracy, which initially emerged in far-right, White supremacist places, are much more widely known across the American public. While demographic determinism is anchored in partisan perceptions of politics, I assert that the idea extends much further outside of overt party consideration because of the consistent prodding of fear within the mass public. The salience of racial threat poses a danger to democracy because erosion can happen even when the threat isn't intentionally discussed.

A Changing Nation and a Changing View of Democracy

The consistent prodding of the racial threat through the diversification of the United States, I assert, has become embedded in American political and cultural discourse. Party elites have used these ideas, and Americans discuss them among themselves and over social media. To some, the ideas exist in forms as far-reaching as the Great Replacement, while to others, they are more moderated and operate in the forms of "changing American culture and ideas." Ultimately, the chronic salience of racial threat explains how it takes very scant and sometimes unintentional descriptions of the changing country to generate strong negative, anti-democratic reactions.

This sits outside of the context of racial messaging and its deleterious effects on attitudes. A host of research in political science on racial messaging finds that when elites use messages that implicitly evoke race, these messages are significantly more effective than explicit messages in generating negative sentiment across the mass White public. Examples of this would be using the term *urban crime* to intentionally and subtly refer to Black Americans, as opposed to simply saying *Black crime*. Formally, this idea has come to be known as the IE model. Defining this dynamic, Valentino, Wayne, and Oceno write the following:

> The IE model predicts that racial attitudes will be active in memory when there are subtle racial cues in the environment, but these attitudes will be suppressed when citizens are consciously confronted with hostile or racist arguments for or against a given policy or candidate. The reason for this shift away from racial judgment criteria in the face of explicit cues is that, at least at the time the theory was proposed, many whites seemed profoundly ambivalent about race.
>
> (2018)

The concept of chronically salient threat sits outside of the bounds of this model because it describes how ideas about race can be so activated across the White public that the rhetoric needs no intention to elicit a threatened reaction. Stimuli that are "out there" in the world generally can still work well to activate threatened sentiment and thereby drive up anti-democratic views. In the IE model, there is a notion about "priming" or activating the ideas in the minds of White Americans that would then connect to their latent racially resentful attitudes. Chronic threat suggests that the information environment is so pervasively steeped in these resentful ideas that certain content that is not intended to work in this implicitly racist way still works. Then, by extension, these threatened ideas will lead to further erosion of American democracy.

Expectations

Formally, my main expectation is that racial threat is now chronically salient in the minds of White Americans (H1). I will describe this as *chronic racial threat*, and the central function of this concept comes in the way racial threat is generated. Lightly calling to any and all dimensions related to racial demographic change, I expect, will drive sentiments that are motivated by demographic determinism. Overall, I expect that, irrespective of the different narratives about the country changing, the threatening feelings will still altogether be accessible in White Americans' minds external to the specific framing of the ideas. Demographic determinism has become so deeply embedded in the American public that Americans need only to think about demographic changes to generate it. The three *P*'s will come to mind even when conceptually different forms of content about demographic change are shown to White Americans. The content of narratives about racial demographic change will thus not matter; the only important component of them will be that they tap into the discussion of diversification in the United States.

Beyond simply activating these ideas of the three *P*'s and the way that they motivate demographic determinism, I further expect that this chronic threat will lead to existential considerations about the US democratic system—under the condition that it is perceived to be beneficial to the Democratic Party (H2). This will come in the form of increased skepticism of democratic elections, political violence, and an overarching distrust of democratic norms. Importantly, this impact is contingent on the Democratic Party being the perceived beneficiary; in effect, this means that Republican elections and candidates will not be called into question.

The Perpetual Democratic Erosion from Chronic Racial Threat

My first test of chronic threat is expansive in scope. I test ideas about racial demographic change in ways that validate its existence and allow me to investigate what is at the top of Americans' minds. Previously, I have used this same test on the diversification of the United States, but in this iteration I ask how the prime works to drive anti-democratic views. I have used this same prime in previous studies in chapters 5–7 and used it to better validate the existence of the *P*'s in demographic determinism. With this following test, I go one step further to ask about how it generates threat that drives anti-democratic ideas about the future of politics in the United States. My previous tests utilize a variety of contexts, yet they offer little to say about the deterministic aspects of threat from the big flip. I conduct this study with more than 1,400 respondents (Lucid Fulcrum; N = 1,435, Table 8.2). The two conditions in this study allow for more than sufficient statistical power. The outcome variables presented in this study assess support for different qualities in a candidate running for office in 2024. These qualities are either pro- or anti-democratic in their scope (respect for democracy, bipartisanship, and support for political violence).

I will first analyze the overall effect of the prime through "difference in means" tests. This approach provides a larger perspective on what the simple prime of racial diversification does to Americans' emotions, senses of threat, and attitudes toward democracy. I then follow this analysis with a deeper dive into *what* respondents articulate about racial demographic change.

Up to this point, research on the political implications of the country's racial diversification has almost exclusively addressed the question through the use of vignettes. While these are useful, they only provide a static perspective of how racial threat is processed (i.e., we only know how respondents are reacting to the very specific framing of the changes in the vignette).

Chronic Threat from Minimal Prompting

The prime I use is a light touch—the same that I have used in chapters 5–7:

> You may have heard about the diversification of the United States. Tell us what immediately comes to mind when you think about racial demographic change within the US.

I randomly assign respondents to this question; the control group does not receive this question and simply moves on to the outcome variables. Again, I measure respondents' open-ended reactions to the prompt to capture qualitative ideas. Overall, I find an overwhelmingly negative, threatened reaction among respondents. A host of answers to this prime refer directly to Black

Americans, again reaffirming the second *P* in demographic determinism—that Americans infer that people of color are Black Americans.

When qualitatively evaluating the responses to the prime, again the same themes of threat and violent reactions come to the fore. Some threatened Americans express ideas that diversification is fundamentally changing the dynamics of the country. For example, one participant articulates, "The balance is being tipped toward Blacks. The violence of Blacks in this society accomplishes little. All it does is ruin people's lives." This response directly attributes the United States' changing demographics to Black Americans—the second *P*, from chapter 6. The comment on the balance of the country tipping toward Blacks clearly demonstrates a sentiment of changing cultural or political dynamics leading to Black Americans gaining power. The light touch of the prime on diversification helpfully presents how chronically the racial threat is functioning in the mind of this American. The questions about the country's diversification *do not at all*, explicitly or implicitly, refer to Black Americans.

On the most extreme responses, I again find inflammatory comments that capture the chronic threat and its erosion of democratic ideals. Some respondents even go as far as to articulate support for eugenics and violence:

> America is "Browning." While that is not necessarily a bad thing, it may cause the slow extinction of the white race. While I disagree with eugenics, I understand why it was implemented in the past.
>
> To this American, the diversifying country is a direct threat to White Americans, and in order to curb it, they explicitly describe a sympathy toward the use of eugenics to prevent these changes from continuing to happen. This idea connects closely with the White supremacist idea that has driven domestic terrorism and fueled conspiracy theories like the Great Replacement—this is the interpretation of the shrinking White population as a type of casualty for White Americans.
>
> (Belew 2018)

Other responses highlight this same violent orientation toward the changing country:

> Everything these days is anti-white. Seriously sick of it. You're poking the bear. American people will not like the results if they keep poking us hard enough.
>
> They play the victim; they will someday regret what they [have] done.

These responses present implicitly violent responses to the minimal prime about diversification. The assertion about "poking the bear" alludes to White Americans eventually becoming violent toward racial minorities. Affirming the ideas surrounding emotions about racial threat, some assert that the changing country explicitly scares them:

> White people will soon be a minority in their own country. The USA will then be ruled by malignant nonwhites and democrat speakers. This is very horrifying to think about.

This series of responses evokes the idea that the violent, conflict-driven attitudes White Americans hold might be latent in their minds. These ideas could exist under the surface of their general attitudes and simply need to be primed slightly. Specifically, this could be a sentiment of violence that simply needs to be drawn out by active sentiments of racial threat, and once White Americans consider it, they become significantly more violent. Overall, I find this to be a strong first validation of the idea of chronic racial threat in the mass public. But does it extend more comprehensively beyond the scope of qualitative responses from some threatened Americans?

As a further test of how extensively connected the threat is to violent attitudes, I investigate closed-ended responses that are measured immediately after this prime. Because the prime splits the sample into two groups (one treatment and one control group), there are roughly seven hundred respondents in each group. This two-condition design provides more than enough statistical power to detect the small effects of the treatment.[1] My measures capture anti-democratic support, emotions about diversification, and expressions of racial threat.

[1] The following are the results from a power analysis: n = 393.4057; d = 0.2; sig. level = 0.05; power = 0.8.

Chronic Threat Increasing Support for Anti-Democratic Candidates

Turning to a forward-looking measurement of anti-democratic views and their connection to chronic threat, I show that priming chronic threat through the diversification prime drives up support. The measures I use in this case are quite specific and propose scenarios of candidates running for office in 2024. They do not specify who is running, which at the time of the study (2022) was unknown, but the ideas these measures propose remain. They pose ideas to respondents about presidential candidates running for office in 2024 supporting ideas of political violence or democracy. These are among the most overt measures of anti-democratic attitudes I test because political violence and support for democracy are stated explicitly.

Think of a candidate running for the presidency in 2024. To what extent do you agree that they should have the following qualities (Strongly Disagree to Strongly Agree):

- Respect for democracy
- Support for political violence

In this same study, I show that this same prime causes Americans to express anger ($p = 0.037$) and worry ($p = 0.031$) about racial demographic change (appendix 3). Moreover, in another validation of the threat expressed in the open-ended responses, I find that primed Americans feel a greater sense of racial threat in the present and future from Black Americans specifically. I also include measures for threats from other groups, and significantly more threat is expressed about Black Americans than about any other group.

Elaborating on the mechanism behind the chronic threat, I show that the expressed fear of Black Americans mediates the causal connection between the prime and Americans' anti-democratic attitudes. Both the negative emotions about the country's diversification and the expressed threat from Black Americans in the present and future significantly mediate anti-democratic attitudes (appendix 4). The strongest connection between these sentiments and anti-democratic views is in how they motivate support for a violent candidate running for office in 2024, Donald Trump seizing voting machines in 2020, and the January 6 insurrectionists.

These mediation tests, not without their drawbacks (Green, Ha, and Bullock 2010), provide further tapestry to the story of chronic racial threat.

Again, they further validate the idea that racial threat has a deep connection to how Americans think about democracy. I show that threat increases support for both forward- and backward-oriented anti-democratic ideas. Also, within this study, I show that Americans presume strongly that racial demographic changes will result in an increase in the Black American population on a national level.

Chronic Threat and Highly Salient Political Attitudes

While in this first test of chronic threat I detect a shift in support for democracy at large, what I have identified could still simply be a set of abstract ideas about democracy. By this, I mean that Americans could simply dislike an idea of democracy but not express or act on anti-democratic sentiment. To ground chronic threat in relevant, salient political ideas, I turn to two additional outcomes that are contemporary evaluations of politics. These ideas are captured as (1) support for the January 6 insurrectionists and (2) support for the idea of Donald Trump using the military to seize voting machines in the 2020 presidential election. These measures are checks on the function of anti-democratic support as well as extensions to the idea of chronic threat. The previous anti-democratic measures on 2024 candidate qualities are forward-looking, while these measures concerned immediate, contemporary interpretations of anti-democratic events, which, at the time of this study, were actively discussed in politics.

On these contemporary views of politics, chronic threat works all the same. It increases support for the January 6 insurrectionists, patriots taking the law into their own hands, and Trump's hypothetical military interference in the 2020 election. Threat causes a great increase in support for these grounded anti-democratic ideas that contest the legitimacy of American democracy and the rule of law.[2] I find roughly a 4-percentage-point increase in support for these ideas collapsed in a single scale ($p = 0.045$).

Here, I further show that chronic threat alters how Americans interpret and reinterpret previous political events and their perceptions of the legitimacy of the rule of law. Support for the January 6 insurrectionists and the idea of Trump seizing voting machines are recent evaluations of historical events. So, pairing these findings with the qualities of a candidate running

[2] Within these regression analyses, I use the same controls as in the previous analyses with robust standard errors.

in 2024, chronic threat poses a problem for both forward- and backward-looking evaluations of anti-democratic ideas. When it is primed—even with minimal stimuli, as I show here—it shifts how Americans think about the future role of government and about past events that have eroded institutions of American democracy.[3]

One major limitation of this study is that it works only with the ideas that come to mind immediately among Americans. So, as I show with my open-ended priming approach, I am exclusively able to detect the ideas that are top of mind. To follow this priming approach, I use a series of specific frames about racial demographic change to test the potency of chronic threat.

The three *P*'s of demographic determinism appear in the responses to the prime in this study, which is national in scope. As another vital test of chronic threat, I turn briefly to whether it varies across states. To do this, I utilize the same prime in a series of state-specific studies designed to capture ideas about which groups are projected to increase in size. The intention behind these following studies is to further validate whether the threat from demographic determinism is seemingly contingent on the location.

Is Chronic Threat State-Contingent?

The United States is an excessively large country. When considering changes to its demographic landscape, Americans might be making inferences that are either interpreted through their localities or conditioned on the racial environments in which they exist. In a brief but vital set of studies, I look at five widely different states: Iowa, Georgia, Mississippi, Florida, and California. The main intention behind the selection of these different states is that their racial compositions differ drastically from one to another.

Georgia and Florida are selected because they are battleground states, experiencing racial demographic change in distinct ways (Gringlas 2022). Florida is diversifying from mostly an increasing Cuban population. Georgia

[3] Interestingly, the effect of threat on support for Trump and the January 6 insurrectionists is not conditional on party identification. I find consistency regardless of party identification (appendix 2).

is also diversifying but through an increasing Black population. Mississippi's population has steadily been changing, but less so relative to Florida's and Georgia's (Castro 2022); its population mostly consists of Black and White Americans, with smaller amounts of other racial groups interspersed. California has a distinct demographic nature, as it was one of the first states in the country to undergo a majority-minority flip (Rodd 2019). Finally, Iowa is a predominately White state and is not experiencing as much demographic change relative to all of our other cases. I present our summarized rationale for selecting states in table 8.1.

I assess the extent to which priming national demographic changes generates similar sentiments among residents of each state. Then, I look to see if Black Americans are considered throughout these cases in relation to other racial minority groups.

First, in evaluating the responses to the national prime, I find clear examples of racial threat felt across state contexts. Among the most extreme of these qualitative responses comes in from a White woman who identifies as a Republican-leaning Independent in Iowa and writes, "White is right. Kill the niggers."

Despite the vague language used in the prime, thinking about the United States racially changing leads this respondent to become anti-Black to the point of asserting violence toward Black Americans. This response is direct in its racist orientation. It is by far the most anti-Black assertion in reaction to the national prime and, I show next, is mirrored in other degrees across the four other states I investigate.

Table 8.1 Demographic descriptions of each state

Iowa	Georgia	Mississippi	Florida	California
• Predominately White state • Small Black population	• Diversifying state • Largely Black American	• Demographically more stable • Mostly White-Black split	• Rapidly diversifying • Sizable Black population, but mostly the Latino (particularly Cuban) population is growing	• Has been diversifying • Mixture of racial groups • Flipped state with a predominantly Latino and Asian American population

Another example within a different state context comes via a White man who identifies as a strong Republican in Georgia. In response to the prime, he writes, "I am sorry, but I think the black population feels they are entitled." The judgment articulates the idea that there are problems with Black American entitlement, but importantly it also has no immediate pertinence to the racial demographic change prime, which does not explicitly prompt respondents to think of how racial groups feel. In a similar fashion, a White woman, also a strong Republican, living in Mississippi, responds to the prime by saying, "I don't think there will ever be true change. The black community will never be satisfied." This respondent seems to have interpreted the prompt's term *change* as normative changes in American society, but her conclusion is similar to the Georgia response in its criticism of the Black community.

Outside of the South, we also see this anti-Black sentiment mirrored in California, a crucial state for describing the national scope of the big flip. It is well outside of the Black Belt, where the aforementioned Georgia and Mississippi respondents reside, but it is also the first state in the United States to have experienced a majority-minority flip. Here, a Hispanic woman who identifies as a strong Democrat articulates that "Black lives matter and what it stands for, I think . . . was a big mistake because now all blacks think that they have a right for everything." Entitlement of Black Americans again is referenced in a drastically different demographic and political setting.

Throughout these states, I observe fundamentally political and extreme reactions to the diversification question. These reactions, on their own, are noteworthy in confirming the idea of chronic threat, sans state-level context. But they do even more to describe just how deeply held national views about Black Americans and the diversification of the country are. Using a secondary measure, I couple these qualitative findings, among others, with a second set of measures, which captures the projected increasing size of groups. In the next analyses, I show numerically that Black Americans are overwhelmingly the most referenced group, which is an initial validation of the Black dimension of the POC expectation in demographic determinism. I show this in the following graphs (Figures 8.1–8.5):

I show above, consistently, that threat from Black Americans is at the top of participants' minds regardless of the state I am evaluating. Threat from Black Americans can thereby be portable over state context and less dependent on the state-level composition.

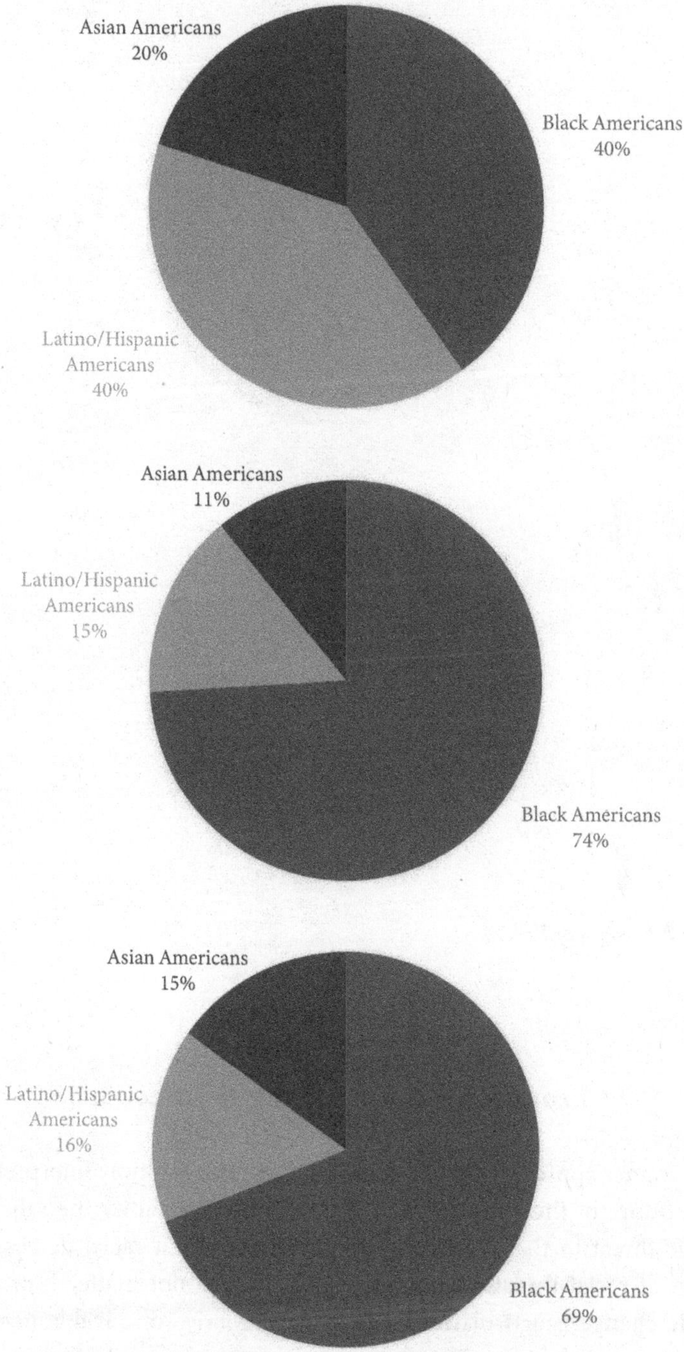

Figure 8.1–8.5 Pie charts on state-level responses to diversification prime.

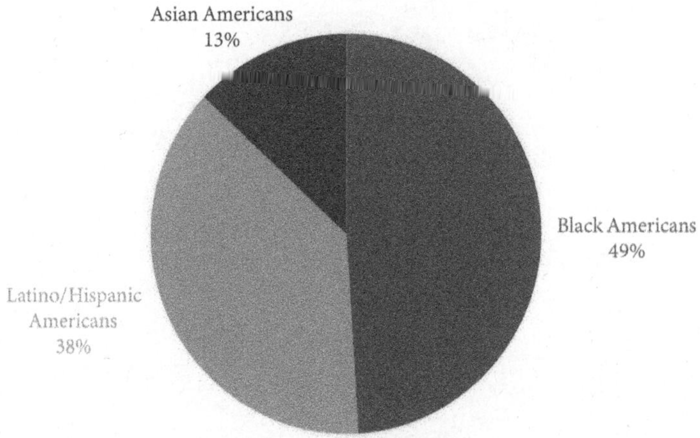

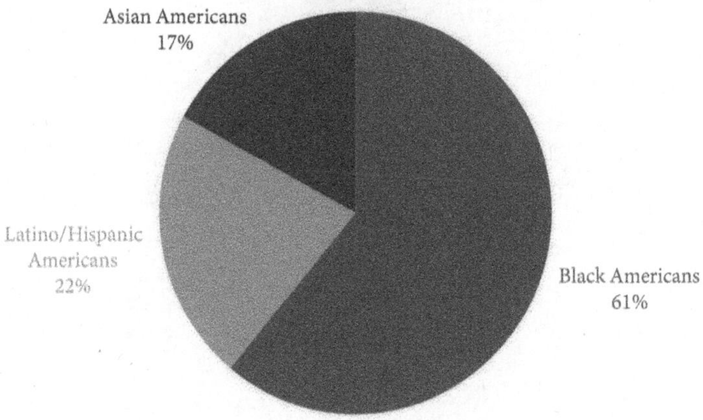

Figure 8.1–8.5 *continued*

Chronic Threat from Multiple Directions

These frames approach demographic change from multiple interpretations of the future of the United States. Next, I seek to identify the saliency of chronic threat in the face of variant narratives about racial demographic change. If racial threat is chronic, then it should not matter how demographic change is articulated. I use three similarly conceivable narratives about these predictions. These are all competing frames in that they lead to different outcomes within the racial composition of the United States.

The first narrative is the most common: that racial minorities will become the numerical majority and White Americans will be the minority by mid-century (Craig and Richeson 2017, 2018; Krosch et al. 2022). The second narrative articulates the exact same idea as the first but also mentions that Whites will not lose their status (Mutz 2018). Status threat among White Americans is a key driver of their racial threat, so the intention behind this narrative is to lessen that concern. The third and final narrative I utilize articulates that White Americans will maintain their majority amid changing racial demographics. This narrative has been previously shown to assuage threat and has also been argued to be a reasonable expectation for demographic change (Alba 2018a; Levy and Myers 2021). I use a placebo article for the control group. Below I show each of the conditions. To further test for the potency of chronic threat, I test it two times—first the initial reactions to the treatment, then again nearly three weeks after the first exposure. Using this approach, I can test for the staying power of threat. If it is chronic, then it should not diminish slowly after it is activated. Next, I present the conditions (figures 8.6–8.8).

First, to validate the consistency in the function of chronic threat, I test the effect of each narrative on the perceived threat from Black Americans. I use a pre/post design to assess this level of threat with more certainty, which amounts to testing outcomes before and after exposure to the treatment (Clifford, Sheagley, and Piston 2021). Ultimately, under my framework, the idea of chronic threat would be validated if racial threat is elicited from every one of the conditions, which is exactly what I find.[4]

The majority-minority flip narrative ($p = 0.07$), majority-minority narrative + no status threat ($p = 0.03$), and majority maintenance narrative ($p = 0.01$) all induce stronger senses of racial threat from Black Americans. These findings are made even more robust through the pre/post design approach because it provides me with an assessment of the extent to which threatened attitudes shift in the midst of the study. I find that, regardless of the narrative, all discussion of racial demographic change generates a stronger sense of threat from Black Americans in participants than in those who do not read any narrative.

As seen in figures 8.6–8.8, there are no overt mentions of Black Americans growing in any of the primes I design and implement, yet they still work

[4] Along with no significant differences in the effect of each narrative, meaning each causes a similar level of threat (appendix 3).

U.S.

U.S. Census Bureau Sees Whites Falling to Minority in a More Racially Diverse America

1-20-2022

Washington, D.C. – Detailed new projections from the U.S. Census Bureau find that the U.S. population will become more racially diverse in coming decades.

The largest increase in racial diversity will be seen among younger generations while older Americans remain predominantly non-Hispanic white. Altogether, between 2016 and 2045, the country's Hispanic and Asian populations will rise 74% and 82% respectively, accounting for most of U.S. population growth during that period.

Over the same period, the older white population will stop growing altogether. Already, for the first time, whites are in the minority among children under the age of 5 and will be a minority of all young people under the age of 18 before the end of the decade. By 2044, whites will be a minority of the entire population.

According to Dr. Robert Manning, a sociologist at the University of Kansas' Center for the Study of Demography, "This is without historical precedent. Whites are becoming a minority in the U.S. as a whole, and the former minorities are going to be the new majority, as they are in some parts of the country already."

U.S.

U.S. Census Bureau Sees White Americans Falling to Minority in a More Racially Diverse America

1-20-2022

Washington, D.C. – Detailed new projections from the U.S. Census Bureau find that the U.S. population will become more racially diverse in coming decades.

The largest increase in racial diversity will be seen among younger generations while older Americans remain predominantly non-Hispanic white. Altogether, between 2016 and 2045, the country's Hispanic and Asian populations will rise 74% and 82% respectively, accounting for most of U.S. population growth during that period.

Over the same period, there will also be a major rise in the number of Americans with mixed-race ancestry that includes a white parent or grandparent. Many such people identify themselves as white, often in combination with another race or ethnicity. As a result, white Americans will continue to make up about three-quarters (74%) of the U.S. population through 2060, the last year for which projections are available.

According to Dr. Robert Manning, a sociologist at the University of Kansas' Center for the Study of Demography, "This is without historical precedent. Whites are becoming a minority in the U.S. as a whole, and the former minorities are going to be the new majority, as they are in some parts of the country already. They will, however, maintain their status in society as the most influential racial group."

Figure 8.6–8.8 Treatments used in experiment.

to cause the sentiments of Black threat. These same tests replicate the same effect of my first priming study with the same measure of Black threat. This further validates the idea that the threat felt from racial demographic change is cohesive and deeply related to Black Americans. My results here show that the threat that emerges from extant ideas about diversification mimics other, more specific primes about demographics changing (even when they are projected *not* to change). This second test strengthens the idea that

U.S.

U.S. Census Bureau Expects Enduing White Majority in a More Racially Diverse America

1-20-2022

Washington, D.C. – Detailed new projections from the U.S. Census Bureau find that the U.S. population will become more racially diverse in coming decades.

The largest increase in racial diversity will be seen among younger generations while older Americans remain predominantly non-Hispanic white. Altogether, between 2016 and 2045, the country's Hispanic and Asian populations will rise 74% and 82% respectively, accounting for most of U.S. population growth during that period.

Over the same period, the older white population will stop growing altogether. Already, for the first time, whites are in the minority among children under the age of 5 and will be a minority of all young people under the age of 18 before the end of the decade. There are, however, mixed race individuals and racial groups who may likely identify as white in the coming future. A new idea of white identity could mean whites will maintain their majority status past the midcentury, some argue.

According to Dr. Robert Manning, a sociologist at the University of Kansas' Center for the Study of Demography, "This is with historical precedent. Irish Americans, who were once identified as non-white, became incorporated into white Americans in the early 20th century. White Americans will maintain their majority group status in the U.S. through midcentury."

Figure 8.6–8.8 *continued*

threat may be chronically salient. That is, racial threat from Black Americans could be so top of mind for Americans that multiple approaches to articulating racial demographic change lead to the exact same outcome—heightened racial threat from Black Americans. In this study, the mock articles describe Asian American and Hispanic American populations increasing and the White American population decreasing; Black Americans are completely absent from this discussion.

Of course, the absence of Black Americans in the mock articles could be interpreted as an implicit (i.e., outside of awareness) or explicit yet understated connection between Black Americans and the changing demographics of the United States. In chapter 6, I provide an explanation for how this might be at play in the ways Americans historically think about race.

A Chronic Threat to the Legitimacy of Democracy?

I expect that the chronic nature of racial threat is directly tied to the antidemocratic ideas within the big flip. When it is activated among White Americans, it will directly affect how they think about American democracy. Moreover, most concerningly so, the chronic nature of the threat means that there are minimal bounds on which ideas can generate it.

I show that, when it is primed, the threat from the big flip connects to forward-looking ideas *and* retrospective evaluations of democratic politics. To expand on my investigation of chronic threat's effect on democratic attitudes, I assess support for the legitimacy of the American government and democratic practices, insofar as they are perceived to benefit the Democratic Party. This takes the form of outcome measures that test Americans' support for vigilantism and skepticism of recent presidential elections. Ultimately, I expect that chronic threat will generate more support for vigilantism; decrease the perceived legitimacy of recent Democratic elections (namely the elections of Barack Obama and Joe Biden), which are purported to advance the diversification of the United States; and increase support for the legitimacy of recent Republican elections.

Across all conditions, I find that the threat leads Americans to become more supportive of vigilantism ($p = 0.035$) and recent Republican presidential elections—particularly Donald Trump's 2016 victory ($p = 0.0002$), shown in figure 8.9. I use a pre/post design to measure these outcomes, as I do with threat above. Within the following coefficient plot, I collapse all three conditions together. For the legitimacy of Republican presidential elections, I measure perceptions of George Bush's election in 2004[5] and Donald Trump's in 2016. For Democrats, I measure perceptions of Barack Obama's election in 2012 and Joe Biden's election in 2020. (See appendix 6 for regressions for each condition.)

[5] I opt to use this because of the contentious conclusion of the 2000 election, so perceptions of legitimacy could be less driven by a threat connecting to partisanship and more to institutional ideas.

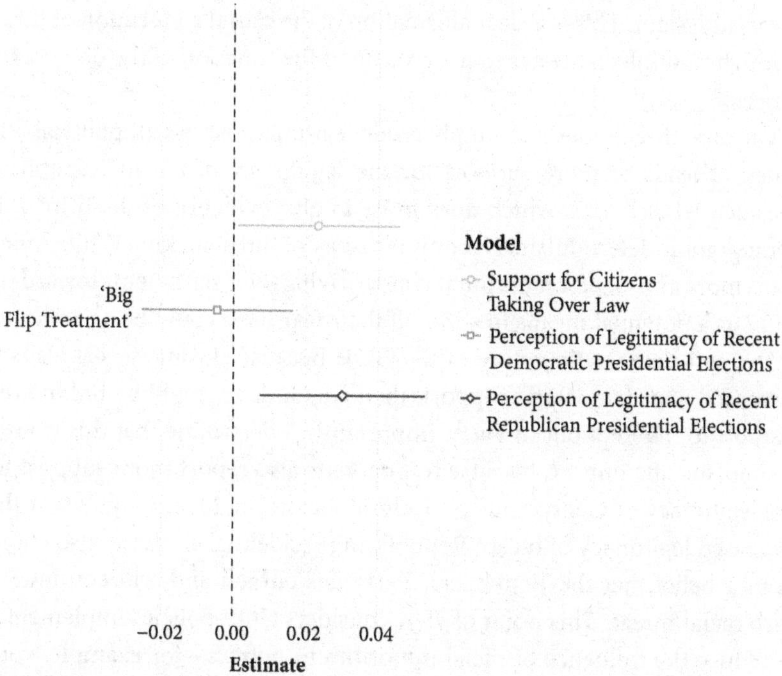

Figure 8.9 Coefficient plot of effect of treatment on support for anti-democratic attitudes and legitimacy of Democratic and Republican electoral victories.

I find that threats from different narratives of racial demographic change have a similar delegitimizing effect on the rule of law as it currently stands—which also replicates the same effect of the minimal prime in study 1 increasing support for vigilantism. Threat also increases the perceived legitimacy of Republican presidential victories (both Trump and Bush). These effects are generated irrespective of the narrative about demographic change (all three of the mock articles above cause a threat), thereby indicating that these sentiments of racial threat are less connected to the outcome of the racial demographic shift; they instead stem from the general discussion of racial demographic change. White Americans can maintain their majority, but this narrative does not assuage these views nor their downstream consequences on democratic legitimacy. As to the increased support for patriotic vigilantism, my findings here show that a perceived threat drives a decreased legitimacy of the function of the law. Chronic threat decreases support for the law and the idea that "patriotic Americans" are not represented within the legal system. This is a clear affirmation of the causal connection of threat through multiple pathways to the erosion of the function of the democratic process.

Chronic threat does not simply erode legitimacy across all political attitudes; it leads to more support for the legitimacy of recent Republican presidential elections, which does more to give evidence of the third *P* in demographic determinism. Not only is a sense of threat making White Americans more anti-democratic, but it is also driving their sentiments toward the GOP as a potential means to stave off their fear. This could be an indicator of the anti-democratic nature of the GOP. Because chronic threat leads to increased anti-democratic support, then respondents could be linking this support to the Republican Party. Importantly, I determine that this is not a Trump-specific impact, because respondents also report more support for the legitimacy of George Bush's electoral victory in 2004. I argue that this increased legitimacy of recent Republican presidential elections also comes from a belief that the Republican Party has curbed and will continue to curb racial threat. This point of view considers GOP policies implemented to reduce the influence of racial minorities in politics—for example, voter ID laws. The increased support for the legitimacy of Republican elections also comes from an increased expression of conservative ideology. By testing ideology pre- and posttreatment, I find that those who are exposed to the variant demographic change narratives express significantly more conservative ideology ($p = 0.041$; see appendix 7 for results).

The null finding of chronic threat's effect on Democrats' recent presidential elections, I find, likely comes from both the perceived role of the Democratic Party and an interpretation of the question wording. This null finding affirms the idea that Democrats are being perceived to advance the diversification of the United States. On the question wording, I do not ask respondents if they think the other candidate should have won. Given the competitive, typically binary nature of elections, support for Republicans' legitimacy is likely drawing away legitimacy from Democrats, if even on an implicit level.

The Reverberations of Chronic Threat

Given racial threat's high salience, I expect that, once it is primed, it will sustain itself over time in the American consciousness. To test this theory, I follow up with the same respondents in study 2 three weeks after they are initially primed, measuring the anti-democratic sentiments on legitimacy again.

In this follow-up, respondents are *not* primed again, yet those exposed three weeks prior still express support for the legitimacy of recent Republican elections at nearly the same magnitude. The outcome variables are, again, patriotic vigilantism and the legitimacy of Republican and Democratic presidential elections. I take my assessment of chronic threat one step further here, testing the respondents' confidence in democracy. If racial threat is chronic, then priming it should have a long-lasting impact on confidence in democracy over time.

Over time, threat enduringly shifts the perceived legitimacy of the law and recent Republican presidential elections. In short, I find stability in chronic threat over time. Support for vigilantism is robust and at a similar level to the measurement weeks prior ($p = 0.07$), as is the perception of the legitimacy of recent Republican elections ($p = 0.008$). On the latter, I find suggestive evidence of an *increase* in this perception of legitimacy over the three-week period (figure 8.10).

The stability in attitudes over time is a shocking finding that affirms the existence of chronic threat. I show that exposure to narratives about racial demographic change generates a strong sense of racial threat that sustains over a long period. It cannot be understated that two of the frames I use are to intentionally reduce racial threat and have been shown to reduce threat in previous studies (Levy and Myers 2021). Threat, I show, is intimately tied to ideas about democracy. When it is primed marginally (through the light-touch prime) and unintentionally (by attempting to curb it using an ostensibly unthreatening narrative), the same outcome occurs—support for democracy erodes, and the perceived legitimacy of elites who allegedly curb racial demographic change increases.

The implications of chronic threat abound. With narratives pushed by news outlets and misinformation on social media, Americans are consistently inculcated with a sense of threat. While there are media that intentionally present threatening narratives, I show here that the current political discourse and information environment in the United States facilitate a chronic sense of threat in many Americans' minds. Views of the future of the country's demographics are intimately tied to anti-democratic ideas, and the stability of these attitudes over time represents a crucial stickiness of these attitudes.

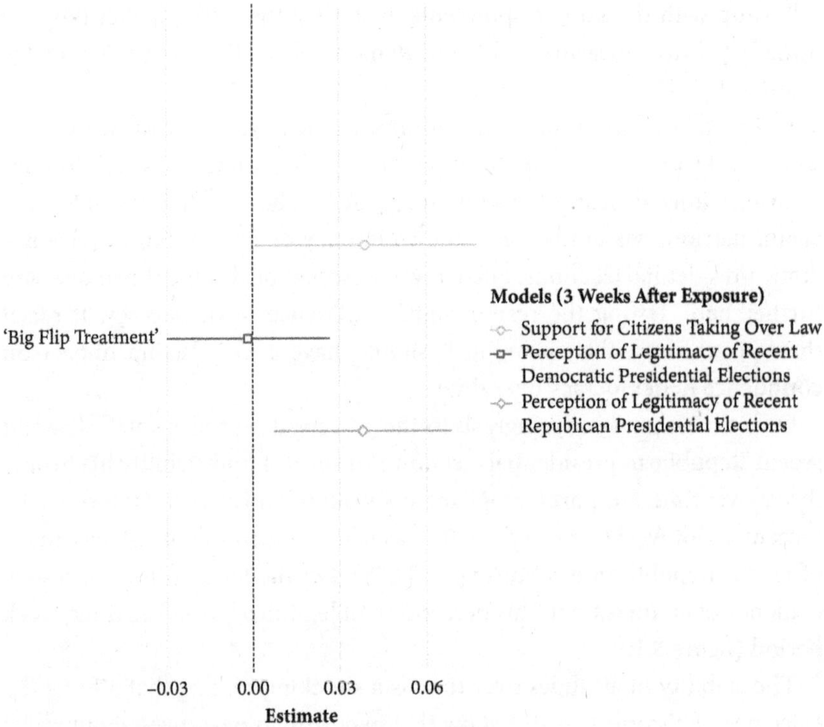

Figure 8.10 Coefficient plot of effect of treatment on support for anti-democratic attitudes and legitimacy of Democratic and Republican electoral victories, reinterviewed three weeks after exposure.

Once chronic threat is activated, it does not dissipate over time. This could be because these threatened views are well-established or repeated messages in Americans' consumption of media. On the whole, the mere maintenance of democratic erosion over time is quite dangerous for democratic norms among the public. It even erodes confidence in democracy as a system. In one final overall test of chronic threat, I test the extent to which primed Americans express confidence in democracy relative to the control group. Collectively, these primed Americans express less confidence in democracy ($p = 0.07$; figure 8.11).

A chronic sense of threat in the public can move the needle of democratic support. The implications that stem from this movement are immense. This final confirmation is important in and of itself because it was not tested in the original study. Threat from these primes has such a strong

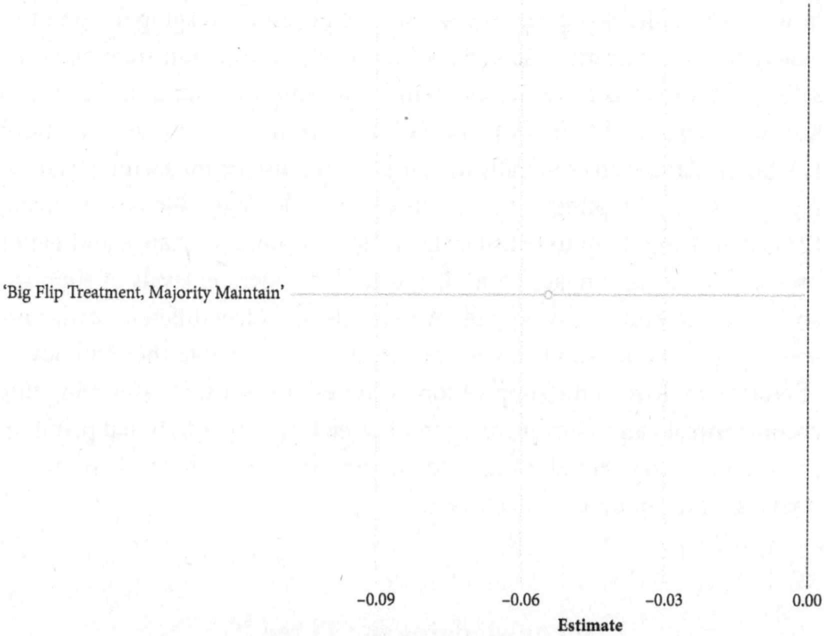

Figure 8.11 Coefficient plot of effect of treatment on confidence in democracy.

effect on attitudes that it shifts overall confidence in democracy roughly three weeks after exposure.

In effect, I find that not only can racial threat from demographic change be generated quickly and from minimal information, but also, once generated from even countervailing messages, it seems to maintain itself in the minds of the most threatened Americans.

Trying to Assuage Chronic Threat

Previously, I show consistently that presenting countervailing narratives about how the country is diversifying and simply priming ideas about changes still drive up threat and erosion among White Americans. From the onset, the assertion I have made is that racial threat is chronically salient among these Americans. This, in effect, means that we ought to consider the racial messaging displayed intentionally to prompt threat as a second-order factor to a grander story. Earlier iterations of American politics allow us to make causal inferences about where racial threat comes from and even how to correct it. However, now we may be beyond assuaging the point of assuaging this concern. The series of tests I display demonstrate just how salient the threat is from demographic determinism. Taking the series of tests together reveals a bleak picture of the current state of public opinion: (1) Asking Americans generally to consider and discuss the changing country leads to a prompting of the the three *P*'s of demographic determinism, (2) encouraging them to consider how race is bound to change and is not predictable has *no* impact on their racial or democratic levels of support, and (3) these same ideas pervade Americans in widely different state contexts, all generating similar types of threat. They generate the same levels of erosion of democratic support too. And I even show that prompting this chronic threat can last over the span of weeks without additional priming. Next, putting together all of these dynamics of chronic threat, I conduct a final test of the bounds of its efficacy.

Acknowledging the Three *P*'s

In a study that covers the whole country, I test reactions to correcting the Three *P*'s of demographic determinism. Specifically, I bring each of these terms (prediction, POC, and partisanship) to the fore, stating the uncertainty present within each of the ideas. Then I use this within the form of the prime I utilized on the diversification of the country. This means I am also able to gauge reactions to this same prime in qualitative ways by evaluating how Americans respond.

Overall, I expect that these three *P*'s, primed together, will still continue to increase anti-democratic sentiments (H1) and that responses will be rife with anti-Black sentiment (H2) despite explicit attempts to assuage these concerns. This study brings together a series of disparate aspects of chronic threat in a single study:

1) The effect of priming the three *P*'s on anti-democratic sentiments (support for political violence, electoral skepticism, use of weapons against the government).
2) A direct test of demographic determinism as an outcome variable.
3) An expansive investigation of the mass public through a sizable, high-quality probability sample.
4) Republican versus Democratic reactions to the priming.

This study works to activate ideas about the three *P*'s, describing how, despite projections, there is no way to be certain of the country will change, especially within politics. The prime acknowledges presumptions about the Democratic Party gaining advantages from demographic changes, but it iterates that this is impossible to know because of how parties adapt to changes. This assertion is fundamentally different from the previous chapter because it does not project so much as introduce uncertainty. I fielded this study with NORC of the University of Chicago in May 2023, utilizing a sample of 1,015 Americans benchmarked to the census.

In this nationally representative sample, I look specifically at White Americans' reactions to information. The prime I utilize is framed to assuage their threatened concerns. But despite this intention, I expect that, conforming to the idea of chronic threat, they will express greater levels of threat and anti-democratic views. With the individual-level reactions to the prime *and* the collective responses, I confirm that threat from the changing country is chronically salient on a mass level across the White public.

Across the White Americans within this study (N = 670), when I prime demographic changes while also reassuring them with the three *P*'s, they still express a greater sense of threat along the lines of demographic determinism. First, I find, by and large, that they become more expressively anti-Black (4 percentage point decrease; $p = 0.04$). This does not, coextensively, also function as an increase in positive feelings toward White Americans, where I find null results ($p = 0.76$); see figure 8.12.

Table 8.2 Sample composition

Gender	**49% Female** **51% Male**
Race	72% White 9% African American 2% Asian American 12% Latino 2% Native American 3% Other
Household income (median)	$50,000–$59,000
Age (median)	54
Education Level	Less than high school (4%) High school graduate or equivalent (17%) Some college or associate's degree (38%) Bachelor's degree (22%) Postgraduate study/professional degree (18%)

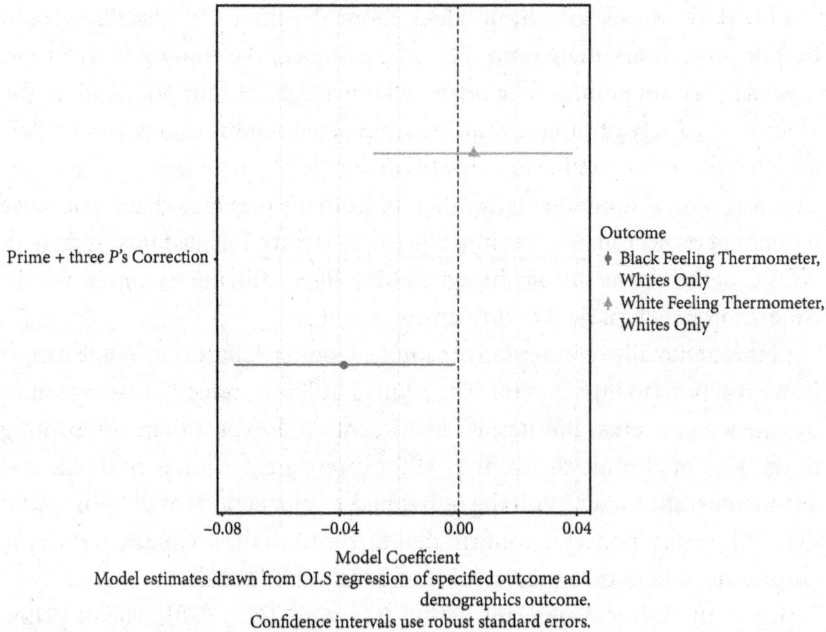

Figure 8.12 (1) Majority-minority flip
Coefficient plot of effect of treatment on demographic determinism and support for political violence, Whites only.

So, in effect, priming the idea of there being *no* party advantage from the coming majority-minority flip still increases anti-Black sentiment among White Americans.

These sentiments and inferences about Black Americans are reflected in the responses to this prompt; many respondents make direct links to the Democratic Party. One respondent, a sixty-three-year-old White man who identifies as a strong Republican, writes the following:

> Democrats believe it will change for them. It is more racially divided than they want blacks to believe it is, and yes it is a democratic plot to change to socialist and make blacks believe it is better for them.

Another respondent, a seventy-nine-year-old White woman who also identifies as a strong Republican, responds with this:

> Stop immigration to the US. Stop transgender bullshit—it is a mental problem. Stop blacks from asking for reparations. Also stop calling blacks

> African-Americans. They're not from Africa for hundreds of years, they're black Americans just like I am a white American.

There are clear linkages made between political parties and Black Americans within these responses. White Americans assume Black Americans will make gains in tandem with the demographic changes to the country. The two respondents above are older Americans, but I also find that these views pervade generations of White Americans. The following response comes from a thirty-year-old White woman who identifies as a Republican-leaning Independent:

> African-Americans have and will become more dominant within American culture, both politically and socially. Also, Native Americans will be considered one of the biggest minorities in American culture. And lastly, Asian American populations will have increased tremendously!

The multiple themes that emerge in these responses give further context to the sharp decrease in warmth toward Black Americans. White Americans here are expressing concern over Black influence and power in light of demographic changes, as I anticipate in the second *P*. They take a step further and describe concern over the Democratic Party making power gains through an increasing Black influence. This is a clear validation of the chronic salience of racial threat—there are inferences made about Black Americans and the Democratic Party despite the prime articulating that there will not be an influence. Directionally, this is a crucial finding because it does well to show that these threatened Americans cannot be convinced otherwise about their concerns.

Beyond the chronic nature of anti-Black sentiments, I look next into the extent to which these motivate overt anti-democratic support and ideas of demographic determinism. Measuring demographic determinism and violent political support through a closed-ended item, I find that attempting to assuage sentiments of threat still activates support for these same views. White Americans primed with the correction still become more violent (~ 4 percentage points; $p = 0.02$) and anticipate even more that the Democratic Party will be at an advantage as the country changes (2 percentage points; $p = 0.04$); see figure 8.13.

Compared to my previous sets of findings on the priming of racial threat and anti-democratic views, I find high levels of consistency. Recall within

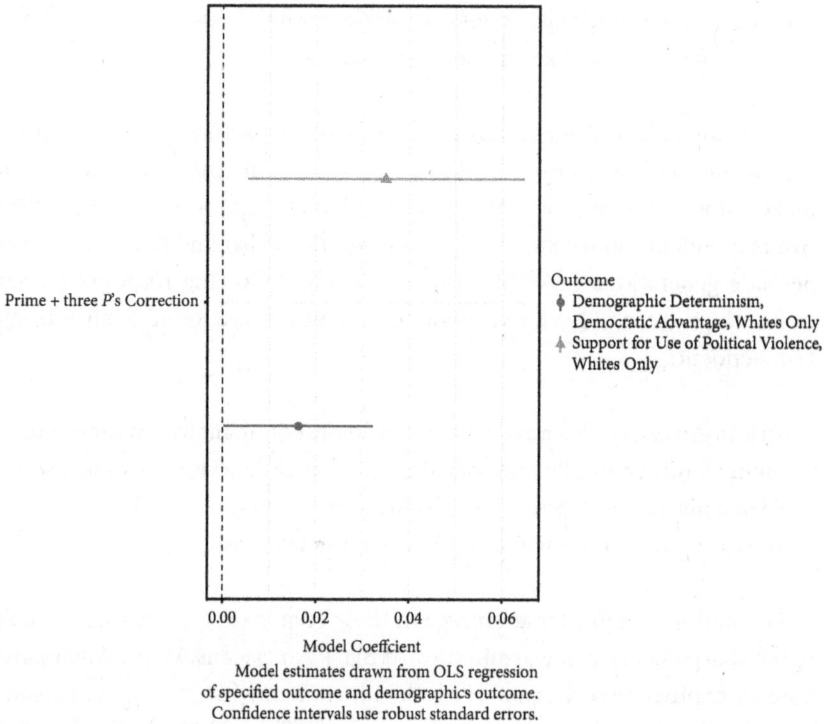

Figure 8.13 Majority-minority flip
Coefficient plot of effect of treatment on Black and White Feeling thermometers, Whites only.

the first study of this chapter, the basic prime of diversification of the United States prompts a 4-percentage-point increase in support for a 2024 presidential candidate who endorses political violence. The consistency in effect size here does not suggest that these two sets of findings directly mirror one another; rather, it offers support to the notion that the chronic threat captured from multiple, varying primes leads to similarity in the upticks of violent views.

Across the board, we see the activation of chronic threat in variant forms. The most crucial dimension of my findings across these multiple studies is that the prompting of threat is not content-contingent; instead, it is more dependent on the inferences White Americans are making through that content. More specifically, White Americans do not care nor think significantly differently about where racial threat is coming from—regardless of the information they are provided with. In certain respects, they cannot be convinced otherwise.

This final nationally representative study validates the idea of chronic threat in the strongest way relative to all previous studies. I show that (1) threat is not limited in its scope across a broad swath of White Americans, and (2) activating ideas meant to assuage concerns about demographic determinism by addressing the uncertainty in the three *P*'s is unsuccessful—it actually backfires.

A Chronic Issue?

The big flip, messaging about it from elites, and public sentiment about the threat it poses for White Americans have created a pervasive environment of fear and anxiety across the public. In contrast to previous political moments that involved the intentional use of racial messages to shift attitudes, I show, in a variety of instances, that even seemingly innocuous information about demographic changes generates a sense of threat. Moreover, this threat is not contained in even the subjects of interest, however incorrect the thought is that Black Americans are a growing racial group—the threat reaches directly and immediately into eroding support for democracy. Crucially, I show that this erosion looks like shifting support for abstract ideas of democracy and shifting interpretations of political moments along the lines of electoral legitimacy. It also works to embed itself in the minds of the most threatened Americans, lasting weeks later with no further priming. Racial threat from the big flip is chronically salient among the mass public.

The processes I describe and evaluate diagnose just how potent, powerful, and salient racial threat is in shifting support for democratic norms. But what exactly does it mean to shift norms? How should democratic erosion be considered, as it is clearly facilitated through threat?

Empirical scholars who have investigated the extent to which support for violence and anti-democratic ideas pervades the public have speculated about how to think of these changes. The problem in describing these aspects of change is twofold: (1) the extent to which they exist is an interpretable question, and (2) even if they do exist, it is difficult to discuss how they may manifest in politics. The big flip, and specifically the threat felt from perceived shifting racial status and the threat from Black Americans, provides a great example of just how erosion could look over time and materialize—we have already witnessed it unfolding in real time.

From a crucial theoretical perspective, eroding democratic norms are ethereal, abstract, hotly contested, and difficult to observe. There is slow erosion, often imperceptible to many in the same way that water erodes rock. Levitsky and Ziblatt (2018) describe this explicitly: "The backsliding of democracy is often gradual, its effects unfolding slowly over time" (187). Where I will give attention is what the erosion looks like on a public level. Citizens can act as bulwarks of democracy or facilitators of its erosion, for example based on how they react to instances of authoritarianism or political violence. Permissiveness of violence can lead to more violence *because* of the outward perception that those actions are reasonable in politics. We will call this "moving the needle."

Moving the Needle

The needle represents the permissible norms and practices in politics. As an institution, the public essentially sets the tone of what democratic norms look like, which then provides the bounds to what is and is not permitted. These democratic boundaries are never fixed. They move and adjust with shifts to politics. I use a scale as a metaphor for the existence and function of norms.

Visualized in figure 8.14, these norms represent the general support the public gives to democratic or authoritarian ideas. One can think of the needle as capturing the actions and ideas that are permitted. Put another way, this scale represents the actions and ideas in politics that are permitted among the public. Overall, public acceptance determines such things as the political actions of fellow citizens, the candidates who are suitable for office, what those candidates can say, and which other nations the state affiliates with. When we evaluate the citizenry and their political views, we encounter where the needle is *at that point in time*. We do not capture how norms might be shifting or could be moved by certain shocks. Extending our political analysis over time, we then are better able to theorize what the shifts are or could be, and we are better able to identify how they have gradually been altered. If a leader, group of citizens, or an individual visibly engages in anti-democratic or authoritarian actions, they are then perceived

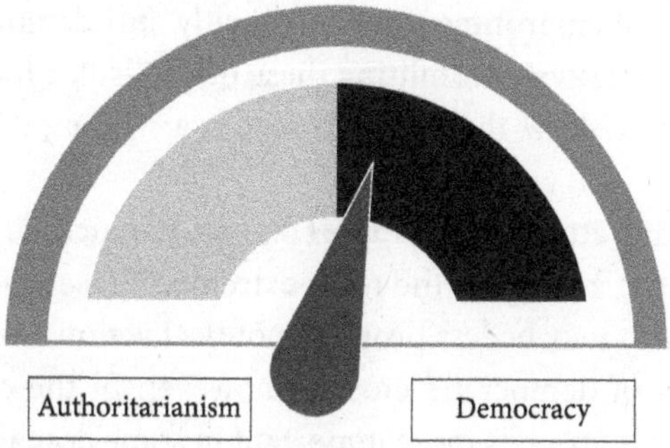

Figure 8.14 (2) Majority-minority flip + no status threat
Figure of needle, identifying authoritarianism and democracy.

by others, and how those onlookers interpret those actions sets the terms for what is viable in politics.

On erosion or moving the needle, if a political actor says or does something anti-democratic and it is *not* sanctioned by others, then this tacitly endorses the action. In effect, it moves the political needle, even if for a moment. Over time, consistent pushing of norms of political discourse can gradually and robustly move those norms.

Let us use examples from the findings in this chapter, where I show that chronic threat affects the views of a potential 2024 candidate. I do not use their party affiliation or a specific name intentionally to allow the Americans participating in the study to think abstractly about the candidate. When they are primed to think about the country's diversification, White Americans generally become more supportive of a candidate who endorses political violence and coextensively less supportive of a candidate who explicitly endorses democracy. Threat leads White Americans to turn away from democratic norms when they think of who ought to run for office in 2024. I show this in a single instance; consider it over time. Images and content, some intentional and others unintentional, generate a sense of threat, all the while, these same Americans are becoming more supportive of authoritarian candidates. With a groundswell of support, these candidates are elected into office on national, state, or local stages, and perceive that their positions are winning strategies. Other candidates, less committed to the same anti-democratic views but ambitious nonetheless, enter the political fray advocating for similar ideas because they know it will aid in their political success. Repeat the process, and over time, you have a reshaped political environment with explicitly anti-democratic, violence-endorsing representatives. Permitting these qualities in candidates is a step in that direction. I show that racial threat is a major catalyst in starting this support.

Too often, paying attention to support for anti-democratic or violent views means tracking the actions of the most extreme. Those who fall below the most extreme, who may be less prone to political action, are no less important to the story of democratic erosion, however. In the consideration of shifting norms, this group is more important in some domains because they can help to set the bounds of what extremism is. There are greater numbers of people with extreme views who can explain away anti-democratic views or violence as unimportant or not threatening to the function of American democracy. We see examples of how this can operate, especially over a long time horizon.

In one case, citizens who are becoming more extreme can rhetorically attribute anti-democratic actions to "both sides" of the political spectrum. This would involve stating that extremism is held equally in both political camps, thereby justifying their actions as reasonable because political opposition also holds similarly extreme views. Leaders who engage in "both-sidesism" might find more support from a more extreme public because their rhetorical side-stepping could work to rationalize its extremity. A clear example of this comes from Donald Trump identifying that "there are very fine people on both sides" in the wake of White supremacist violence in Charlottesville in 2017 (Gray 2017).

Another clear case of how the public can shift the discourse of violent actions comes in how Americans could justify burgeoning acts of domestic terrorism as a series of "lone wolf" acts instead of perceiving trends within these actions.

Crucially, I empirically show the importance of a set of perceptions that exist in the general public. They are about the future of American society, many of which either are or teeter on the edge of being false. Black Americans are currently not a drastically increasing racial group, yet this belief is still held. This belief, in and of itself, stands as an important driver that ought to be taken seriously because it branches into ideas of violence, particularly the motivators of terrorism.

Within comparative examinations of the motivations of terrorism, the mere perception of group status decline is a standalone predictor of engagement in violence and terrorism. Miodownik and Nir (2016) describe how the multiple pathways of subjective perceptions of grievance and group status threat can intimately connect to violent support across the mass public. They write that threat leads to two sets of normative implications:

> The first concerns risks of misinformation and misperceptions. . . . Such conditions might be conducive to mobilization attempts by irresponsible, self-interested leaders who agitate discontent among group members by harping on grievances, even when objective conditions of the group are better than others. The second normative issue concerns genuine inclusivity and representation in power-sharing agreements. The feeling that the government treats one's group unfairly, even—or especially—if this group is included in the power structure, leads to greater grievances and readiness for violence (p. 39).

White Americans' positionality is vital to their susceptibility toward violence. A leader could fan the flames of violent support by covering for those who commit the acts and providing reasons and responses for those who are partial to the actions. Additionally, the high status of White Americans adds to the concern that they could lose that status in light of the big flip. Taken to its most extreme framing, this is the sentiment behind "White genocide." White grievance over the changing country is not only about the perception of Americans of color achieving a higher status; it also concerns White Americans losing their status. Objective conditions do not always map the observation of them (Langer and Smedts 2013). Americans of color might be increasing in size across the United States, but the sense of threat that is intimately tied to the perceptions of the ongoing changes are (falsly) about Black Americans. Shown below is an example of the violent sentiment behind the perception of White grievance—the banner of a White supremacist website headlined by the phrase "Voice of the new embattled *White* minority!" Changing status is viewed and framed as conflict (figure 8.15).

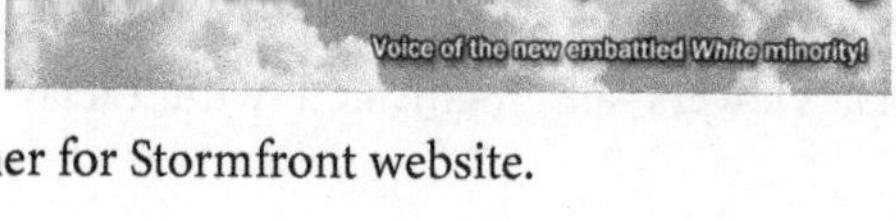

Figure 8.15 Banner for Stormfront website.

Importantly, this functions outside of the bounds of what the relative decrease in status is or could look like. What this means, in essence, is that any potential status threat is viewed as an existential problem. It leads to ideas of defending that status by any means necessary, and as I have shown in a variety of tests, these anti-democratic, violent responses to the perceptions of the big flip are not only embedded in these extremist circles. Elites may inflame and activate these ideas, but the chronic salience of racial threat shows there to be less content-contingent eroding effects in the White public. Intimations of the big flip work just as well to break down trust and care for American democracy.

The central dynamic to the big flip, demographic determinism, and the outgrowth of chronic racial threat that emerges from it is the centrality of perceptions. I show across the three *P*'s that these views are built off of uncertainty, yet they have an importance and reality to them because of the number of Americans who buy into the ideas. Causally, they drive democratic erosion; they drive support for political violence; they drive extreme attitudes. In short, they can work to move the needle. I go further to show that when racial threat is tapped, it has a staying power in the minds of Americans. It shifts support for anti-democratic extensions from the January 6 insurrection and for the legitimacy of recent Republican elections.

The needle of public support for democratic norms is crucial for future political activity. It does not simply describe the amount of support toward democratic and anti-democratic ideas in the present, but it also gives insight into who can run for office and what ideas will be allowed as time goes on. To put this into the context of the results shown above, when a violent leader is elected to office, their tacit or active support of violence will set new political norms into motion. These leaders move the needle further in the authoritarian direction, and as time progresses, more violent leaders will be accepted.

Racial threat has a direct bearing on the needle of democratic norms, as I show. Once activated, it does not decrease as time elapses. Importantly, my studies involve one stimulus among each of the treated groups. Minimal information about the diversification of the United States affects Americans' racially threatened sentiments—but this is not the environment in which Americans view and process their news. In certain information environments, viewers are inculcated with racial threat messages on a daily basis, which is to say, my results here are a snapshot of a wider, prevalent issue. If one-off exposure to messages or one-off prompts regarding demographic change leads to the real-time and longer-term erosion of democratic attitudes, then the repeated exposure to similar ideas likely has a lasting effect on how Americans think about democracy.

9
The Future of Multiracial American Democracy

Demographic determinism pervades the American public. In a variety of contexts, the three *P*'s bear out in Americans' minds, and I consistently validate their function. Americans consistently assume to know the future of race, inferring that people of color are mostly Black Americans, and therefore assume that Democrats will benefit from the big flip. All three of these misperceptions feed into demographic determinism, which namely makes Republicans feel a sense of threat that motivates their anti-democratic sentiments.

The idea of demographic determinism taps into these important ideas about the future of the United States and has shaped how all Americans consider the system of democracy. Racial threat from anticipations about the country's future has shaped Americans' views of democracy so strongly that it now operates on a chronic level, as I show in chapter 8.

Priming any sort of ideas about racial demographic change, even in non-threatening ways, accentuates senses of threat, conservative shifts in attitudes, and movement away from democratic ideals. These shifts happen distinctly outside of the strong influence of partisanship or ideology. As a concept, chronic racial threat poses a massive problem for American democracy. I show that there are few ways to reverse or quell this type of threat. If there are no potential ways to curb racially threatened sentiments—and, by extension, the eroding democratic attitudes from them—then counter-messaging on these changes is effectively bunk. Threatening messages continue to be so over time and likely can only deepen. Media coverage of demographic change of any sort is likely to be more threatening. Extending from my focus in this book, the erosion prompted by racial threat could open doors to other domains—such as ideas of gender.

As I described at the onset of this book, demographic determinism has been a long-standing idea that has driven political violence in the Buffalo massacre, the Charleston massacre, and a host of others. In chapter 2, I show

The Big Flip. Andrew Ifedapo Thompson, Oxford University Press. © Oxford University Press (2026).
DOI: 10.1093/9780197822173.003.0009

that commentators who describe these sentiments as new fail to capture that this political violence is historically rooted in concern and fear of Black enfranchisement. Since the Civil War and Reconstruction, there has been a clear anti-democratic and violent motivation to quell Black political enfranchisement that is mirrored in the big flip. In chapters 5, 6, and 7, I show consistently that the racial threat from these sentiments not only radicalizes the most extreme Americans but can also shift opinions of more moderate Americans in extreme directions. It can make them more supportive of anti-democratic ideas like voter obstruction, restricting freedom of speech, and supporting authoritarian leadership. The major implication of this effect on moderates is that demographic determinism can shift norms of political behavior over time. Chronic threat can move the needle of legitimate political action in such a way that it increases public support for political violence. Given the causal role of racial threat, increased support for violence could look like more Americans becoming unconcerned by mass shootings motivated by racist, White supremacist ideas.

The current anti-democratic reaction the United States is facing amounts to a second Redemption era. This new period arises from deep anti-Black anxiety about the future of American politics. As I chart in the long history of racial struggle and conflict, Barack Obama brought about a representational revolution in US politics, which was driven by the perceived position of Black Americans. His legacy connects to the long arc of the civil rights struggle, which harkens even further back to Reconstruction. He was a monumental figure in the American presidency that completely reoriented what Americans considered was possible in government. To some Americans, he was a new horizon of what politics could look like, while for others Obama also brought about a new threat. He was the realization of the concern of many others about the future of the country. This threat was the idea of further Black enfranchisement and gains of political power; Obama, to these fearful Americans, was the big flip embodied.

The outgrowth of overt racially threatened sentiment led to a contingent of Americans supporting Donald Trump. Ideas of "taking the country back" have been dog whistles to many of these Americans about regaining their power after having lost it under Obama. Under threat, they felt as though they needed to recapture their power from increasing Black power—demographic determinism that, in their minds, took the form of a future of perpetual Democratic Party victories, further deepening the control of Black Americans and other people of color. Initially these appeared to be innocuous ideas, but eventually they took the form of reactions toward democracy. Questions arose about the efficacy of elections, the intention of candidates, the use of violence toward fellow citizens, and even whether democracy is a useful form of government at all.

Beyond demographic determinism as a concept, there are two crucial takeaways from this book for American politics. The first, which requires consistent emphasis, is how central race is to US politics. Across every chapter in this book, I show that racial attitudes have had an immense bearing on how Americans consider the entire system of democracy. I am not simply identifying a disparate effect of racial threat on politics; I show through a variety of evidence that race is a crucial feature of the American system. Even more importantly, I show that Americans infer a great deal about race: They think primarily of Black Americans when they think of people of color and racial minorities (chapter 5).

Black Americans are central to how all Americans process race, and so when thinking about the big flip, Black Americans are considered to be the group that is significantly increasing in size. This misperception is what drives all of demographic determinism. Black Americans are vital to the politics of race *even when they are not mentioned.* This dimension of the importance and function of race in American politics has, thus far, not been explicated or accounted for. My argument is ultimately that when race is considered in any context within the United States, it is analytically important to consider how views about Black Americans might be related to and influencing these views. Moreover, from these inferences, I show that threat from Black Americans makes many non-Black Americans willingly engage in anti-democratic views. Thus, the pervasiveness of Black Americans in American politics cannot be understated. Their perceived position in the American polity leads to different evaluations of the entire system of American democracy. The misperception here leads to the second major takeaway from this book.

I show that for a broad swath of Americans, much of their support for democracy is seemingly based upon who they think will be able to win. That is, they are *contingent democrats.* Their attitudes about the future of American politics shift based on their inferences about Black Americans. The moment when they are informed that they will not win, which manifests in the form of *demographic determinism* for Republicans, they strongly turn away from the system of democracy. From this effect, I suggest that under a system of democracy, there could be a variety of citizens who are "contingent democrats" or people who support the system of democracy insofar as they perceive that they can win. The moment they believe they cannot win, their support for the system goes by the wayside.

Looking forward, this is a vital point for all supporters of and scholars of democracy. The idea that democratic values are not unconditional is strongly concerning. How contingent on victory is this support for democracy? Does it simply require convincing citizens that their current party will be unable to win to erode it? How long does this diminishment of support last? For all people who care about the system of democracy, this question, in a comparative context, deserves a great deal of attention. With what appears to be a mass level of erosion of support for democratic norms and support around the world, contingent support for democracy could be a helpful rationale for what is happening. It could also be a potential avenue for reducing this eroding support.

In a final study, I seek to test the extent to which the three *P*'s work in motivating pro-democratic sentiment. I introduce the uncertainty of the future of American politics—that is, we are unaware of how politics is likely to change. Specifically, I seek to prime the three *P*'s among Americans, articulating that prediction, people of color, and partisanship are uncertain into the future. In short, I use the three *P*'s together to correct perceptions of demographic determinism.

Through a final experiment, I prime racial demographic change again.[1] I then randomly assign respondents to receive the following additional prime, which articulates the ideas of the three *P*'s:

> Interestingly, the projected groups growing in size are expected to be Hispanic Americans and Asian Americans. A large proportion of Americans presume these changes to be about Black Americans, but this is incorrect. African Americans, in all projections of demographic change, are not projected to grow significantly.
>
> Also, given the social function of race, it is actually very difficult to predict how the future racial demographics of the country will look. They are simply estimates, but cannot anticipate how racial groups will change in their identification.
>
> Lastly, the demographic changes of the country are not expected to benefit any one political party. American political parties adjust their

[1] I use the following open-ended prompt: "You may have heard about the diversification of the United States. Tell us what immediately comes to mind when you think about racial demographic change within the US. (Please tell us in at least three sentences.)"

platforms as times change, so Democrats, Republicans or any other political party is not slated to be at an advantage as the United States racially shifts.

I assess the effects of this prime on anti-democratic support in the mass public,[2] particularly support for overturning elections and the use of political violence.[3] In my analyses, I give attention to partisans generally, but I give special attention to Republicans' anti-democratic support. Overall, I find that introducing the uncertainty behind the three *P*'s is effective in robustly reducing anti-democratic support among Republicans. In figure 9.1, the use of the three *P*'s prime drastically reduces the support for overturning elections, effectively exclusive among Republicans.

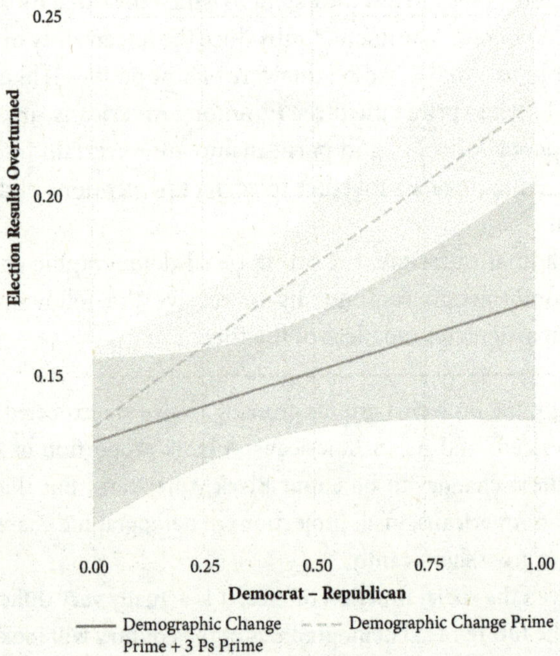

Figure 9.1 Interaction plot depicting the effect of treatment on electoral skepticism posttreatment across Democrats to Republicans. Upon receiving the three *P*'s treatment, Republicans become less skeptical of election results.

[2] Both of these I measure pre and post (Clifford, Sheagley, and Piston 2021).

[3] Two measures collapsed into a single scale: (1) support for using violence against political opposition, and (2) support for the idea that "if my party were to lose an election, citizens should prepare weapons to resist the federal government in their communities."

I find the same effect of the three *P*'s on support for political violence. Introducing the idea to Republicans drastically reduces their violent attitudes to a level akin to Democrats (figure 9.2).

The big flip is central to the future of American democracy. It drives anti-democratic views, such as support for violence and authoritarian leaders. It rests on a set of misperceptions that have been driven so deeply into the American political mind that they are now chronically salient. Historically I chart where these ideas come from, and just like the first *P* in demographic determinism, we cannot predict how the emergent threat from the big flip will affect American politics. We have indications from mass shootings and a failed insurrection that the threat is a crucial determinant of current democratic backsliding. But the future of politics is not determined. As I show in the priming study, simply introducing the basic ideas of the three *P*'s can work to reduce these negative, anti-democratic sentiments in the mass public. Ideas of demographic determinism from the big flip pervade

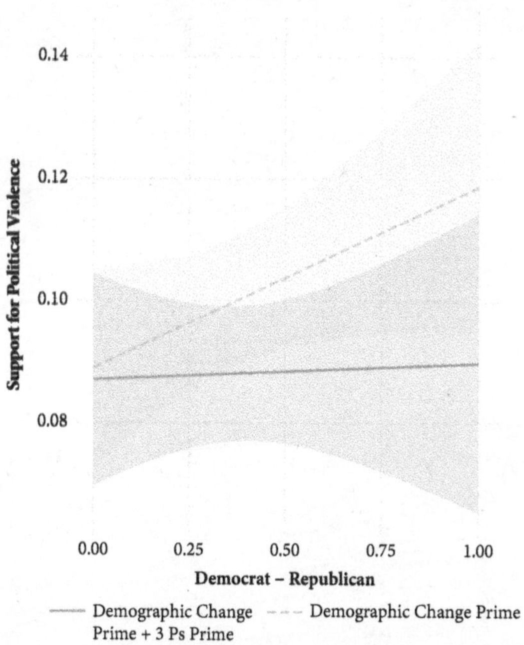

Figure 9.2 Interaction plot depicting the effect of treatment on support for political violence posttreatment across Democrats to Republicans. Upon receiving the three *P*'s treatment, Republicans become less supportive of political violence.

the American public, but I show that correcting for them leads to a more pro-democratic public. In this book, I help to diagnose one of the major problems for Americans' contemporary anti-democratic attitudes and, from this point, open avenues for developing practices to curb the threat. Misperceptions of the big flip are a central concern for democratic backsliding in the United States. It will take a coordinated effort of practitioners, researchers, policymakers, and American citizens to work to alter these misperceptions. The future of American democracy depends on it.

Appendices

Chapter 6, Appendix 1—Demographic composition of samples

AGE	BLACK AMERICANS	LATINX AMERICANS	CENSUS
Age 18–24	10.3%	9.3%	12.8%
Age 25–34	23.0%	28.1%	17.7%
Age 35–44	24.9%	26.6%	16.5%
Age 45–54	19.9%	18.8%	17.7%
Age 55–64	15.7%	12.2%	16.4%
Age 65+	6.1%	4.7%	18.9%
Base Size	1,204	1,202	N/A

REGION	BLACK AMERICANS	LATINX AMERICANS	CENSUS
Northeast	15.4%	18.7%	17.6%
Midwest	20.6%	10.9%	21.2%
South	52.6%	38.9%	37.6%
West	11.4%	31.5%	23.6%
Base Size	1,202	1,198	N/A

Chapter 6, Appendix 2—Specific racial group importance

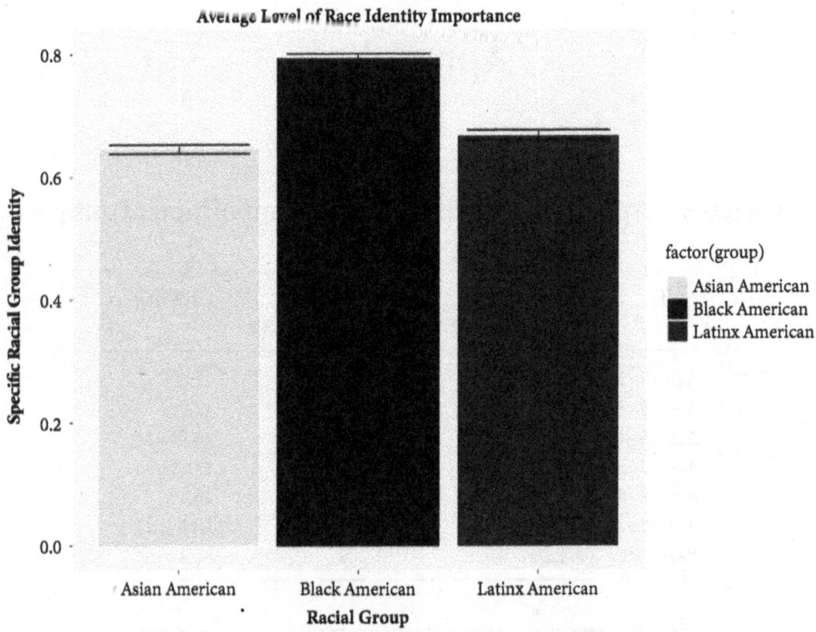

Chapter 6, Appendix 3—Specific racial group-linked fate

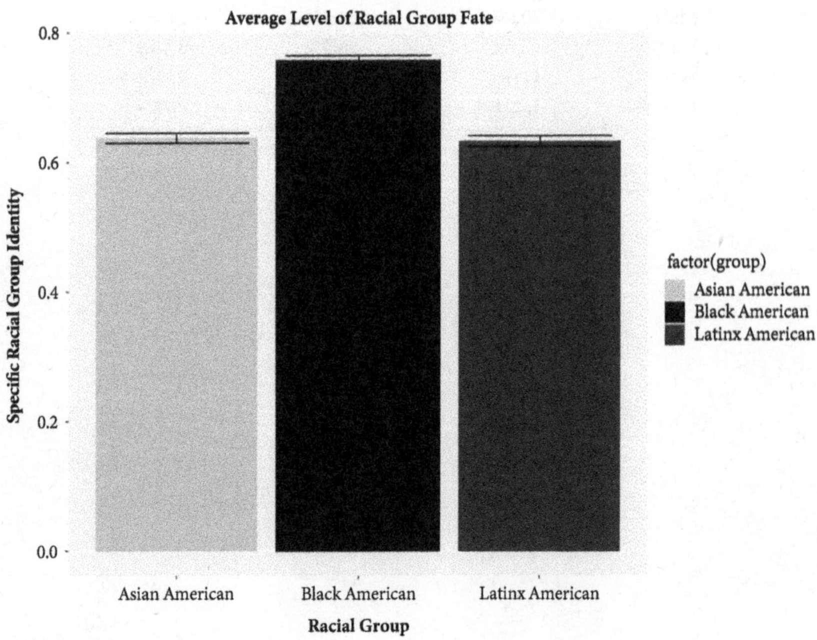

Chapter 6, Appendix 4—Expectations of groups increasing in size

All respondents

Condition	hispanic_ inclusive	black_ inclusive	asian_ inclusive	white_ inclusive	hispanic_ only	black_ only	asian_ only	white_ only
Pure Control	72.19	26.51	15.56	16.83	47.12	6.87	4.06	10.51
POC Treatment	66.51	64.79	35.66	7.94	20.56	21.33	1.24	5.45
Diverse Treatment	87.55	8.71	7.74	6.77	78.69	3.45	2.48	5.53

White respondents (1,655 observations)

Condition	hispanic_ inclusive	black_ inclusive	asian_ inclusive	white_ inclusive	hispanic_ only	black_ only	asian_ only	white_ only
Pure Control	73.97	24.59	13.54	19.25	48.30	4.99	1.96	12.29
POC Treatment	66.60	65.05	34.94	8.30	21.04	21.42	0.77	5.59
Diverse Treatment	87.84	8.33	6.59	6.77	80.20	3.47	2.08	5.38

Non-White respondents (540 observations)

Condition	hispanic_ inclusive	black_ inclusive	asian_ inclusive	white_ inclusive	hispanic_ only	black_ only	asian_ only	white_ only
Pure Control	69.47	30.00	21.05	6.84	47.89	12.63	10.52	3.68
POC Treatment	69.37	63.12	38.12	6.25	20.62	19.37	2.50	4.37
Diverse Treatment	86.84	11.57	11.57	7.36	73.15	3.68	3.15	5.78

Black respondents (222 observations)

Condition	hispanic_ inclusive	black_ inclusive	asian_ inclusive	white_ inclusive	hispanic_ only	black_ only	asian_ only	white_ only
Pure Control	69.33	48.00	16.00	10.66	36.00	20.00	2.67	4.00
POC Treatment	48.57	77.14	24.28	11.42	10.00	38.57	0.00	8.57
Diverse Treatment	81.81	18.18	6.49	10.38	64.93	7.79	1.29	9.09

Non-Black respondents (1,857 observations)

Condition	hispanic_ inclusive	black_ inclusive	asian_ inclusive	white_ inclusive	hispanic_ only	black_ only	asian_ only	white_ only
Pure Control	72.72	23.98	15.51	17.55	48.43	5.32	4.23	11.28
POC Treatment	68.70	63.28	37.06	7.51	21.85	19.23	1.39	5.06
Diverse Treatment	88.23	7.58	7.89	6.34	80.34	2.94	2.63	5.10

Chapter 7, Appendix 1, Treatment Conditions

Conditions	Description
0	Pure control
1	Majority-minority flip
2	Majority-minority flip + Republican frame
3	Majority-minority flip + Democratic frame

Chapter 7, Appendix 2, Concern and worry about racial demographic change

	Dependent variable			
	WORRIED		CONCERNED	
	(1)	(2)	(3)	(4)
demographic_change_ democrats	0.057 (0.063)		−0.061 (0.063)	
demographic_change_ republicans		0.130** (0.054)		0.045 (0.054)
PID	0.291*** (0.081)	0.338*** (0.077)	0.188** (0.081)	0.225*** (0.078)
IDEO	0.106 (0.073)	0.013 (0.069)	0.111 (0.074)	(0.074) (0.070)
EDU	0.060 (0.072)	−0.084 (0.067)	−0.006 (0.072)	−0.109 (0.067)
MEDIA	−0.036 (0.056)	0.053 (0.052)	0.018 (0.056)	0.062 (0.053)
AGE	−0.0003 (0.001)	0.0002 (0.001)	0.0001 (0.001)	−0.0004 (0.001)
GENDER	0.021 (0.036)	0.048 (0.033)	0.011 (0.036)	0.038 (0.033)
RACE1	0.017 (0.041)	−0.056 (0.035)	−0.013 (0.041)	−0.076** (0.035)
demographic_change_ democrats:PID	−0.093 (0.106)		0.074 (0.107)	
demographic_change_ republicans:PID		−0.238** (0.097)		−0.205** (0.097)
Constant	0.252*** (0.073)	0.307*** (0.070)	0.404*** (0.073)	0.483*** (0.071)
Observations	255	287	255	287
R^2	0.132	0.105	0.112	0.085
Adjusted R^2	0.100	0.075	0.080	0.055
Residual Std. Error	0.275 (df = 245)	0.267 (df = 277)	0.277 (df = 245)	0.270 (df = 277)
F Statistic	4.138*** (df = 9; 245)	3.593*** (df = 9; 277)	3.449*** (df = 9; 245)	2.852*** (df = 9; 277)

Note: $^{*}p<0.1$; $^{**}p<0.05$; $^{***}p<0.01$

Chapter 7, Appendix 3, POC, BLM, Feelings about immigrants, Study 1

	Dependent variable					
	feeling_racial_minorities		BLM		feeling_immmigrants	
	(1)	(2)	(3)	(4)	(5)	(6)
demographic_change_democrats	0.011 (0.064)		−0.061 (0.063)		−0.050 (0.063)	
demographic_change_republicans		−0.056 (0.055)		−0.085 (0.058)		−0.079 (0.054)
PID	−0.161* (0.082)	−0.185** (0.078)	−0.419*** (0.081)	−0.407*** (0.083)	−0.262*** (0.081)	−0.272*** (0.077)
IDEO	−0.139* (0.075)	−0.149** (0.070)	−0.383*** (0.073)	−0.322*** (0.074)	−0.220*** (0.073)	−0.154** (0.069)
MEDIA	0.120 (0.074)	0.014 (0.068)	−0.113 (0.073)	0.013 (0.072)	−0.030 (0.073)	0.089 (0.067)
GENDER	−0.017 (0.058)	0.103* (0.054)	0.051 (0.057)	0.114** (0.057)	0.037 (0.057)	0.141*** (0.053)
SOUTH	−0.0005 (0.001)	0.0002 (0.001)	−0.003*** (0.001)	−0.004*** (0.001)	−0.001 (0.001)	−0.002 (0.001)
AGE	0.038 (0.037)	0.021 (0.034)	0.024 (0.036)	0.003 (0.036)	0.014 (0.036)	0.004 (0.033)
RACE1	−0.034 (0.042)	0.004 (0.035)	0.002 (0.041)	−0.040 (0.038)	−0.034 (0.041)	−0.001 (0.035)

demographic_change_democrats:PID	0.013 (0.108)		0.029 (0.106)		0.051 (0.106)	
demographic_change_republicans:PID		0.212** (0.099)		0.199* (0.105)		0.209** (0.097)
Constant	0.701*** (0.074)	0.657*** (0.072)	1.044*** (0.073)	0.983*** (0.076)	0.869*** (0.073)	0.738*** (0.071)
Observations	243	273	243	273	243	273
R^2	0.127	0.091	0.461	0.350	0.230	0.178
Adjusted R^2	0.094	0.060	0.440	0.328	0.201	0.150
Residual Std. Error	0.275 (df = 233)	0.268 (df = 263)	0.270 (df = 233)	0.284 (df = 263)	0.270 (df = 233)	0.263 (df = 263)
F Statistic	3.781*** (df = 9; 233)	2.942*** (df = 9; 263)	22.166*** (df = 9; 233)	15.764*** (df = 9; 263)	7.750*** (df = 9; 233)	6.336*** (df = 9; 263)

Note: *p<0.1; **p<0.05; ***p<0.01

Chapter 7, Appendix 4, Concern and worry about racial demographic change, POC feelings, Study 2

	Dependent variable					
	CONCERNED		WORRIED		POC_feeling	
	(1)	(2)	(3)	(4)	(5)	(6)
demographic_change_democrats	−0.035 (0.035)		−0.047 (0.036)		0.029 (0.027)	
demographic_change_republicans		0.073** (0.036)		0.071* (0.037)		−0.028 (0.028)
PID	0.164*** (0.053)	0.153*** (0.055)	0.167*** (0.055)	0.120** (0.056)	−0.213*** (0.041)	−0.194*** (0.043)
IDEO	0.215*** (0.052)	0.226*** (0.057)	0.106** (0.054)	0.182*** (0.058)	−0.219*** (0.040)	−0.241*** (0.044)
MEDIA	−0.037 (0.033)	−0.042 (0.035)	−0.056 (0.034)	−0.031 (0.035)	0.029 (0.026)	0.025 (0.027)
GENDER	−0.017 (0.022)	0.026 (0.022)	−0.029 (0.022)	−0.003 (0.022)	−0.027 (0.017)	−0.021 (0.017)
SOUTH	0.016 (0.022)	0.012 (0.022)	0.045** (0.023)	0.029 (0.023)	0.006 (0.017)	0.011 (0.017)
AGE	0.177** (0.070)	0.168** (0.071)	0.104 (0.073)	0.091 (0.073)	−0.207*** (0.055)	−0.208*** (0.055)
RACE1	−0.017 (0.023)	−0.011 (0.024)	0.005 (0.024)	0.019 (0.024)	−0.047*** (0.018)	−0.072*** (0.019)

demographic_change_democrats:PID	0.140**		0.144**		−0.002	
	(0.060)		(0.062)		(0.047)	
demographic_change_republicans:PID		−0.133**		−0.133**		0.083*
		(0.061)		(0.062)		(0.047)
Constant	0.216***	0.200***	0.258***	0.218***	0.872***	0.886***
	(0.042)	(0.042)	(0.043)	(0.043)	(0.032)	(0.033)
Observations	630	622	630	622	630	622
R^2	0.233	0.138	0.167	0.086	0.349	0.326
Adjusted R^2	0.222	0.125	0.154	0.072	0.340	0.316
Residual Std. Error	0.270	0.271	0.278	0.276	0.210	0.210
	(df = 620)	(df = 612)	(df = 620)	(df = 612)	(df = 620)	(df = 612)
F Statistic	20.891***	10.899***	13.770***	6.389***	36.953***	32.937***
	(df = 9; 620)	(df = 9; 612)	(df = 9; 620)	(df = 9; 612)	(df = 9; 620)	(df = 9; 612)

Note: *p < 0.1; **p < 0.05; ***p < 0.01

Chapter 7, Appendix 5, Effect of partisan frame on anti-democratic support, Study 1

	Dependent variable	
	ad_scale	
	(1)	(2)
demographic_change_democrats	−0.011 (0.031)	
demographic_change_republicans		0.018 (0.030)
PID	0.094** (0.047)	0.057 (0.045)
IDEO	0.006 (0.045)	0.081* (0.046)
MEDIA	−0.070** (0.029)	−0.062** (0.028)
GENDER	0.016 (0.019)	0.028 (0.018)
SOUTH	0.009 (0.019)	0.017 (0.018)
AGE	−0.228*** (0.062)	−0.241*** (0.058)
RACE1	−0.023 (0.020)	−0.057*** (0.019)
demographic_change_democrats:PID	−0.033 (0.052)	
demographic_change_republicans:PID		−0.105** (0.049)
Constant	0.364*** (0.036)	0.357*** (0.034)
Observations	630	622
R^2	0.064	0.100
Adjusted R^2	0.050	0.086
Residual Std. Error	0.236 (df = 620)	0.220 (df = 612)
F Statistic	4.704*** (df = 9; 620)	7.520*** (df = 9; 612)

Note: *p < 0.1; **p < 0.05; ***p < 0.01

Chapter 7, Appendix 6, Effect of partisan frame on preventing minorities from participating in politics, Study 1

	Dependent variable	
	Prevent minorities	
	(1)	(2)
demographic_change_democrats	−0.229	
	(0.228)	
demographic_change_republicans		−0.394*
		(0.226)
PID	−1.675***	−1.211***
	(0.341)	(0.340)
ideo	−0.116**	−0.236***
	(0.056)	(0.059)
media	0.084***	0.078**
	(0.031)	(0.031)
gender	0.069	0.183
	(0.134)	(0.126)
region	0.040	−0.072
	(0.070)	(0.067)
age	0.009**	0.011***
	(0.004)	(0.004)
demographic_change_democrats:PID	0.636	
	(0.387)	
demographic_change_republicans:PID		1.364***
		(0.377)
Constant	5.425***	5.715***
	(0.421)	(0.413)
Observations	630	622
R^2	0.145	0.149
Adjusted R^2	0.134	0.138
Residual Std. Error	1.743 (df = 621)	1.680 (df = 613)
F Statistic	13.131*** (df = 8; 621)	13.382*** (df = 8; 613)

Note: *p<0.1; **p<0.05; ***p<0.01

Chapter 7, Appendix 7, Effect of partisan frame on anti-democratic support and effect of prime on support for political violence, Study 3

	Dependent variable			
	Concerned	Worried	Angry	Anxious
	(1)	(2)	(3)	(4)
demo_prime	−0.145	−0.128	−0.184*	−0.147
	(0.124)	(0.120)	(0.109)	(0.121)
PID	1.689***	1.639***	1.111***	1.248***
	(0.165)	(0.160)	(0.145)	(0.161)
edu	−0.097***	−0.109***	−0.097***	−0.113***
	(0.030)	(0.029)	(0.026)	(0.029)
region	−0.034	−0.007	−0.043	−0.061*
	(0.033)	(0.032)	(0.029)	(0.032)
income	−0.030**	−0.023*	−0.030***	−0.019
	(0.012)	(0.012)	(0.011)	(0.012)
gender	−0.072	−0.057	−0.203***	−0.035
	(0.075)	(0.073)	(0.066)	(0.073)
demo_prime:PID	0.459**	0.374*	0.685***	0.434*
	(0.232)	(0.225)	(0.205)	(0.226)
Constant	3.396***	3.156***	2.995***	3.465***
	(0.227)	(0.220)	(0.200)	(0.222)
Observations	2,118	2,118	2,118	2,118
R^2	0.130	0.127	0.114	0.091
Adjusted R^2	0.127	0.124	0.111	0.088
Residual Std. Error (df = 2110)	1.759	1.701	1.548	1.713
F Statistic (df = 7; 2110)	44.865***	43.875***	38.776***	30.091***

Note: *p < 0.1; **p < 0.05; ***p < 0.01

	Dependent variable
	Violence_against_opposition_Post
Demo_prime	−0.029**
	(0.014)
PID	0.027
	(0.019)
violence_against_opposition_pre	0.405***
	(0.014)

	Dependent variable
	Violence_against_opposition_Post
edu	0.001
	(0.003)
income	−0.007***
	(0.001)
region	0.002
	(0.004)
gender	−0.019**
	(0.009)
demo_prime:PID	0.045*
	(0.026)
Constant	0.119***
	(0.026)
Observations	1.966
R^2	0.309
Adjusted R^2	0.306
Residual Std. Error	0.193 (df = 1957)
F Statistic	109.435*** (df = 8; 1957)

Note: *p < 0.1; **p < 0.05; ***p < 0.01

Chapter 7, Appendix 8—Power analysis

Sample required for detecting small effect
Two-sample t-test power calculation
n = 393.4057 d = 0.2 sig.level = 0.05 power = 0.8 alternative = two.sided

Chapter 7, Appendix 9—Regression table, violence support

	Dependent variable
	reasonable_violence
minorities_v_poc_trend	0.045*** (0.017)
EDU	0.126*** (0.041)
GENDER	−0.074*** (0.017)
PID	0.055 (0.045)
IDEO	−0.034 (0.050)
INCOME	−0.058* (0.031)
MEDIA	−0.082** (0.034)
raceAsian or Asian American	0.092 (0.238)
raceBlack or African American	0.121 (0.236)
raceHawaiian or Pacific Islander	−0.005 (0.288)
raceHispanic/Latino(a)	0.024 (0.238)
raceMiddle Eastern or North African	−0.101 (0.289)
raceMultiracial	0.098 (0.239)
raceWhite	0.037 (0.235)
Constant	0.083 (0.238)
Observations	798
R^2	0.065
Adjusted R^2	0.048
Residual Std. Error	0.235 (df = 783)
F Statistic	3.878*** (df = 14; 783)

Note: *p < 0.1; **p < 0.05; ***p < 0.01

Appendix 7, Appendix 10 —Regression table, hard to trust elections

	Dependent variable
	hard_to_trust_elections
minorities_v_poc_trend	0.044**
	(0.022)
EDU	−0.073
	(0.054)
GENDER	0.003
	(0.022)
PID	0.228***
	(0.059)
IDEO	0.381***
	(0.065)
INCOME	−0.062
	(0.041)
MEDIA	−0.127***
	(0.044)
raceAsian or Asian American	−0.022
	(0.312)
raceBlack or African American	0.071
	(0.311)
raceHawaiian or Pacific Islander	0.160
	(0.379)
raceHispanic/Latino(a)	−0.070
	(0.313)
raceMiddle Eastern or North African	−0.035
	(0.380)
raceMultiracial	−0.062
	(0.314)
raceWhite	−0.082
	(0.309)
Constant	0.333
	(0.312)
Observations	798
R^2	0.253
Adjusted R^2	0.240
Residual Std. Error	0.308 (df = 783)
F Statistic	18.973*** (df = 14; 783)

Note: $^{*}p<0.1$; $^{**}p<0.05$; $^{***}p<0.01$

Chapter 7, Appendix 11—Open-ended responses

Orientation (Positive/negative)	Content
Negative	The balance is being tipped toward Blacks. The violence of Blacks in this society accomplishes little. All it does is ruin people's lives.
Negative	BLM is racist and so are blacks and they get everything free.
Negative	Whites are becoming the minority. Blacks want too many handouts. Non-whites want things without having to work for them.
Negative	Blacks feel they are targeted for crimes. They feel they are owed something. Whites are because the minority.
Negative	White people will soon be a minority in their own country. The USA will then be ruled by malignant nonwhites and hispanic speakers. This is very horrifying to think about.
Positive	There are more minorities. More hispanics and blacks. Good that this is happening.
Negative	I see more racism than ever before. It scares me because I don't know what the future holds for us as a country especially when it seems that all Republicans are racists.
Negative	Blacks can riot and have no consequences, whites can die with a knee on their neck and no rioting, minorities can get subsidies and yet whites can not.
Negative	Everything these days is anti-white. Seriously sick of it. You're poking the bear. American people will not like the results if they keep poking us hard enough.
Negative	We are letting race take over in this country. Things, such as "Black Lives Matter" are causing demographic changes. The Asian people are taking over our eateries. [*sic*]
Negative	I think they cheated; they play the victim; they will someday regret what they got done.
Negative	I think people take this too far! People constantly say blacks are oppressed but they are the most racist ones! I myself am biracial and have strong Hispanic values and I am treated no different as long as I live an upstanding lifestyle!
Negative	Racial demographic change is the number of people in an area or region. A communication [*sic*] which was all white now is fifty percent black and fifty percent white. The number of a particular race increased in different areas
Neutral	In the 60's when I was in grade school I read an article about the "Browning of America" so that was 60 years ago and it true then and true now. It's the way it is get over it—I'm white but it is what it is to quote a former president.
Neutral	I believe the demographics are changing so that most people will be of color. The resistant white oligarchs do not like this idea. Hence, battling equal voting rights and rights in general.

Orientation (Positive/negative)	Content
Positive	The country is becoming more diverse. That is likely a good thing. I'm not afraid of the diversity.
Negative?	I THINK WE ARE NOT AGAINST BLACK PEOPLE THAT ARE LAW BIDING CITIZENS I ALSO FEEL THAT IT IS NOT RACIALY MOVITIVE ABOUT ILLEGAL EMAGRENTS CROSSING OUR BORDER DO IT RIGHT BY THE LAW.
Negative	I do not agree with the diversification. US is going to hell. If people don't get together and fight for what is right we will go to war.
Negative	Conditions have improved for blacks. A lot of prejudice has disappeared. However, I think blacks may have more problem with upward mobility.
Negative	Omg it's only the white people vs. the world. If they not white they not racist. If they are dude they racist. God made everybody human in many shape sizes and that includes color. White people just disclose blacks cuz idk maybe they feel threaten but if people didn't beat them they wouldn't seem such a threat. Racism is very much alive!!! Like seriously it's a problem.
Negative	Blacks are taking over. Blacks want something for nothing. The Mexican are invading us.
Negative	Black lives matter. Blacks are rioting and causing a ruckus under the premise that their great, great, great, great, great, great ancestors were wronged. The nation has bent so much to cater blacks that whites are now the minority who are discriminated against. Whites can't speak their minds openly out of fear. Whites can't have a "white history month," or we'd be seen as racist, yet blacks can have black history month, NAACP, specific awards, and get a job because of their race and it's perfectly acceptable.
Positive	It makes me happy. I'm glad blacks are getting treated better. We need this change.
Negative	I see many colored people moving to las vegas and cities like this once they get stimulus checks. I know because I got screwed out of my stimulus checks and was washing their clothes.
Negative	I agree black people gets everything.
Negative	America is "Browning." While that is not necessarily a bad thing, it may cause the slow extinction of the white race. While I disagree with eugenics, I understand why it was implemented in the past.
Negative	White people getting screwed. Big money checks going to minorities. And a lot of unfairness overall!
Negative	The movement of black lives matter has derailed the way the civil rights movement is supposed to work. When the authorities cannot use the power they are given to prevent crime, the system suffers. The concept is correct, the execution of it was wrong.

Chapter 8, Appendix 1—Support for citizens taking law into their own hands + Trump legitimacy, study 2

	Dependent variable	
	patriots_law_in_hands_post	Trump_election_legitimate
	(1)	(2)
big_flip	0.025**	0.026***
	(0.012)	(0.007)
patriots_law_in_hands_pre	0.655***	
	(0.016)	
Trump_election_legitimate_pre	0.870***	
	(0.011)	
Constant	0.034***	0.076***
	(0.011)	(0.010)
Observations	1,966	1,959
R^2	0.468	0.773
Adjusted R^2	0.467	0.772
Residual Std. Error	0.221 (df = 1963)	0.130 (df = 1956)
F Statistic	862.621*** (df = 2; 1963)	3,324.830*** (df = 2; 1956)

Note: *p < 0.1; **p < 0.05; ***p < 0.01

	Dependent variable		
	patriots_law_in_hands_post		
	(1)	(2)	(3)
white_minority	0.025*		
	(0.014)		
white_minority_no_loss	0.011		
	(0.014)		
white_maintain_majority	0.037***		
	(0.013)		
patriots_law_in_hands_pre	0.631***	0.645***	0.671***
	(0.023)	(0.022)	(0.021)
Constant	0.041***	0.037***	0.028**
	(0.013)	(0.012)	(0.012)

	Dependent variable		
	patriots_law_in_hands_post		
	(1)	(2)	(3)
Observations	952	955	1,011
R^2	0.449	0.475	0.499
Adjusted R^2	0.448	0.474	0.498
Residual Std. Error	0.221 (df = 949)	0.214 (df = 952)	0.214 (df = 1008)
F Statistic	386.272*** (df = 2; 949)	430.858*** (df = 2; 952)	501.223*** (df = 2; 1008)

Note: *p < 0.1; **p < 0.05; ***p < 0.01

	Dependent variable		
	Trump_election_legitimate		
	(1)	(2)	(3)
white_minority	0.031*** (0.008)		
white_minority_no_loss	0.013 (0.009)		
white_maintain_majority	0.031*** (0.008)		
Trump_election_legitimate_pre	0.892*** (0.015)	0.894*** (0.016)	0.899*** (0.014)
Constant	0.060*** (0.012)	0.059*** (0.013)	0.055*** (0.012)
Observations	946	952	1,007
R^2	0.801	0.774	0.805
Adjusted R^2	0.800	0.774	0.805
Residual Std. Error	0.126 (df = 943)	0.136 (df = 949)	0.124 (df = 1004)
F Statistic	1,895.654*** (df = 2; 943)	1,626.044*** (df = 2; 949)	2,071.328*** (df = 2; 1004)

Note: *p < 0.1; **p < 0.05; ***p < 0.01

Chapter 8, Appendix 2—Regressions for anti-democratic support, study 1

	Dependent variable
	Trump_use_military_seize_voting
demo_prime	0.035**
	(0.017)
PID	0.061**
	(0.030)
IDEO	0.045
	(0.036)
edu	−0.004
	(0.006)
income	0.011***
	(0.003)
media	−0.025***
	(0.004)
REGION	−0.031
	(0.023)
FEMALE	−0.037**
	(0.018)
race_id	0.00000**
	(0.00000)
Constant	0.400***
	(0.037)
Observations	1,435
R^2	0.058
Adjusted R^2	0.052
Residual Std. Error	0.330 (df = 1425)
F Statistic	9.703*** (df = 9; 1425)

Note: *p < 0.1; **p < 0.05; ***p < 0.01

	Dependent variable
	support_Jan_6
DEMO_PRIME	0.032*
	(0.017)
PID	0.081***
	(0.029)
IDEO	0.072**
	(0.034)
edu	0.004
	(0.006)
income	0.014***
	(0.003)
media	−0.028***
	(0.003)
REGION	−0.030
	(0.022)
FEMALE	−0.044**
	(0.017)
race_id	0.00000**
	(0.00000)
Constant	0.345***
	(0.036)
Observations	1,435
R^2	0.083
Adjusted R^2	0.077
Residual Std. Error	0.317 (df = 1425)
F Statistic	14.308*** (df = 9; 1425)

Note: *p < 0.1; **p < 0.05; ***p < 0.01

Chapter 8, Appendix 3—Emotions about diversification, study 1

	Dependent variable	
	demo_feelings_angry	demo_feelings_worried
	(1)	(2)
demo_prime	0.034**	0.035**
	(0.016)	(0.015)
PID	0.045*	0.072***
	(0.027)	(0.027)
IDEO	0.060*	0.059*
	(0.032)	(0.032)
EDU	−0.022***	−0.018***
	(0.006)	(0.006)
income	0.007***	0.007***
	(0.003)	(0.003)
media	−0.015***	−0.009***
	(0.003)	(0.003)
REGION	−0.036*	−0.029
	(0.021)	(0.020)
FEMALE	−0.015	0.002
	(0.016)	(0.016)
race_id	−0.00000	−0.00000
	(0.00000)	(0.00000)
Constant	0.505***	0.514***
	(0.033)	(0.033)
Observations	1,435	1,435
R^2	0.046	0.041
Adjusted R^2	0.040	0.035
Residual Std. Error (df = 1425)	0.295	0.291
F Statistic (df = 9; 1425)	7.715***	6.779***

Note: *p < 0.1; **p < 0.05; ***p < 0.01

Chapter 8, Appendix 4—Emotions and threat mediating anti-democratic support, study 1

Anger and anxiety mediating support for violent 2024 candidate

Causal Mediation Analysis

Estimate 95% CI Lower 95% CI Upper p-value

Quasi-Bayesian Confidence Intervals

ACME	0.01423	0.00297	0.03	0.013 *
ADE	0.02457	−0.00768	0.06	0.140
Total Effect	0.03880	0.00422	0.07	0.023 *
Prop. Mediated	0.35653	0.06680	1.44	0.036 *
—				
Signif. Codes:	0 "***"	0.001 "**"	0.01 "*"	0.05 "."

Sample Size Used: 1435

Simulations: 2000

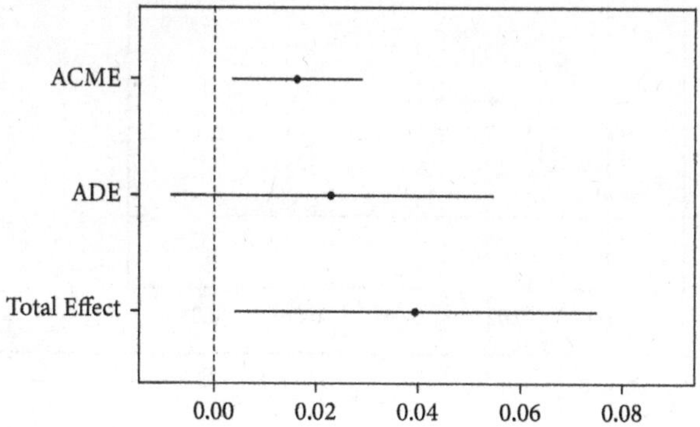

Present threat from Black Americans mediating support for candidate who supports violence

Estimate 95% CI Lower 95% CI Upper p-value

Causal Mediation Analysis

Quasi-Bayesian Confidence Intervals

	Estimate	95% CI Lower	95% CI Upper	p-value
ACME	0.01622	0.00265	0.03	0.015 *
ADE	0.02266	−0.00917	0.05	0.163
Total Effect	0.03888	0.00414	0.07	0.028 *
Prop. Mediated	0.40297	0.02750	1.65	0.043 *

—

Signif. codes: 0 "***" 0.001 "**" 0.01 "*" 0.05 "." 0.1 ' ' 1

Sample Size Used: 1435

Simulations: 2000

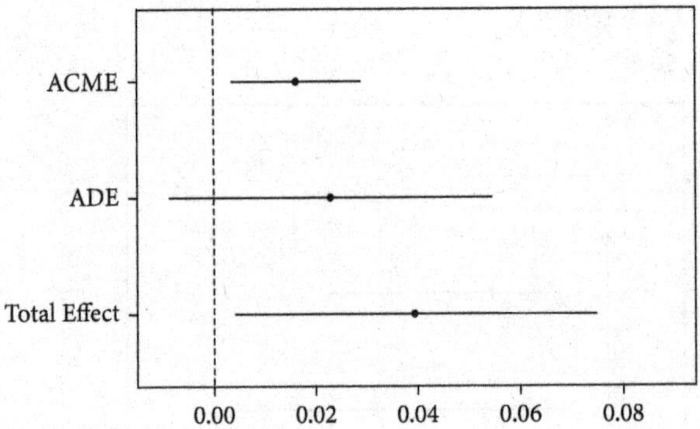

Future threat from Black Americans mediating support for candidate who supports violence
Estimate 95% CI Lower 95% CI Upper p-value
Causal Mediation Analysis

Quasi-Bayesian Confidence Intervals

Acme	0.011865	0.000158	0.02	0.048 *
Ade	0.027324	−0.004135	0.06	0.096 .
Total Effect	0.039189	0.005093	0.08	0.026 *
Prop. Mediated	0.291847	−0.031238	1.18	0.064 .

—

Signif. codes: 0 "***" 0.001 "**" 0.01 "*" 0.05 "." 0.1 ' ' 1

Sample Size Used: 1435

Simulations: 2000

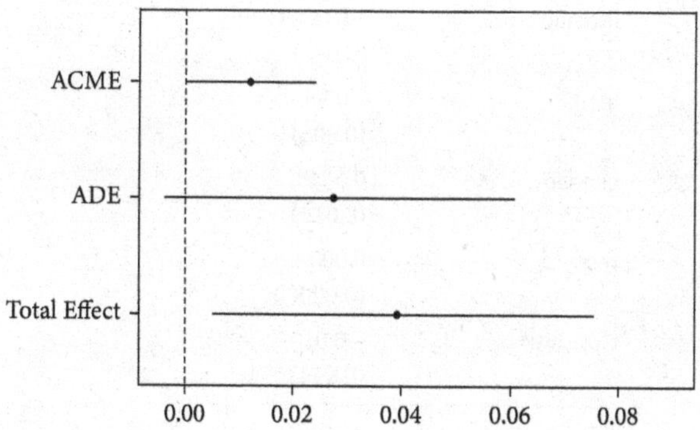

Chapter 8, Appendix 5—Differences in threat across conditions, study 2

	Condition 1	Condition 2	Condition 3
Average threat from Black Americans	0.1663098	0.1749460	0.1820513
P-values for differences between conditions	Conditions 1 vs. 2 p = 0.6345	Conditions 1 vs. 3 p = 0.3751	Conditions 2 vs. 3 p = 0.6945

Chapter 8, Appendix 6—Posttreatment evaluation of ideology, study 2

	Dependent variable
	ideo_post
big_flip	0.033**
	(0.016)
ideo	0.959***
	(0.007)
pid	0.031***
	(0.006)
edu	−0.001
	(0.005)
income	−0.0004
	(0.002)
media	0.003
	(0.003)
gender	0.014
	(0.014)
race_id	0.000
	(0.00000)
Constant	−0.018
	(0.044)
Observations	1,952
R^2	0.971
Adjusted R^2	0.971
Residual Std. Error	0.303 (df = 1943)
F Statistic	8,236.883*** (df = 8; 1943)

Note: *p < 0.1; **p < 0.05; ***p < 0.01

References

"1–1:03 p.m.: Session Begins." n.d. *American Oversight* (blog). Accessed June 17, 2024. https://www.americanoversight.org/timeline/pr-1pm.

"The 2016 SNL Election Special," Saturday Night Live, NBC, aired November 3, 2016, television special. Accessed December 15, 2025. https://www.imdb.com/title/tt6545172/.

Abascal, Maria. 2020. "Contraction as a Response to Group Threat: Demographic Decline and Whites' Classification of People Who Are Ambiguously White." *American Sociological Review* 85 (2): 298–322. https://doi.org/10.1177/0003122420905127.

Acharya, Avidit, Matthew Blackwell, and Maya Sen. 2016. "The Political Legacy of American Slavery." *The Journal of Politics* 78 (3): 621–41. https://doi.org/10.1086/686631.

Ahmed, Amel. 2022. "Is the American Public Really Turning Away from Democracy? Backsliding and the Conceptual Challenges of Understanding Public Attitudes." *Perspectives on Politics* (July): 1–12. https://doi.org/10.1017/S1537592722001062.

Ajinkya, Julie. 2012. "Right-Wing Extremists Aren't the Lone Wolves They Seem to Be." *Center for American Progress* (blog). https://www.americanprogress.org/article/right-wing-extremists-arent-the-lone-wolves-they-seem-to-be/.

Alba, Richard. 2018a. "What Majority-Minority Society? A Critical Analysis of the Census Bureau's Projections of America's Demographic Future." *Socius* 4 (January): 2378023118796932. https://doi.org/10.1177/2378023118796932.

Alba, Richard. 2018b. "What Majority-Minority Society? A Critical Analysis of the Census Bureau's Projections of America's Demographic Future." *Socius* 4 (January): 2378023118796932. https://doi.org/10.1177/2378023118796932.

Alba, Richard, Brenden Beck, and Duygu Basaran Sahin. 2018. "The Rise of Mixed Parentage: A Sociological and Demographic Phenomenon to Be Reckoned With." *The Annals of the American Academy of Political and Social Science* 677 (1): 26–38. https://doi.org/10.1177/0002716218757656.

Alcoff, Linda Martín. 2003. "Latino/as, Asian Americans, and the Black–White Binary." *The Journal of Ethics* 7 (1): 5–27. https://doi.org/10.1023/A:1022870628484.

Anderson, Bryan. 2021. "Critical Race Theory Is a Flashpoint for Conservatives, but What Does It Mean?" PBS NewsHour. November 2. https://www.pbs.org/newshour/education/so-much-buzz-but-what-is-critical-race-theory.

Anderson, Tonnia L. 2019. "Herrenvolk Democracy: The Rise of the Alt-Right in Donald Trump's America." In *Critical Theory and the Humanities in the Age of the Alt-Right*, edited by Christine M. Battista and Melissa R. Sande. Springer International Publishing. https://doi.org/10.1007/978-3-030-18753-8_5.

Biesecker, Michael. 2022. "Ashli Babbitt, Jan. 6 Insurrectionist Portrayed as Martyr by Some, Had Violent Past." PBS News Hour. January 3. https://www.pbs.org/newshour/nation/ashli-babbitt-jan-6-insurrectionist-portrayed-as-martyr-by-some-had-violent-past.

Badger, Emily. 2017. "Immigrant Shock: Can California Predict the Nation's Future?" The Upshot. *New York Times*, February 1. https://www.nytimes.com/2017/02/01/upshot/strife-over-immigrants-can-california-foretell-nations-future.html.

Bakker, Bert N., Yphtach Lelkes, and Ariel Malka. 2020. "Understanding Partisan Cue Receptivity: Tests of Predictions from the Bounded Rationality and Expressive Utility Perspectives." *The Journal of Politics* 82 (3). https://doi.org/10.1086/707616.

Bakker, Bert N., Gijs Schumacher, and Matthijs Rooduijn. 2021. "Hot Politics? Affective Responses to Political Rhetoric." *American Political Science Review* 115 (1): 150–64. https://doi.org/10.1017/S0003055420000519.

Banks, Antoine J. 2016. "Are Group Cues Necessary? How Anger Makes Ethnocentrism among Whites a Stronger Predictor of Racial and Immigration Policy Opinions." *Political Behavior* 38 (3): 635–57. https://doi.org/10.1007/s11109-016-9330-3.

Baram, Marcus. 2008. "Racism, Security Threats Issues for Obama." *ABC News*, May 23. https://abcnews.go.com/Politics/story?id=4918487&page=1.

Barbour, Henry, Sally Bradshaw, Ari Fleischer, Zori Fonalledas, and Glenn McCall. 2013. "Growth & Opportunity Project."(Report). Republican National Committee.

Barnett, Ida B. Wells. 2002. "Lynching, Our National Crime." In *African-American Philosophy: Selected Readings*, edited by Tommy Lee Lott, 420. Hoboken, New Jersey: Prentice-Hall.

Barr, Andy. 2010. "The GOP's No-Compromise Pledge." *Politico*, October 28. https://www.politico.com/story/2010/10/the-gops-no-compromise-pledge-044311.

Bartels, Larry M. 2020a. "Ethnic Antagonism Erodes Republicans' Commitment to Democracy." *Proceedings of the National Academy of Sciences* 117 (37): 22752–9. https://doi.org/10.1073/pnas.2007747117.

Bartels, Larry M. 2020b. "Ethnic Antagonism Erodes Republicans' Commitment to Democracy." *Proceedings of the National Academy of Sciences* 117 (37): 22752–9. https://doi.org/10.1073/pnas.2007747117.

Bartels, Larry M. 2022. "Democracy Erodes from the Top: Public Opinion and Democratic 'Backsliding' in Europe." In *Democracy in Times of Crises: Challenges, Problems and Policy Proposals*, edited by Emmanouil M. L. Economou, Nicholas C. Kyriazis, and Athanasios Platias, 41–67. Cham: Springer International Publishing. https://doi.org/10.1007/978-3-030-97295-0_3.

Beals, Monique. 2022. "Buffalo Shooting Pushes 'Great Replacement Theory' into National Spotlight." *The Hill* (blog), May 16. https://thehill.com/policy/national-security/3489423-buffalo-shooting-pushes-great-replacement-theory-into-national-spotlight/.

Belew, Kathleen. 2018. *Bring the War Home: The White Power Movement and Paramilitary America*. Cambridge, MA: Harvard University Press.

Bernstein, Lenny, Sari Horwitz, and Peter Holley. 2015. "Dylann Roof's Racist Manifesto: 'I Have No Choice.'" *Washington Post*, June 20, sec. National. https://www.washingtonpost.com/national/health-science/authorities-investigate-whether-racist-manifesto-was-written-by-sc-gunman/2015/06/20/f0bd3052-1762-11e5-9ddc-e3353542100c_story.html.

Blake Masters (@bgmasters). 2021. "This reconciliation bill isn't about a budget. It's about mass amnesty for illegal immigrants and unlimited cheap labor for big corporations. Https://T.Co/OsgV1AG6XN." Twitter (now X), October 28. https://twitter.com/bgmasters/status/1453872421249826817.

Blalock, Hubert M. 1967. *Toward a Theory of Minority-Group Relations*. New York: Wiley.

Blum, Rachel M. 2020. *How the Tea Party Captured the GOP: Insurgent Factions in American Politics*. Chicago, IL: University of Chicago Press.

Blumer, Herbert. 1958. "Race Prejudice as a Sense of Group Position." *Pacific Sociological Review* 1 (1): 3–7. https://doi.org/10.2307/1388607.

Bonikowski, Bart. 2017. "Ethno-Nationalist Populism and the Mobilization of Collective Resentment." *The British Journal of Sociology* 68 (S1): S181–213. https://doi.org/10.1111/1468-4446.12325.

Boyd, James. 1970. "Nixon's Southern Strategy." *New York Times*, May 17, sec. Archives. https://www.nytimes.com/1970/05/17/archives/nixons-southern-strategy-its-all-in-the-charts.html.

Brader, Ted, and George E. Marcus. 2013. "Emotion and Political Psychology." In *The Oxford Handbook of Political Psychology*, 2nd ed., edited by Leonie Huddy, David O. Sears, and Jack S. Levy, 165–204. New York: Oxford University Press.

Brader, Ted, Nicholas A. Valentino, and Elizabeth Suhay. 2008. "What Triggers Public Opposition to Immigration? Anxiety, Group Cues, and Immigration Threat." *American Journal of Political Science* 52 (4): 959–78.

Brookover, Wilbur B. 1993. "Education in Prince Edward County, Virginia, 1953–1993." *The Journal of Negro Education* 62 (2): 149–61. https://doi.org/10.2307/2295190.

Bruni, Frank. 2015. "Opinion: The Scary Specter of Ted Cruz." *New York Times*, October 21, sec. Opinion. https://www.nytimes.com/2015/10/21/opinion/the-scary-specter-of-ted-cruz.html.

Budiman, Abby, and Neil G. Ruiz. 2021. "Asian Americans Are the Fastest-Growing Racial or Ethnic Group in the U.S." *Pew Research Center* (blog), April 9. https://www.pewresearch.org/fact-tank/2021/04/09/asian-americans-are-the-fastest-growing-racial-or-ethnic-group-in-the-u-s/.

Burns, Peter, and James G. Gimpel. 2000. "Economic Insecurity, Prejudicial Stereotypes, and Public Opinion on Immigration Policy." *Political Science Quarterly* 115 (2): 201–25. https://doi.org/10.2307/2657900.

Cadava, Geraldo L. 2015. "Jeb Bush's Complicated Relationship with Latino Voters." *Atlantic*, September 1. https://www.theatlantic.com/politics/archive/2015/09/jeb-bush-inadequate-latino-ties/402748/.

Caputo, Marc. 2022. "Poll: Hispanics Aren't Flocking to the GOP, but Democrats Still Have Problems." NBC News, March 21. https://www.nbcnews.com/politics/elections/poll-hispanics-arent-flocking-gop-democrats-still-problems-rcna20794.

Carey, John M., Gretchen Helmke, Brendan Nyhan, Mitchell Sanders, and Susan Stokes. 2019. "Searching for Bright Lines in the Trump Presidency." *Perspectives on Politics* 17 (3): 699–718. https://doi.org/10.1017/S153759271900001X.

Carlson, Tucker. 2022. "Tucker Carlson: The Great Replacement Is an Electoral Strategy." *Fox News*, July 19. https://www.foxnews.com/opinion/tucker-carlson-great-replacement-electoral-strategy.

Carter, Dan T. 1999. *From George Wallace to Newt Gingrich: Race in the Conservative Counterrevolution, 1963–1994*. Rev. ed. Baton Rouge: Louisiana State University Press.

Castro, Gina. 2022. "More than 15% of Black Mississippi Residents Permanently Barred from Voting." Center for Public Integrity. October 6, 2022. http://publicintegrity.

org/politics/elections/who-counts/more-than-15-of-black-mississippi-residents-permanently-barred-from-voting/.

Census. 2011. "2010 Census Shows America's Diversity, 2010 Census, Newsroom, U.S. Census Bureau." https://www.census.gov/newsroom/releases/archives/2010_census/cb11-cn125.html.

Chan, Michael D. 2004. "Alexander Hamilton on Slavery." *The Review of Politics* 66 (2): 207–31.

Chow, Kat. 2017. "'Model Minority' Myth Again Used as a Racial Wedge between Asians and Blacks." NPR, April 19. https://www.npr.org/sections/codeswitch/2017/04/19/524571669/model-minority-myth-again-used-as-a-racial-wedge-between-asians-and-blacks.

Citrin, Jack, Donald P. Green, Christopher Muste, and Cara Wong. 1997. "Public Opinion Toward Immigration Reform: The Role of Economic Motivations." *The Journal of Politics* 59 (3): 858–81. https://doi.org/10.2307/2998640.

Clarke, Chavez. 2020. "BIPOC: What Does It Mean and Where Does It Come From?" *CBS News*, July 2. https://www.cbsnews.com/news/bipoc-meaning-where-does-it-come-from-2020-04-02/.

Clifford, Scott, Geoffrey Sheagley, and Spencer Piston. 2021. "Increasing Precision without Altering Treatment Effects: Repeated Measures Designs in Survey Experiments." *American Political Science Review* 115 (3): 1048–65. https://doi.org/10.1017/S0003055421000241.

Coates, Ta-Nehisi. 2017. "My President Was Black." *Atlantic*, January/February. https://www.theatlantic.com/magazine/archive/2017/01/my-president-was-black/508793/.

Cohen, William. 1969. "Thomas Jefferson and the Problem of Slavery." *The Journal of American History* 56 (3): 503–26. https://doi.org/10.2307/1904203.

Cohn, D'vera. 2010. "Race and the Census: The 'Negro' Controversy." *Pew Research Center's Social & Demographic Trends Project* (blog), January 21. https://www.pewresearch.org/social-trends/2010/01/21/race-and-the-census-the-negro-controversy/.

Cohn, Nate. 2015. "Why Marco Rubio's Chances Are Rising." *New York Times*, October 6, sec. The Upshot. https://www.nytimes.com/2015/10/06/upshot/why-marco-rubio-is-rising.html.

Cohn, Nate. 2016. "The Biggest Danger for Donald Trump: Florida." The Upshot. *New York Times*, July 6. https://www.nytimes.com/2016/07/07/upshot/the-biggest-danger-for-donald-trump-florida.html.

Craig, Maureen, and Jennifer Richeson. 2014a. "More Diverse Yet Less Tolerant? How the Increasingly Diverse Racial Landscape Affects White Americans' Racial Attitudes." *Personality and Social Psychology Bulletin* 40 (6): 750–61. https://doi.org/10.1177/0146167214524993.

Craig, Maureen, and Jennifer Richeson. 2014b. "On the Precipice of a 'Majority-Minority' America: Perceived Status Threat from the Racial Demographic Shift Affects White Americans' Political Ideology." *Psychological Science* 25 (6): 1189–97. https://doi.org/10.1177/0956797614527113.

Craig, Maureen, and Jennifer Richeson. 2017. "Information about the US Racial Demographic Shift Triggers Concerns about Anti-White Discrimination among the Prospective White 'Minority.'" *PLOS ONE* 12 (9): e0185389. https://doi.org/10.1371/journal.pone.0185389.

Craig, Maureen, and Jennifer Richeson. 2018. "Hispanic Population Growth Engenders Conservative Shift among Non-Hispanic Racial Minorities." *Social Psychological and Personality Science* 9 (4): 383–92. https://doi.org/10.1177/1948550617712029.

Craig, Maureen, Julian Rucker, and Jennifer Richeson. 2018. "The Pitfalls and Promise of Increasing Racial Diversity: Threat, Contact, and Race Relations in the 21st Century." *Current Directions in Psychological Science* 27 (3): 188–93. https://doi.org/10.1177/0963721417727860.

Crespino, Joseph. 2016. "Opinion | Why Hillary Clinton Might Win Georgia." Opinion. *New York Times*, August 22. https://www.nytimes.com/2016/08/22/opinion/campaign-stops/why-hillary-clinton-might-win-georgia.html.

Crowder, Kyle. 2000. "The Racial Context of White Mobility: An Individual-Level Assessment of the White Flight Hypothesis." *Social Science Research* 29 (2): 223–57. https://doi.org/10.1006/ssre.1999.0668.

Crowder, Kyle, and Scott J. South. 2008. "Spatial Dynamics of White Flight: The Effects of Local and Extralocal Racial Conditions on Neighborhood Out-Migration." *American Sociological Review* 73 (5): 792–812. https://doi.org/10.1177/000312240807300505.

Davidson, Kizha. 2024. "Why We Use BIPOC." YWCA Seattle, March 12. https://www.ywcaworks.org/blogs/ywca/wed-04062022-0913/why-we-use-bipoc.

Davis, Darren W., and David C. Wilson. 2023. "'Stop the Steal': Racial Resentment, Affective Partisanship, and Investigating the January 6th Insurrection." *The Annals of the American Academy of Political and Social Science* 708 (1): 83–101. https://doi.org/10.1177/00027162241228400.

Dawson, Michael C. 1995. *Behind the Mule: Race and Class in African-American Politics.* Princeton, NJ: Princeton University Press.

Dawson, Michael C., and Lawrence D. Bobo. 2009. "One Year Later and the Myth of a Post-Racial Society." *Du Bois Review: Social Science Research on Race* 6 (2): 247–9. https://doi.org/10.1017/S1742058X09990282.

Day, John Kyle. 2015. *The Southern Manifesto: Massive Resistance and the Fight to Preserve Segregation*. Repr. ed. Jackson, Mississippi: University Press of Mississippi.

Debenedetti, Gabriel. 2016. "They Always Wanted Trump." *Politico Magazine*, November 7. https://www.politico.com/magazine/story/2016/11/hillary-clinton-2016-donald-trump-214428.

Delgado, Richard, and Jean Stefancic. 1998. *The Latino/a Condition: A Critical Reader.* New York, NY: New York University Press.

Dixon, Jeffrey C. 2006. "The Ties That Bind and Those That Don't: Toward Reconciling Group Threat and Contact Theories of Prejudice." *Social Forces* 84 (4): 2179–204. https://doi.org/10.1353/sof.2006.0085.

Domínguez, Arturo. 2022. "Blaming Latinos for Democratic Political Losses Just Needs to Stop (OPINION)." *Latino Rebels* (blog), June 21. https://www.latinorebels.com/2022/06/21/blaminglatinosforpoliticallosses/.

Douthat, Ross. 2017. "Opinion | The Democrats in Their Labyrinth." Opinion. *New York Times*, October 21. https://www.nytimes.com/2017/10/21/opinion/sunday/democrats-alabama-doug-jones.html.

Druckman, James, Erik Peterson, and Rune Slothuus. 2013. "How Elite Partisan Polarization Affects Public Opinion Formation." *American Political Science Review* 107 (1): 57–79.

Du Bois, W. E. B. 2015. *The Problem of the Color Line at the Turn of the Twentieth Century: The Essential Early Essays*. New York, NY: Fordham University Press. https://doi.org/10.2307/j.ctt1287g49.

Du Bois, W. E. B., ed. 2017. *Black Reconstruction in America: Toward a History of the Part Which Black Folk Played in the Attempt to Reconstruct Democracy in America, 1860–1880*. New York: Routledge. https://doi.org/10.4324/9781315147413.

Eatwell, Roger, and Matthew Goodwin. 2018. *National Populism: The Revolt Against Liberal Democracy*. London, England: Penguin UK.

Eidgahy, Kaumron, and Efrén O. Pérez. 2022. "How Wide Is the Arc of Racial Solidarity? People of Color and Middle Easterners and North Africans." *Political Research Quarterly*, March, 10659129221076143. https://doi.org/10.1177/10659129221076143.

Enten, Harry. 2015. "Pols and Polls Say the Same Thing: Jeb Bush Is a Weak Front-Runner." *FiveThirtyEight* (blog), June 15. https://fivethirtyeight.com/features/pols-and-polls-say-the-same-thing-jeb-bush-is-a-weak-front-runner/.

Epperly, Brad, Christopher Witko, Ryan Strickler, and Paul White. 2020. "Rule by Violence, Rule by Law: Lynching, Jim Crow, and the Continuing Evolution of Voter Suppression in the U.S." *Perspectives on Politics* 18 (3): 756–69. https://doi.org/10.1017/S1537592718003584.

Federal Writers' Project, Regional Staff. 2016. *These Are Our Lives*. Chapel Hill, NC: University of North Carolina Press Books.

Feinberg, John S., and Harold O. J. Brown. 2006. *No One Like Him*. Wheaton, IL: Crossway.

Fenno, Richard F., and John R. Hibbing. 2002. *Home Style: House Members in Their Districts*. Longman Classics ed. New York: Pearson College Div.

Folmsbee, Stanley J. 1949. "The Origin of the First 'Jim Crow' Law." *The Journal of Southern History* 15 (2): 235–47. https://doi.org/10.2307/2197999.

Foner, Eric. 1987. "Rights and the Constitution in Black Life during the Civil War and Reconstruction." *The Journal of American History* 74 (3): 863–83. https://doi.org/10.2307/1902157.

Fortuna, Alan. 2019. "3. Makers vs. Takers: Polarizing Rhetoric in the Tea Party Oratorical Network." In *3. Makers vs. Takers: Polarizing Rhetoric in the Tea Party Oratorical Network*, 102–66. Berlin, Germany: De Gruyter. https://doi.org/10.1515/9783110664775-004.

Fossett, Mark, and Jill Kiecolt. 1989. "The Relative Size of Minority Populations and White Racial Attitudes." *Social Science Quarterly* 70 (4): 820–35.

Frankenberg, Ruth. 1993. *White Women, Race Matters: The Social Construction of Whiteness*. NED-New ed. Minneapolis, MN: University of Minnesota Press. https://www.jstor.org/stable/10.5749/j.ctttsnhh.

Franke-Ruta, Garance. 2013. "What You Need to Read in the RNC Election-Autopsy Report." *Atlantic*, March 18. https://www.theatlantic.com/politics/archive/2013/03/what-you-need-to-read-in-the-rnc-election-autopsy-report/274112/.

Frey, William H. 1979. "Central City White Flight: Racial and Nonracial Causes." *American Sociological Review* 44 (3): 425–48. https://doi.org/10.2307/2094885.

Frey, William H. 2012. "Census Projects New 'Majority Minority' Tipping Points." *Brookings* (blog). https://www.brookings.edu/opinions/census-projects-new-majority-minority-tipping-points/.

Fuchs, Lawrence H. 1990. *The American Kaleidoscope: Race, Ethnicity, and the Civic Culture*. Middletown, CT: Wesleyan University Press. http://archive.org/details/americankaleidos00fuch_0.

Gaines, James R. 1993. "From The Managing Editor: Nov. 18, 1993." *Time*, December 2. https://time.com/archive/6724351/from-the-managing-editor-nov-18-1993/.

Gandhi, Jennifer. 2019. "The Institutional Roots of Democratic Backsliding." *The Journal of Politics* 81 (1): e11–16. https://doi.org/10.1086/700653.

Garand, James C., Ping Xu, and Belinda C. Davis. 2017. "Immigration Attitudes and Support for the Welfare State in the American Mass Public." *American Journal of Political Science* 61 (1): 146–62. https://doi.org/10.1111/ajps.12233.

Gaskin, R. 1993. "Conditionals of Freedom and Middle Knowledge." *The Philosophical Quarterly (1950–)* 43 (173): 412–30. https://doi.org/10.2307/2219983.

Gates, Henry Louis. 2019. *Stony the Road: Reconstruction, White Supremacy, and the Rise of Jim Crow*. New York: Penguin Press.

German, Michael. 2022. "Hearing: Domestic Extremism in America: Examining White Supremacist Violence After Recent Attacks." Brennan Center for Justice at New York University Law School.

Gilens, Martin. 1995. "Racial Attitudes and Opposition to Welfare." *The Journal of Politics* 57 (4): 994–1014. https://doi.org/10.2307/2960399.

Gilens, Martin. 1996. "'Race Coding' and White Opposition to Welfare." *American Political Science Review* 90 (3): 593–604. https://doi.org/10.2307/2082611.

Gilens, Martin, Paul M. Sniderman, and James H. Kuklinski. 1998. "Affirmative Action and the Politics of Realignment." *British Journal of Political Science* 28 (1): 159–83. https://doi.org/10.1017/S0007123498000143.

Giles, Micheal W., and Kaenan Hertz. 1994. "Racial Threat and Partisan Identification." *American Political Science Review* 88 (2): 317–26. https://doi.org/10.2307/2944706.

Gittinger, Ted, and Allen Fisher. 2004. "LBJ Champions the Civil Rights Act of 1964." National Archives. https://www.archives.gov/publications/prologue/2004/summer/civil-rights-act.

Glaser, James M. 1994. "Back to the Black Belt: Racial Environment and White Racial Attitudes in the South." *The Journal of Politics* 56 (1): 21–41. https://doi.org/10.2307/2132344.

Gold, Susan Dudley. 2009. *Lyndon B. Johnson*. Tarrytown, NY: Marshall Cavendish.

Goldman, Russell. 2010. "President Obama's Morning After 2010 Midterm Election Results." *ABC News*, November 3. https://abcnews.go.com/Politics/president-obama-morning-after-vote-2010-election-results/story?id=12045687.

Gonzalez-Sobrino, Bianca, and Devon R. Goss. 2019. "Exploring the Mechanisms of Racialization beyond the Black–White Binary." *Ethnic and Racial Studies* 42 (4): 505–10. https://doi.org/10.1080/01419870.2018.1444781.

Graham, Matthew H., and Milan W. Svolik. 2020. "Democracy in America? Partisanship, Polarization, and the Robustness of Support for Democracy in the United States." *American Political Science Review* 114 (2): 392–409. https://doi.org/10.1017/S0003055420000052.

Gray, Rosie. 2017. "Trump Defends White-Nationalist Protesters: 'Some Very Fine People on Both Sides.'" Politics. *The Atlantic*, August 15. https://www.theatlantic.com/

politics/archive/2017/08/trump-defends-white-nationalist-protesters-some-very-fine-people-on-both-sides/537012/.

Green, Donald P., Shang E. Ha, and John G. Bullock. 2010. "Enough Already about 'Black Box' Experiments: Studying Mediation Is More Difficult than Most Scholars Suppose." *The Annals of the American Academy of Political and Social Science* 628 (1): 200–8. https://doi.org/10.1177/0002716209351526.

Grieco, Elizabeth. 2001. "Census 2000 Shows America's Diversity. Census 2000. Newsroom U.S. Census Bureau." https://www.census.gov/newsroom/releases/archives/census_2000/cb01cn61.html.

Gringlas, Sam. 2022. "Step aside, Florida and Ohio. Georgia Is Ready to Be a Political Battleground." *NPR*, December 16, 2022, sec. Politics. https://www.npr.org/2022/12/16/1143194218/step-aside-florida-and-ohio-georgia-is-ready-to-be-a-political-battleground.

Hacker, Andrew. 2003. *Two Nations: Black and White, Separate, Hostile, Unequal.* Repr. ed. New York: Scribner.

Hall, Jacquelyn Dowd. 2005. "The Long Civil Rights Movement and the Political Uses of the Past." *The Journal of American History* 91 (4): 1233–63. https://doi.org/10.2307/3660172.

Hamilton, Alexander, James Madison, and John Jay. 2008. *The Federalist Papers.* Oxford, England: OUP Oxford.

Hamilton, Charles V., and Kwame Ture. 1992. *Black Power: Politics of Liberation in America.* New York, NY: Knopf Doubleday.

Hancock, Ange-Marie. 2004. *The Politics of Disgust: The Public Identity of the Welfare Queen.* New York, NY: New York University Press.

Hanley, Seán, and Milada Anna Vachudova. 2018. "Understanding the Illiberal Turn: Democratic Backsliding in the Czech Republic." *East European Politics* 34 (3): 276–96. https://doi.org/10.1080/21599165.2018.1493457.

Harris, Paul, and Ewen MacAskill. 2010. "US Midterm Election Results Herald New Political Era as Republicans Take House." *The Guardian*, November 3, sec. US news. https://www.theguardian.com/world/2010/nov/03/us-midterm-election-results-tea-party.

Helderman, Rosalind S., and Jon Cohen. 2012. "As Republican Convention Emphasizes Diversity, Racial Incidents Intrude." *Washington Post*, August 29, sec. Politics. https://www.washingtonpost.com/politics/2012/08/29/b9023a52-f1ec-11e1-892d-bc92fee603a7_story.html.

Hill, Lee. 2010. "GOP Pressured to End 'Tea Party Racism.'" NPR, March 25, sec. The Tea Party in America. https://www.npr.org/sections/tellm2011/01/25/03/gop_pressured_to_end_tea_party.html.

Hill, Seth J., Daniel J. Hopkins, and Gregory A. Huber. 2019. "Local Demographic Changes and US Presidential Voting, 2012 to 2016." *Proceedings of the National Academy of Sciences* 116 (50): 25023–8. https://doi.org/10.1073/pnas.1909202116.

Hirano, Shigeo, James M. Snyder, and Michael M. Ting. 2009. "Distributive Politics with Primaries." *The Journal of Politics* 71 (4): 1467–80. https://doi.org/10.1017/S0022381609990247.

Hochschild, Arlie Russell. 2016. *Strangers in Their Own Land: Anger and Mourning on the American Right.* New York: The New Press.

Hoefer, Carl. 2023. "Causal Determinism." In *The Stanford Encyclopedia of Philosophy*, edited by Edward N. Zalta and Uri Nodelman, Spring. Metaphysics Research

Lab, Stanford University. https://plato.stanford.edu/archives/spr2023/entries/determinism-causal/.

Holpuch, Amanda. 2021. "US Capitol's Last Breach Was More than 200 Years Ago." *The Guardian*, January 7, sec. US news. https://www.theguardian.com/us-news/2021/jan/06/us-capitol-building-washington-history-breach.

Hooker, Juliet. 2023. *Black Grief/White Grievance: The Politics of Loss*. Princeton, NJ: Princeton University Press.

Hopkins, Daniel J. 2021. "The Activation of Prejudice and Presidential Voting: Panel Evidence from the 2016 U.S. Election." *Political Behavior* 43 (2): 663–86. https://doi.org/10.1007/s11109-019-09567-4.

Horowitz, Juliana Menasce, Kiley Hurst, and Dana Braga. 2023. "1. Views on the Black Lives Matter Movement." *Pew Research Center* (blog), June 14. https://www.pewresearch.org/social-trends/2023/06/14/views-on-the-black-lives-matter-movement/.

Horwitz, Joshua, and Casey Anderson. 2009. "The Civil War and Reconstruction." In *Guns, Democracy, and the Insurrectionist Idea*, 118–36. Ann Arbor, MI: University of Michigan Press. https://doi.org/10.2307/j.ctv3znzcm.9.

Hughes, Langston, and Arnold Rampersad. 1993. *The Big Sea: An Autobiography*. 2nd ed. New York: Hill and Wang.

Husain, Atiya. 2019. "Moving beyond (and Back to) the Black–White Binary: A Study of Black and White Muslims' Racial Positioning in the United States." In *The Mechanisms of Racialization beyond the Black/White Binary*. Oxfordshire, UK: Routledge.

Ignatiev, Nole. 2008. *How the Irish Became White*. New York: Routledge. https://doi.org/10.4324/9780203473009.

Jacoby, Tamar. 2009. *Reinventing the Melting Pot: The New Immigrants and What It Means To Be American*. New York, NY: Basic Books.

Jardina, Ashley. 2019. *White Identity Politics*. Cambridge, England: Cambridge University Press.

Johnson, Lyndon B. 2014. "A Force of Nature." In *Effective Presidency*, 2nd ed. Oxfordshire, UK: Routledge.

Jonsson, Patrik. 2008. "After Obama's Win, White Backlash Festers in US." *Christian Science Monitor*, November 17. https://www.csmonitor.com/USA/Politics/2008/1117/p03s01-uspo.html.

Kalmoe, Nathan P., and Lilliana Mason. 2022. *Radical American Partisanship: Mapping Violent Hostility, Its Causes, and the Consequences for Democracy*. Chicago, IL: University of Chicago Press.

Karpowitz, Christopher F., J. Quin Monson, Kelly D. Patterson, and Jeremy C. Pope. 2011. "Tea Time in America? The Impact of the Tea Party Movement on the 2010 Midterm Elections." *PS: Political Science & Politics* 44 (2): 303–9. https://doi.org/10.1017/S1049096511000138.

Katz, Andrew. 2017. "Scenes from the Deadly Unrest in Charlottesville." *Time*. https://time.com/charlottesville-white-nationalist-rally-clashes/.

Key, Valdimer Orlando, and Alexander Heard. 1984. *Southern Politics in State and Nation*. Knoxville, Tennessee: University of Tennessee Press.

Kilbride, Daniel. 2006. Review of *New York Burning: Liberty, Slavery, and Conspiracy in Eighteenth-Century Manhattan*, by Jill Lepore. *Pennsylvania History: A Journal of Mid-Atlantic Studies* 73 (2): 263–65.

Killingsworth, Silvia. 2015. "How Hispanic Is Jeb Bush?." *New Yorker*, April 6. https://www.newyorker.com/news/news-desk/how-hispanic-is-jeb-bush.

Kim, Claire Jean. 1999. "The Racial Triangulation of Asian Americans." *Politics & Society* 27 (1): 105–38. https://doi.org/10.1177/0032329299027001005.

Kinder, Donald R., and Tali Mendelberg. 1995. "Cracks in American Apartheid: The Political Impact of Prejudice among Desegregated Whites." *The Journal of Politics* 57 (2): 402–24. https://doi.org/10.2307/2960313.

King, Ledyard. 2015. "Republicans Need More than a Marco Rubio Primary Win to Win over Hispanics." *USA Today*, updated October 16. https://www.usatoday.com/story/news/politics/elections/2015/10/16/marco-rubio-gop-trouble-winning-hispanic-vote/74013866/.

King, Ryan D., and Darren Wheelock. 2007. "Group Threat and Social Control: Race, Perceptions of Minorities and the Desire to Punish." *Social Forces* 85 (3): 1255–80. https://doi.org/10.1353/sof.2007.0045.

Kistner, Tyler. 2022. "PolitiFact: Claims That Biden Is 'Secretly' Flying Immigrants into U.S. Cities Ignore Key Facts." @politifact, March 16. https://www.politifact.com/factchecks/2022/mar/16/tyler-kistner/claims-biden-secretly-flying-immigrants-us-cities-/.

Klar, Samara. 2014. "Identity and Engagement among Political Independents in America." *Political Psychology* 35 (4): 577–91. https://doi.org/10.1111/pops.12036.

Klar, Samara, and Yanna Krupnikov. 2016. *Independent Politics*. Cambridge, England: Cambridge University Press.

Klar, Samara, Yanna Krupnikov, and John Barry Ryan. 2022. "Who Are Leaners? How True Independents Differ from the Weakest Partisans and Why It Matters." *The Forum* 20 (1): 155–67. https://doi.org/10.1515/for-2022-2048.

Knowles, Eric D., Linda R. Tropp, and Mao Mogami. 2022. "When White Americans See 'Non-Whites' as a Group: Belief in Minority Collusion and Support for White Identity Politics." *Group Processes & Intergroup Relations* 25 (3): 768–90. https://doi.org/10.1177/13684302211030009.

Kraus, Joe. 1999. "How The Melting Pot Stirred America: The Reception of Zangwill's Play and Theater's Role in the American Assimilation Experience." *MELUS* 24 (3): 3–19. https://doi.org/10.2307/468036.

Krosch, Amy R., Suzy J. Park, Jesse Walker, and Ari R. Lisner. 2022. "The Threat of a Majority-Minority U.S. Alters White Americans' Perception of Race." *Journal of Experimental Social Psychology* 99 (March): 104266. https://doi.org/10.1016/j.jesp.2021.104266.

Kuhn, Thomas S. 1996. *The Structure of Scientific Revolutions*. 3rd ed. Chicago: University of Chicago Press.

Kuziemko, Ilyana, and Ebonya Washington. 2018. "Why Did the Democrats Lose the South? Bringing New Data to an Old Debate." *American Economic Review* 108 (10): 2830–67. https://doi.org/10.1257/aer.20161413.

Lahut, Jake. 2022. "Trump Said 'I Don't Effing Care That They Have Weapons. They're Not Here to Hurt Me' as an Angry Mob Avoided Metal Detectors at His January 6 Speech: Ex-Aide Testimony." *Business Insider*, June 28. https://www.businessinsider.com/trump-weapons-january-6-crowd-dont-fucking-care-2022-6.

Langer, Arnim, and Kristien Smedts. 2013. "Seeing Is Not Believing: Perceptions of Horizontal Inequalities in Africa." *Centre for Research on Peace and Development (CRPD) Working Paper* 16.

"Leaders Say Blacks Want to Be Called 'African-Americans.'" n.d. *AP News*. Accessed December 19, 2022. https://apnews.com/article/089fc3ab25b86e14deeefae3adb7a5ad.

Lee, Robert G. 2010. "14. The Cold War Origins of the Model Minority Myth." In *14. The Cold War Origins of the Model Minority Myth.*, 256–71. New Brunswick, NJ: Rutgers University Press. https://doi.org/10.36019/9780813549330-016.

Lee, Taeku. 2011. "Somewhere Over the Rainbow? Post-Racial & Pan-Racial Politics in the Age of Obama." *Daedalus* 140 (2): 136–50. https://doi.org/10.1162/DAED_a_00083.

"Letter from Thomas Jefferson to John Holmes, April 22, 1820. U.S. Capitol: Visitor Center." n.d. Accessed April 18, 2023. https://www.visitthecapitol.gov/artifact/letter-thomas-jefferson-john-holmes-april-22-1820.

Levitsky, Steven, and Daniel Ziblatt. 2018. *How Democracies Die*. New York, NY: Crown.

Levy, Morris, and Dowell Myers. 2021. "Racial Projections in Perspective: Public Reactions to Narratives about Rising Diversity." *Perspectives on Politics* 19 (4): 1147–64. https://doi.org/10.1017/S1537592720003679.

Logan, Rayford W. 1997. *The Betrayal of the Negro: From Rutherford B. Hayes to Woodrow Wilson*. New York: Da Capo Press.

Lopez, Ian F. Haney. 2005. "Race on the 2010 Census: Hispanics & the Shrinking White Majority." American Academy of Arts & Sciences. https://www.amacad.org/publication/race-2010-census-hispanics-shrinking-white-majority.

Lopez, Ian F. Haney. 2010. "Is the Post in Post-Racial the Blind in Colorblind." *Cardozo Law Review* 32:807.

Lopez, Mark Hugo, Ana Gonzalez-Barrera, Jens Manuel Krogstad, and Gustavo López. 2016. "4. Latinos and the Political Parties." *Pew Research Center's Hispanic Trends Project* (blog), October 11. https://www.pewresearch.org/hispanic/2016/10/11/latinos-and-the-political-parties/.

Love, Bettina L., and Brandelyn Tosolt. 2010. "Reality or Rhetoric? Barack Obama and Post-Racial America." *Race, Gender & Class* 17 (3/4): 19–37.

Lührmann, Anna, and Staffan I. Lindberg. 2019. "A Third Wave of Autocratization Is Here: What Is New about It?" *Democratization* 26 (7): 1095–113. https://doi.org/10.1080/13510347.2019.1582029.

Ly, Sarah Boxer, Dakin Andone, Laura. 2022. "Buffalo Shooting Suspect Said He Committed Massacre 'for the Future of the White Race' in Note Apologizing to His Family, Affidavit Says." CNN. https://www.cnn.com/2022/06/16/us/buffalo-shooting-suspect-federal-court/index.html.

Lynch, Myles. 2021. "Disloyalty & Disqualification: Reconstructing Section 3 of the Fourteenth Amendment." *William & Mary Bill of Rights Journal* 30 (1): 153.

Maccaskill, Nolan, and Connor Sheets. 2022. "'Another Dylann Roof . . . Another Emmett Till': Buffalo Reels from Racist Mass Shooting." *Los Angeles Times*, May 15. https://www.latimes.com/world-nation/story/2022-05-15/another-dylann-roof-another-emmett-till-buffalo-reeling-from-racist-attack-at-market.

Major, Brenda, Alison Blodorn, and Gregory Major Blascovich. 2018. "The Threat of Increasing Diversity: Why Many White Americans Support Trump in the 2016 Presidential Election." *Group Processes & Intergroup Relations* 21 (6): 931–40. https://doi.org/10.1177/1368430216677304.

Maletz, Donald J. 2002. "Tocqueville's Tyranny of the Majority Reconsidered." *The Journal of Politics* 64 (3): 741–63. https://doi.org/10.1111/1468-2508.00148.

Manby, Bronwen. 1995. "South Africa: Minority Conflict and the Legacy of Minority Rule." *The Fletcher Forum of World Affairs* 19 (1): 27–52.

Marcus, G. E. 2000. "Emotions in Politics." *Annual Review of Political Science* 3 (1): 221–50. https://doi.org/10.1146/annurev.polisci.3.1.221.

Marinov, Nikolay, and Maria Popova. 2021. "Will the Real Conspiracy Please Stand Up: Sources of Post-Communist Democratic Failure." SSRN Scholarly Paper ID 3845517. Rochester, New York: Social Science Research Network. https://doi.org/10.2139/ssrn.3845517.

Martin, Ben L. 1991. "From Negro to Black to African American: The Power of Names and Naming." *Political Science Quarterly* 106 (1): 83–107. https://doi.org/10.2307/2152175.

Martin, Rod. 2015. "Seven Things That Mattered in the 2012 Election." *Fox News*, March 9. https://www.foxnews.com/opinion/seven-things-that-mattered-in-the-2012-election.

Mason, Lilliana. 2018. *Uncivil Agreement: How Politics Became Our Identity*. Illustrated ed. Chicago: University of Chicago Press.

Mason, Lilliana, Julie Wronski, and John V. Kane. 2021. "Activating Animus: The Uniquely Social Roots of Trump Support." *American Political Science Review*, 1–9. https://doi.org/10.1017/S0003055421000563.

Mayhew, David R. 2004. *Congress: The Electoral Connection*. 2nd ed. New Haven, CT: Yale University Press.

McCoy, Jennifer, Tahmina Rahman, and Murat Somer. 2018. "Polarization and the Global Crisis of Democracy: Common Patterns, Dynamics, and Pernicious Consequences for Democratic Polities." *American Behavioral Scientist* 62 (1): 16–42. https://doi.org/10.1177/0002764218759576.

McDonald, Jason J. 2007. *American Ethnic History: Themes and Perspectives*. Rutgers University Press.

McMillen, Neil R. 1990. *Dark Journey: Black Mississippians in the Age of Jim Crow*. Champaign, IL: University of Illinois Press.

Menand, Louis. 2020. "The Changing Meaning of Affirmative Action." *New Yorker*, January 13. https://www.newyorker.com/magazine/2020/01/20/have-we-outgrown-the-need-for-affirmative-action.

Mendelberg, Tali. 2001. *The Race Card: Campaign Strategy, Implicit Messages, and the Norm of Equality*. Princeton, NJ: Princeton University Press.

Miller, Cassie. 2020. "SPLC Poll Finds Substantial Support for 'Great Replacement' Theory and Other Hard-Right Ideas." Southern Poverty Law Center. https://www.splcenter.org/news/2022/06/01/poll-finds-support-great-replacement-hard-right-ideas.

Miller, Kelly. 1937. *Negroes or Colored People?* http://archive.org/details/miller-opportunity-may-1937.

Miodownik, Dan, and Lilach Nir. 2016. "Receptivity to Violence in Ethnically Divided Societies: A Micro-level Mechanism of Perceived Horizontal Inequalities." *Studies in Conflict & Terrorism* 39 (1): 22–45.

Mohamed, Ali Noor. 2022. "Influence of the Supreme Court's *Plessy v. Ferguson* Decision on Southern Editorial Arguments during the 'Massive Resistance' to Integration: Perspective from Alabama." *Howard Journal of Communications* 33 (3): 281–96. https://doi.org/10.1080/10646175.2021.1985660.

Mutnik, Ally, and Sarah Ferris. 2022. "Latino Democrats Vent Their Fury After Foreboding Special Election Loss in Texas." *Politico*. https://www.politico.com/news/2022/06/15/latino-democrats-election-texas-00040057.

Mutz, Diana C. 2018. "Status Threat, Not Economic Hardship, Explains the 2016 Presidential Vote." *Proceedings of the National Academy of Sciences* 115 (19): E4330–39. https://doi.org/10.1073/pnas.1718155115.

Myrdal, Gunnar. 1995. *An American Dilemma: The Negro Problem and Modern Democracy*. New Brunswick, NJ: Routledge.

NAACP. 2010. "The Tea Party Movement: NAACP." https://naacp.org/resources/tea-party-movement.

Nagourney, Adam. 2008. "Obama Elected President as Racial Barrier Falls." *New York Times*, November 5, sec. US. https://www.nytimes.com/2008/11/05/us/politics/05elect.html.

National Advisory Commission on Civil Disorders, and Julian E. Zelizer. 2016. *The Kerner Report*. Princeton, NJ: Princeton University Press.

Neidig, Harper. 2016. "Trump Says 2016 Is the GOP's Last Chance to Win." *The Hill* (blog), September 9. https://thehill.com/blogs/ballot-box/presidential-races/295264-trump-this-will-be-the-last-election-that-the-republicans/.

New-York Daily Tribune. 1860. "The American Experiment." November 27. https://www.historians.org/teaching-and-learning/teaching-resources-for-historians/sixteen-months-to-sumter/newspaper-index/new-york-daily-tribune/the-american-experiment.

Norris, Pippa, and Ronald Inglehart. 2019. *Cultural Backlash: Trump, Brexit, and Authoritarian Populism*. Cambridge, England: Cambridge University Press.

Olver, Christopher. 2011. "Impact of the Tea Party Movement on the 2010 Election." *The Journalist's Resource* (blog), July 6. https://journalistsresource.org/politics-and-government/tea-party-movement-2010-midterm-elections/.

Omi, Michael, and Howard Winant. 2014. *Racial Formation in the United States*. 3rd ed. New York: Routledge.

Pape, Robert A. 2021. "The Jan. 6 Insurrectionists Aren't Who You Think They Are." *Foreign Policy* (blog). https://foreignpolicy.com/2022/01/06/trump-capitol-insurrection-january-6-insurrectionists-great-replacement-white-nationalism/.

Passemiers, Lazlo. 2016. "Safeguarding White Minority Power: The South African Government and the Secession of Katanga, 1960–1963." *South African Historical Journal* 68 (1): 70–91. https://doi.org/10.1080/02582473.2015.1118882.

Patil, Moushmi. 2021. "Affirmative Action, Asian Americans, and the Black/White Binary." SSRN Scholarly Paper. Rochester, New York. https://papers.ssrn.com/abstract=3890197.

Pear, Robert, and Carl Hulse. 2007. "Immigration Bill Fails to Survive Senate Vote." *New York Times*, June 28, sec. Washington. https://www.nytimes.com/2007/06/28/washington/28cnd-immig.html.

Peay, Periloux C., and Tyler Camarillo. 2021. "No Justice! Black Protests? No Peace: The Racial Nature of Threat Evaluations of Nonviolent #BlackLivesMatter Protests." *Social Science Quarterly* 102 (1): 198–208. https://doi.org/10.1111/ssqu.12902.

Peisner, David. 2009. "Why White Supremacists Support Barack Obama." Esquire. June 11. https://www.esquire.com/news-politics/news/a4719/racists-support-obama-061308/.

Pérez, Efrén. 2021. *Diversity's Child: People of Color and the Politics of Identity*. Chicago: University of Chicago Press.

Pérez, Efrén, Crystal Robertson, and Bianca Vicuña. 2022. "Prejudiced When Climbing Up or When Falling Down? Why Some People of Color Express Anti-Black Racism." *American Political Science Review* (June): 1–16. https://doi.org/10.1017/S0003055422000545.

Pérez, Efrén, Bianca V. Vicuña, Alisson Ramos, Kevin Phan, Mariella Solano, and Eric Tillett. 2022. "Bridging the Gaps between Us: Explaining When and Why People of Color Express Shared Political Views." *Political Behavior* (May). https://doi.org/10.1007/s11109-022-09797-z.

Perlstein, Rick. 2009. *Nixonland: The Rise of a President and the Fracturing of America*. Repr. ed. New York: Scribner.

Perlstein, Rick. 2012. "Exclusive: Lee Atwater's Infamous 1981 Interview on the Southern Strategy," November 13. https://www.thenation.com/article/archive/exclusive-lee-atwaters-infamous-1981-interview-southern-strategy/.

Phillips, Amber. 2021. "Analysis: 'They're Rapists.' President Trump's Campaign Launch Speech Two Years Later, Annotated." *Washington Post*, November 25. https://www.washingtonpost.com/news/the-fix/wp/2017/06/16/theyre-rapists-presidents-trump-campaign-launch-speech-two-years-later-annotated/.

Phoenix, Davin L. 2019. *The Anger Gap: How Race Shapes Emotion in Politics*. Cambridge, England: Cambridge University Press.

Pildes, Richard H. 2000. "Democracy, Anti-Democracy, and the Cannon Symposium: The Canon(s) of Constitutional Law." *Constitutional Commentary* 17 (2): 295–320.

Pollack, Jack. 1947. "Literacy Tests: Southern Style." Accessed December 6, 2025. https://storyoftheweek.loa.org/2016/10/literacy-tests-southern-style.html.

Prewitt, Kenneth. 2002. "Demography, Diversity, and Democracy: The 2000 Census Story." *Brookings* (blog). https://www.brookings.edu/articles/demography-diversity-and-democracy-the-2000-census-story/.

PRRI. 2021. "Competing Visions of America: An Evolving Identity or a Culture Under Attack? Findings from the 2021 American Values Survey." *PRRI* (blog). https://www.prri.org/research/competing-visions-of-america-an-evolving-identity-or-a-culture-under-attack/.

Przeworski, Adam. 1991. *Democracy and the Market: Political and Economic Reforms in Eastern Europe and Latin America*. Studies in Rationality and Social Change. Cambridge: Cambridge University Press. https://doi.org/10.1017/CBO9781139172493.

Quillian, Lincoln. 1995. "Prejudice as a Response to Perceived Group Threat: Population Composition and Anti-Immigrant and Racial Prejudice in Europe." *American Sociological Review* 60 (4): 586–611. https://doi.org/10.2307/2096296.

Quillian, Lincoln. 1996. "Group Threat and Regional Change in Attitudes Toward African-Americans." *American Journal of Sociology* 102 (3): 816–60. https://doi.org/10.1086/230998.

Rable, George C. 2007. *But There Was No Peace: The Role of Violence in the Politics of Reconstruction*. Athens, GA: University of Georgia Press.

Raleigh News and Observer. 1898. "The White Declaration of Independence." http://people.uncw.edu/schmidt/Misc/1898/1898WhiteDec.html.

Ray, Rashawn, and Alexandra Gibbons. 2021. "Why Are States Banning Critical Race Theory?" *Brookings* (blog), July 2. https://www.brookings.edu/blog/fixgov/2021/07/02/why-are-states-banning-critical-race-theory/.

Rea, Michael. 2011. *The Oxford Handbook of Philosophical Theology*. Edited by Thomas P. Flint. Repr. ed. Oxford: Oxford University Press.

Reed, Adolph. 2022. *The South: Jim Crow and Its Afterlives*. London: Verso.

Reichelmann, Ashley V., and Matthew O. Hunt. 2021. "The Multidimensionality of Racial Threat: A Consideration of Its Affective Dimension." In *Advances in Group Processes*, edited by Shane R. Thye and Edward J. Lawler, 38:53–74. Emerald Publishing. https://doi.org/10.1108/S0882-614520210000038003.

Rep. Matt Gaetz (@RepMattGaetz). 2020. "There is an attempted cultural genocide going on in America right now. It calls for patriots to stand up and say that America is a great country worthy of our pride and our defense. Https://T.Co/Zhzic8c5qL." Twitter (now X), July 12. https://twitter.com/RepMattGaetz/status/1282320656500174848.

Republican Party (Ill.). Convention (1858: Springfield, Ill), and Abraham Lincoln. 1858. *Proceedings of the Republican State Convention, Held at Spingfield [Sic], Illinois, June 16th, 1858*. Springfield, IL: Bailhache & Baker. http://archive.org/details/proceedingsofr00repu.

Roberts, Dan. 2013. "Ted Cruz Pulls All-Nighter as Marathon Anti-Obamacare Speech Churns On." *The Guardian*, September 25, sec. US news. https://www.theguardian.com/world/2013/sep/25/ted-cruz-marathon-speech-obamacare.

Rodd, Scott. 2019. "California's Population Is Majority-Minority. The Attorneys Who Represent It Are Overwhelmingly White. - Capradio.Org." https://www.capradio.org/articles/2019/06/20/californias-population-is-majority-minority-the-attorneys-who-represent-it-are-overwhelmingly-white/.

Rossell, Christine H. 1975. "School Desegregation and White Flight." *Political Science Quarterly* 90 (4): 675–95. https://doi.org/10.2307/2148750.

Rothschild, Jacob E. 2020. "Identities, Interest Group Coalitions, and Intergroup Relations." *Politics, Groups, and Identities* 0 (0): 1–18. https://doi.org/10.1080/21565503.2020.1756358.

Rothschild, Jacob E., Adam J. Howat, Richard M. Shafranek, and Ethan C. Busby. 2019. "Pigeonholing Partisans: Stereotypes of Party Supporters and Partisan Polarization." *Political Behavior* 41 (2): 423–43. https://doi.org/10.1007/s11109-018-9457-5.

Schickler, Eric. 2016. *Racial Realignment: The Transformation of American Liberalism, 1932–1965*. Princeton, NJ: Princeton University Press.

Schlesinger, Arthur Meier. 1998. *The Disuniting of America: Reflections on a Multicultural Society*. Rev. and enlarged ed. New York: W. W. Norton.

Schlueter, Elmar, and Peer Scheepers. 2010. "The Relationship between Outgroup Size and Anti-Outgroup Attitudes: A Theoretical Synthesis and Empirical Test of Group Threat and Intergroup Contact Theory." *Social Science Research* 39 (2): 285–95. https://doi.org/10.1016/j.ssresearch.2009.07.006.

Schorr, Daniel. 2008. "A New, 'Post-Racial' Political Era in America." NPR, January 28. https://www.npr.org/templates/story/story.php?storyId=18489466.

Schuessler, Jennifer. 2020. "Alexander Hamilton, Enslaver? New Research Says Yes." *New York Times*, November 9, sec. Arts. https://www.nytimes.com/2020/11/09/arts/alexander-hamilton-enslaver-research.html.

Sears, David O., and Victoria Savalei. 2006. "The Political Color Line in America: Many 'Peoples of Color' or Black Exceptionalism?" *Political Psychology* 27 (6): 895–924. https://doi.org/10.1111/j.1467-9221.2006.00542.x.

Shapiro, Herbert. 1964. "The Ku Klux Klan during Reconstruction: The South Carolina Episode." *The Journal of Negro History* 49 (1): 34–55. https://doi.org/10.2307/2716475.

Signer, Michael. 2015. *Becoming Madison: The Extraordinary Origins of the Least Likely Founding Father*. Illustrated ed. New York: PublicAffairs.

Silver, Nate. 2015. "Donald Trump Is the World's Greatest Troll." *FiveThirtyEight* (blog), July 20. https://fivethirtyeight.com/features/donald-trump-is-the-worlds-greatest-troll/.

Smith, Michael A., Kevin Anderson, and Chapman Rackaway. 2015. *State Voting Laws in America*. New York: Palgrave Macmillan US. https://doi.org/10.1057/9781137483584.

Smith, Rogers M. 1993. "Beyond Tocqueville, Myrdal, and Hartz: The Multiple Traditions in America." *American Political Science Review* 87 (3): 549–66. https://doi.org/10.2307/2938735.

Smith, Rogers M. 1997. *Civic Ideals: Conflicting Visions of Citizenship in U.S. History*. New Haven, CT: Yale University Press.

Sohoni, Deenesh. 2022. "The Coming Majority-Minority State?: Media Coverage of U.S. Census Projections, Demographic Threat, and the Construction of Racial Boundaries." *The Sociological Quarterly* 63 (1): 94–113. https://doi.org/10.1080/00380253.2020.1792810.

"Special Message: The American Presidency Project." n.d. Accessed May 4, 2023. https://www.presidency.ucsb.edu/documents/special-message-2071.

Starkes, Taleeb. 2016. *Black Lies Matter: Why Lies Matter to the Race Grievance Industry*. North Charleston, South Carolina: CreateSpace Independent Publishing Platform.

Stewart, Katherine, Timothy Noah, Timothy Noah, Kate Aronoff, Kate Aronoff, Walter Shapiro, Walter Shapiro, et al. 2022. "The Democratic Party Is Shedding Latino Voters. Here's Why." *The New Republic*, May 11. https://newrepublic.com/article/166406/democrats-losing-latino-voters-2022.

Stonecipher, Elliott, and John S. Baker. 2010. "John S. Baker and Elliott Stonecipher: The 2010 Census Will Violate the Constitution." *Wall Street Journal*, August 9. https://www.wsj.com/articles/SB10001424052970204908604574332950796281832.

Swarns, Rachel L. 2008. "Vaulting the Racial Divide, Obama Persuaded Americans to Follow." *New York Times*, November 5, sec. US. https://www.nytimes.com/2008/11/05/us/politics/05race.html.

Takaki, Ronald. 1993. *A Different Mirror: A History of Multicultural America*. Back Bay Books.

Tesler, Michael. 2016. *Post-Racial or Most-Racial?: Race and Politics in the Obama Era. Post-Racial or Most-Racial?* Chicago: University of Chicago Press. https://doi.org/10.7208/9780226353159.

Tesler, Michael, and David O. Sears. 2010. *Obama's Race: The 2008 Election and the Dream of a Post-Racial America*. Illustrated ed. Chicago: University of Chicago Press.

"The Mississippi Constitution of 1890 as Originally Adopted." n.d. Accessed May 9, 2023. https://www.mshistorynow.mdah.ms.gov/issue/mississippi-constitution-of-1890-as-originally-adopted.

Thompson, Andrew Ifedapo, and Ethan C. Busby. 2021. "Defending the Dog Whistle: The Role of Justifications in Racial Messaging." *Political Behavior*, November 30. https://doi.org/10.1007/s11109-021-09759-x.

Thurston, Chloe N. 2018. *At the Boundaries of Homeownership: Credit, Discrimination, and the American State.* Cambridge, England: Cambridge University Press.

Tocqueville, Alexis. 2003. *Democracy in America: And Two Essays on America.* London, UK: Penguin UK.

"Trump's Tweet about Pence Seen as Critical Moment during Riot." n.d. *Wall Street Journal.* Accessed June 17, 2024. https://www.wsj.com/livecoverage/jan-6-hearing-today-trump/card/trump-s-tweet-about-pence-seen-as-critical-moment-during-riot-fmPxoFkeoTKxi0NqPLCL.

"U.S. Constitution: Fifteenth Amendment, Resources, Constitution Annotated, Congress.Gov, Library of Congress." n.d. Accessed December 19, 2022. https://constitution.congress.gov/constitution/amendment-15/.

United States Congress. 1900. *Congressional Record: Proceedings and Debates of the... Congress.* U.S. Government Printing Office.

Vachudova, Milada Anna. 2020. "Ethnopopulism and Democratic Backsliding in Central Europe." *East European Politics* 36 (3): 318–40. https://doi.org/10.1080/21599165.2020.1787163.

Valelly, Richard M. 2004. *The Two Reconstructions: The Struggle for Black Enfranchisement.* American Politics and Political Economy Series. Chicago: University of Chicago Press. https://press.uchicago.edu/ucp/books/book/chicago/T/bo3612558.html.

Valentino, Nicholas A, Carly Wayne, and Marzia Oceno. 2018. "Mobilizing Sexism: The Interaction of Emotion and Gender Attitudes in the 2016 US Presidential Election." *Public Opinion Quarterly* 82 (S1): 799–821. https://doi.org/10.1093/poq/nfy003.

Vargas, Ramon Antonio. 2023. "US Capitol Rioter Who Wore Horned Headdress to Be Released Early." *The Guardian*, March 31, sec. US news. https://www.theguardian.com/us-news/2023/mar/31/jan-6-rioter-qanon-release-jacob-chansley.

Vickery, Kenneth P. 1974. "'Herrenvolk' Democracy and Egalitarianism in South Africa and the U.S. South." *Comparative Studies in Society and History* 16 (3): 309–28. https://doi.org/10.1017/S0010417500012469.

Wallace, D. D. 1896. "The South Carolina Constitutional Convention of 1895." *The Sewanee Review* 4 (3): 348–60.

Warren, Jonathan W., and France Winddance Twine. 1997. "White Americans, the New Minority?: Non-Blacks and the Ever-Expanding Boundaries of Whiteness." *Journal of Black Studies* 28 (2): 200–18.

Weinberger, Eliot. 2008. "Obama v. Clinton: A Retrospective." *London Review of Books*, July 3. https://www.lrb.co.uk/the-paper/v30/n13/eliot-weinberger/obama-v.-clinton-a-retrospective.

Weisman, Jonathan. 2010. "2010 Campaign News: GOP in Lead in Final Lap." *Wall Street Journal*, October 20. https://www.wsj.com/articles/SB10001424052702303550904575562493014465942.

"What It Means To Be Asian in America." 2022. *Pew Research Center Race & Ethnicity* (blog), August 2, 2022. https://www.pewresearch.org/race-ethnicity/2022/08/02/what-it-means-to-be-asian-in-america/.

White, Ismail K., and Chryl N. Laird. 2020. *Steadfast Democrats: How Social Forces Shape Black Political Behavior.* Princeton, NJ: Princeton University Press.

Wildman, Sarah. 2017. "'You Will Not Replace Us': A French Philosopher Explains the Charlottesville Chant." *Vox*, August 15. https://www.vox.com/world/2017/8/15/16141456/renaud-camus-the-great-replacement-you-will-not-replace-us-charlottesville-white.

Williamson, Vanessa, Theda Skocpol, and John Coggin. 2011. "The Tea Party and the Remaking of Republican Conservatism." *Perspectives on Politics* 9 (1): 25–43. https://doi.org/10.1017/S153759271000407X.

Wimmer, Andreas. 2013. *Ethnic Boundary Making: Institutions, Power, Networks.* Illustrated ed. New York: Oxford University Press.

Woldoff, Rachael A. 2011. *White Flight/Black Flight: The Dynamics of Racial Change in an American Neighborhood. White Flight/Black Flight.* Ithaca, NY: Cornell University Press. https://doi.org/10.7591/9780801461033.

Woon, Jonathan. 2018. "Primaries and Candidate Polarization: Behavioral Theory and Experimental Evidence." *American Political Science Review* 112 (4): 826–43. https://doi.org/10.1017/S0003055418000515.

Yokley, Eli. 2021. "Trump Emerges from Impeachment Trial with Sturdy Backing from GOP Voters." *Morning Consult* (blog). https://morningconsult.com/2021/02/16/trump-gop-support-impeachment-poll/.

Zangwill, Israel. 2017. *The Melting-Pot.* Peterborough, Ontario: Broadview Press.

Zeleny, Jeff. 2008. "In Painful Past, Hushed Worry about Obama." *New York Times*, February 25, sec. US. https://www.nytimes.com/2008/02/25/us/politics/25memo.html.

Ziblatt, Daniel. 2017. *Conservative Parties and the Birth of Democracy.* New York: Cambridge University Press.

Index

For the benefit of digital users, indexed terms that span two pages (e.g., 52–53) may, on occasion, appear on only one of those pages.